Accounts Receivable and Inventory Lending

Accounts Receivable and Inventory Lending

How to Establish and Operate a Department

SECOND EDITION

David A. Robinson

Bankers Publishing Company

BOSTON

Copyright © 1977, 1981 by
Bankers Publishing Company
210 South Street
Boston, Massachusetts 02111

First Edition 1977; Second Edition 1981

Printed in the United States of America

Library of Congress Cataloging in Publication Data

Robinson, David Alexander, 1909-
    Accounts receivable and inventory lending.

    Includes index.
    1. Accounts receivable loans. 2. Inventory
loans. I. Title.
HG3752.3.R63 1981   332.1′753′068   80-21097
ISBN 0-87267-036-8

To Mitchell S. (Mike) Lurio, former
President of Walter E. Heller and
Company of New England, Inc. and
John B. Gray, former Vice President of the
First National Bank of Boston, for their
many years of help and friendship.

Contents

Exhibits

Preface

Accounts receivable and inventory lending holds unique advantages for the borrower as well as the lender. It can be a dynamic profit producer for a bank. For the company that is experiencing financial problems or growing rapidly, or for the company with seasonal needs, it is often the ideal form of lending. Nevertheless, many banks do not fully take advantage of the profit potential or the security available in this kind of lending. Some engage in it half-heartedly, without separate departments or trained personnel. Others ignore this kind of lending altogether.

The purpose of this book is to present in detail the procedures and forms that will safeguard the bank's secured position and at the same time promote growth and profitability by making accounts receivable and inventory lending attractive to both present and potential borrowers.

In 1977, many of the procedures and forms still in use were archaic or incomplete. I wrote *Accounts Receivable and Inventory Lending* to fill the need I saw for a careful, comprehensive book on the subject. Now, four years later, I have had to update it to keep it as comprehensive, correct, and useful as possible.

This updated edition reflects the changes in the Bankruptcy Reform Act of 1978 and in Article 9 of the Uniform Commercial Code. I have also added case studies that show how two loans were structured and documented.

In writing this book, I have drawn upon the experiences of my thirty years in commercial finance with James Talcott Company and as Executive Vice President of Walter E. Heller and Company of New England. During this time, I worked closely with many banks handling and developing receivable and inventory lending. I learned a great deal in those years about the risks and rewards of this specialized lending. I hope this book will assist others who are about to enter the field.

I am grateful to the people who so generously gave their time and advice in order to make this book possible: Mr. J. Allen Kerr, Senior Vice President, Walter E. Heller International Corporation; Mr. Norman Veenstra, Vice President, Nytco Services, Inc., Joseph Landis, Esquire; Mr. Morris Weiderhorn, Vice President, Walter E. Heller & Company, of New England, Inc. I am especially grateful to Roger K. Soderberg, Esquire, for his contribution of the section entitled "Bankruptcies and Chapter Proceedings." Special thanks also go to my secretary, Jean Tallberg, who spent many hard hours deciphering my handwriting and assembling my disordered notes.

Accounts Receivable and Inventory Lending

CHAPTER 1

Introduction

GROWTH OF COMMERCIAL FINANCING AND FACTORING

The lending of money on the security of accounts receivable and inventory started in 1905, but the commercial financing industry really has come into its own only within the last four decades. During this period, in the midst of which occurred the enactment of the Uniform Commercial Code in 1954, financing and factoring companies have developed legal and procedural techniques that not only provide them with protection from the many hazards of lending, but also assist them in increasing the volume of their business. At the same time, these developments have benefited borrowers enormously by making more funds available to them on the security of their accounts receivable and inventory than could be borrowed unsecured on the strength of their balance sheets. Volume of this type of financing reached a total of $66.6 billion in 1979! Factoring accounted for an additional $28.1 billion. Obviously, the $94.7 billion thus made available to United States business played a tremendously significant part in our national economy.

Prior to the enactment of the Uniform Commercial Code (UCC or the Code), the lender's legal position was somewhat uncertain because of widely differing state laws governing the recording of liens on accounts receivable and inventory. In addition, most state laws required that the lender maintain strict supervision over all collateral assigned and over all collections of accounts made by the borrower. As a result, commercial finance companies enjoyed a virtual monopoly in this type of business because of the banking industry's apprehension about its legal position, because of its unwillingness to perform the necessary policing, and perhaps because of the stigma associated with this type of lending.

Before the Code, the practice of lending on the security of accounts receivable was based on the Supreme Court ruling in 1925 in the case of *Benedict* v. *Ratner*. In this situation, Benedict was the bankrupt and Ratner was the lender; the Court ruled that Ratner, the assignee, had not exercised sufficient dominion over the accounts receivable assigned to him since he had permitted the bankrupt to collect assigned accounts receivable without reporting collections or substituting new collateral.

The Court ruled that because Ratner had allowed the bankrupt to exercise dominion over the assigned accounts, he was negligent and had acted inconsistently with the maintaining of a good and valid assignment. The Court concluded that it is incumbent upon the lender to exercise complete control of collateral or else the assignment is not good relative to third parties.

The part of the Uniform Commercial Code that deals with secured transactions (Article 9) contrasts sharply with this ruling and states that it is not legally necessary for the lender to exercise dominion over the assigned collateral. Effective with the Code, the borrower may commingle funds received in payment of accounts assigned to the lender with the company's cash resources. It is not necessary for the books of the borrower to be examined, nor does the lender need to exercise control over returned merchandise. Actually, in order to perfect a lien on accounts receivable and inventory, it is only necessary to take three steps:

1. Execute a security agreement with the borrower. (From a legal standpoint, the security agreement requires only the borrower's signature although it is good psychology for the lender to sign also.)
2. Advance cash or other consideration on the security offered.
3. File a financing statement in the places and in the manner prescribed by the law of the state in which the borrower has his or her principal place of business. (Every state in the Union, except Louisiana, has now adopted the Code.) Financing statements must be signed by the borrower but, under a revision of Article 9 adopted by some states, the lender is not required to sign the statement. Your attorney should be consulted on this matter.

After the Code came into being, there was a rapid entry of banks into the field of accounts receivable and inventory lending because of their greatly strengthened legal position. The Code truly does give the lenders greater legal protection. In spite of this, the occurrence of many sizeable losses because of improper policing of collateral or poor documentation leaves little doubt that the principle of dominion over collateral is still necessary from a practical standpoint.

Accounts receivable and inventory lending is a fascinating and rewarding business, but to maximize profits and minimize the risks inherent in this business, constant vigilance is required. Assets, by virtue of purchases, sales, and manufacturing processes, may change daily in both quantity and quality; it is imperative to keep them under constant scrutiny to be sure that they always will provide security, even under the most unfavorable conditions.

THE FLEXIBILITY OF REVOLVING LOANS

Loans made on receivables and inventory are truly *revolving* loans: they are being repaid by customer collections constantly, and are renewed by new advances made against receivables and inventory as these are created. Furthermore, because loans are tied to fluctuating collateral, the amount available for borrowing will increase under normal circumstances with increasing annual or seasonal sales. Conversely, loans will be automatically paid down in an off season when collections from customers exceed advances on new sales. For a graphic representation of the fluid way an accounts receivable and inventory arrangement can work, refer to Exhibit 1. While the name of K. Kringle Manufacturing Company is fictitious, the exhibit is the actual record of a borrower who manufactures various kinds of ornaments for the Christmas season.

K. Kringle's manufacturing process starts about March of each year and, as goods are finished and stored, they are *designated* (pledged) to the lender who makes available to Kringle loans of up to 60 percent of the cost value of the finished goods. With this kind of an arrangement, Kringle can buy supplies and raw materials, meet its payroll, and manufacture enough goods to cover actual and estimated sales.

The shipping season in this industry does not actually start until the end of July, but then goes at a highly accelerated rate through October, with most sales not due for payment until the normal dating period of December 10. As a result, accounts receivable accumulate rapidly and payments against inventory loans have to be made in proportion to the amount of goods shipped.

It is doubtful that any kind of loans so perfectly meet widely fluctu-

EXHIBIT 1

Six Months Summary of Sales, Collections, and Borrowings of
K. Kringle Manufacturing Company

K. KRINGLE MANUFACTURING COMPANY

Month	ACCOUNTS RECEIVABLE					INVENTORY		
	Sales	Accts. Rec. End of Month	Collections	Loan End of Month	Receivable[1] Availability End of Month	Inventory End of Month	Loan End of Month	Inventory[2] Availability End of Month
July	77,600	106,000	33,700	66,500	16,700	458,000	228,000	47,825
August	202,900	283,800	23,900	195,600	30,000	452,300	133,800	137,610
September	238,000	453,442	68,190	315,000	46,400	282,700	33,800	135,833
October	217,900	584,200[3]	86,400	346,600[4]	120,000[5]	142,000	– 0 –	85,192
November	35,000	435,000	183,000	256,700	89,000	130,500	– 0 –	78,301
December	800	93,500	333,800	– 0 –	75,000	– 0 –[6]	– 0 –	– 0 –

NOTE: 1. Loan plus availability based on advance of 80% of face value of accounts receivable within 90 days of invoice date.
2. Loan plus availability based on advance of 60% of cost value of finished goods inventory.
3. Total accounts receivable increased over 500% from July through October.
4. Total loan on accounts receivable increased over 500% from July through October.
5. Peak borrowing power in October was $551,800 including the amount of the loan on receivables plus the amounts available on both receivables and inventory.
6. Inventory is shown as zero at the end of December even though there is always a small carryover at the end of the year. Carryover inventories are not considered to be loanable collateral.

ating seasonal needs as do loans on the security of receivables and inventory. Not only do they provide great flexibility, but also they enable a company to borrow, as in Kringle's case, several times its own net worth. At the time Exhibit 1 was drawn up, Kringle's net worth was $140,000 and its peak borrowing power in October was $551,800.

Exhibit 2 is a daily record for the month of October for K. Kringle Manufacturing Co. and shows one way of keeping track of the frequent transactions involving accounts receivable. In this way, both lender and borrower always will be aware of the amount of collateral and loan outstanding and the amount of money still available to the borrower.

In the case of K. Kringle, the lender allowed an advance of 80 percent of the face value of accounts receivable within ninety days of invoice date. The rate of advance may vary a great deal, depending on the industry, the type of customers, the firmness of credit and collection policies, and other significant factors. The rate of advance on accounts receivable and inventory is a matter of negotiation with a prospective borrower; it should be made clear in all documentation that the rate may be lowered or raised periodically to reflect changes that may take place in the borrower's circumstances, the economy, or the money market.

The four columns on the left of Exhibit 2 keep a running record—in bulk—of the accounts assigned to the lender (Receivables Increase) and of the amounts repaid by customer collections or by the issuance of credits (Receivables Decrease).

The four columns on the right record new advances of funds (Loan Increase), collections from customers (Loan Decrease), a running balance of the loan, and the daily amount of funds available to the borrower.

The recording of inventory is handled much the same as in Exhibit 2. New inventory acquired either by manufacture or purchase may be designated to the lender at frequent intervals and recorded on the lender's books as inventory increases. Decreases of inventory resulting from sales usually are made on the basis of the Cost of Goods Sold. This figure should be agreed upon only after careful discussion with the prospective borrower and his accountant. Daily balances of total inventory, total loan, and availability are computed as in receivable financing.

In this instance, the lender's advance rate of 60 percent of the cost value of Kringle's finished goods inventory is abnormally high. At the start of this lending arrangement, the lender advanced 40 percent against inventory. As the years went by, however, the lender gained

EXHIBIT 2

8

Daily Record of Account with K. Kringle Manufacturing Company

DAILY RECORD OF ACCOUNT WITH C. KRINGLE MANUFACTURING CO.

80% ADVANCE – 90 DAY ACCOUNTS

MONTH OF OCTOBER

Day	ACCOUNTS RECEIVABLE ASSIGNED				LOAN AND AVAILABILITY			
	Receivables Increase	Receivables Decrease	Receivables Balance	Receivables Reserves	Loan Increase	Loan Decrease	Loan Balance	Available to Borrow
1			453,442	1,683	1,420		319,255	42,151
2	8,209	4,275	457,376			4,201	315,054	49,500
3	13,215	1,048	469,543			1,049	314,005	60,283
4					7,500		321,505	52,783
5								
6								
7	3,992	1,294	472,241		12,600	1,288	332,817	43,630
8								
9	19,624	1,247	490,620		8,000	1,244	339,572	51,577
10								
11		872	489,747		4,600	869	343,304	47,147
12								
13								
14								
15	100,458	3,212	586,993		37,456	3,187	377,574	90,674
16	17,058	32,704	571,347		4,500	32,629	349,445	106,286
17					3,001		352,446	103,285
18	5,254	457	576,144		4,500	458	356,488	103,328
19								
20								
21	13,202	4,238	585,107			4,207	352,281	114,706
22					3,001		355,282	111,705
23	12,119	10,062	587,165		9,700	9,799	355,183	113,450
24	10,141	2,636	594,670		9,000	2,564	361,619	113,019
25					6,900		368,519	106,119
26								
27								
28								
29	14,603	3,010	606,263		3,001	2,988	368,532	115,380
30								
31		22,065	584,197	1,683		21,944	346,589	119,671

confidence in the company's management, in the acceptance of the products by Kringle's substantial number of customers, and in the prompt repayment of inventory loans at the end of each season. With the aid of sales forecasts, early orders, and evidence of consistent progress, the advance rate was increased in order to enable Kringle to buy on more advantageous terms and to get an earlier start on building product lines. This, in turn, resulted in the company's being able to reduce back order shipments and to cut down on overtime rates for production workers.

The increase in Kringle's inventory rate was a judgment made with full awareness of the increased risk involved. Any inventory that has to be sold on a liquidation basis is almost always subject to a drastic decrease in value. An additional and considerable risk was taken throughout the time that Kringle was building inventory prior to its being shipped. If, for any reason, the company could not complete the manufacturing of full lines, the lender would be left with inventory that was incomplete with respect to style, size, color, and amount. Kringle's customers are volume buyers who most likely would refuse partial shipments; therefore, whatever inventory was involved would have to be sold to liquidators at disastrous prices.

The violation of conservative advance rates—especially on inventory—should be the rare exception to the rule. On the other hand, the head of the accounts receivable department should be allowed to exercise common sense in enabling a trustworthy customer to attain sensible objectives, even though the element of risk is slightly above normal.

WHEN TO USE ACCOUNTS RECEIVABLE AND INVENTORY FINANCING

Accounts receivable and inventory financing can be especially useful when one or more of the following situations exist:

1. A new business is in such an early stage of its development that there is an insufficient track record for determining its ability to repay an unsecured loan.
2. Larger loans are needed than can be supported by an unsecured loan on the borrower's balance sheet, and such loans may be raised on the security of accounts receivable and inventory.
3. A business is growing rapidly and negotiated loans on balance sheets are time consuming and might be inadequate to meet growing needs. For example, a company may have created a new

product that suddenly catches on, and sales quickly outstrip the finances necessary to carry the receivables that are created and the inventory needed to meet the demand.

4. A company either creates or acquires a sales force with strong marketing and sales ability but has insufficient equity capital to finance rapidly growing sales.

5. A subsidiary company is growing faster than its own capital, and its parent company cannot provide financing without straining its own resources. In such cases, the subsidiary often may be financed independent of the parent.

6. A business is seasonal and borrowing requirements in season exceed normal needs. The many examples of this include manufacturers and wholesalers of: items made especially or primarily for the Christmas trade; clothing or sporting goods for seasonal use; heating oil, coal, or gas, particularly in cold climates; and gardening stock such as trees, shrubs, and related products.

7. A company's working capital has been reduced or is now inadequate due to any of the following circumstances:

   a. Some or all of the company's products have been phased out of the market, either because they have lost popularity or because advancing technology has made them slow-moving or obsolete.

   b. A catastrophe such as a fire or tornado has taken place and has partially or totally destroyed company assets. In such an event, receivables and inventory financing often will buy time until the company is operating smoothly again.

   c. The death of a principal has taken place and the claims of the estate against the business have decreased working capital to the extent that unsecured borrowings are insufficient to meet its normal requirements.

   d. There has been overexpansion, or "conglomeritis," and the company needs more funds than are available to tide it over until it adjusts to its new size and, perhaps, to its new type of operation.

   e. A company or a group of individuals wants to acquire a going concern. In such situations, the assets of either or both are often available to raise a part or all of the purchase price.

ADVANTAGES OF ACCOUNTS RECEIVABLE AND INVENTORY LENDING

Of course, there are hazards in accounts receivable and inventory lending which call for sophisticated credit judgments, not only when the prospect is signed up but frequently during the life of the loan. In most cases, however, the risks are well worth the rewards.

This kind of lending accelerates cash flow by freeing cash that would be otherwise tied up for the number of days of the borrower's normal accounts receivable turnover. In effect, the lender does the waiting while the borrower uses his capital for more profitable purposes. Because cash is immediately available as accounts receivable are created, the borrower increases the leverage of his capital and, as a result, should be able to buy better, handle increasing volume more comfortably, and take cash discounts that are offered.

Accounts receivable and inventory lending is extremely flexible. For example, if a customer is in a seasonal business where sales increase rapidly as the season approaches, his borrowing power automatically can expand with his sales, enabling him to keep suppliers paid satisfactorily, to handle increased payrolls, and to meet other financial demands. In many seasonal situations, growing accounts receivable will provide a sufficient borrowing base to keep creditors happy, but, if not, loans may be made against a build-up of inventory which precedes the selling season.

A receivables and inventory program may also provide the working capital to take care of a business's year-to-year growth—whether normal or rapid.

There is no regular repayment schedule of an accounts receivable loan. Reductions come from application of receivable collections to the loan, and new advances are against sales as they are made. Inventory loans also may revolve, although occasionally it is desirable to institute a gradual reduction program until either the inventory loan is repaid in full or it has been reduced to a point where the possibility of a loss, in the event of liquidation, seems highly improbable.

Customers need not be required to keep any compensating balances; therefore, they get the full use of any funds borrowed. Interest is charged only on a per diem basis so that the borrower is never paying interest for funds not in use.

Accounts receivable and inventory loans may be combined with fixed asset loans to provide a borrower with adequate financing to meet his needs and with a repayment schedule geared to his ability to pay. Furthermore, a receivable and inventory arrangement is simple for the borrower and the bank. Both can tell, on a day-to-day basis, how much may be borrowed; therefore, the borrower can *instruct* the bank to deposit the required amount into his account. This eliminates a great amount of negotiating time for both parties.

Finally, participation with another bank or with a commercial finance company is possible up to any desired percentage of the amount involved. This is usually held to no more than 50 percent of the total loan. In this way, a bank may limit its risk or may use a participation for that portion of the loan over its legal lending limit.

COLLATERAL COMPARISON OF RECEIVABLES AND INVENTORY

When comparing accounts receivable and inventory as collateral, there is no question that the value of accounts receivable can be established more quickly and more accurately than the value of inventory. The outstanding characteristics of receivables are:

1. They are due from specific names located at specific addresses.
2. The goods or services are billed for in specific quantities in clearly stated amounts.
3. The creditworthiness of account debtors usually can be determined easily, by drawing reports on them compiled by credit agencies. Creditworthiness is also frequently indicated by credit ratings published by firms such as Dun & Bradstreet.
4. The existence and value of accounts receivable can be established quickly, by verification procedures as outlined under the heading Verifications in Chapter 6.
5. The flexibility of accounts receivable financing meets the requirements of most financing situations whether they are primarily due to seasonal sales fluctuations, rapid yearly growth, or the need to buy time because a firm has gone through a period of unprofitable operations.
6. Through good and constant administration, accounts receivable collateral can be purified on practically a daily basis, by eliminating from assignments any contra accounts, poor credit risks, or sales to affiliates. In addition, the review and verification of assigned accounts can keep receivables free of disputes and lead to early detection of fraud.

The relative merits of inventory as collateral are spelled out in Chapter 6. As is noted there, inventory may be good collateral, but in order to recoup any loans, a greater degree of policing and good luck is needed than when liquidating receivables.

FACTORING

Although it will not be dealt with in detail in this book, it seems advisable to explain the difference between accounts receivable and inventory financing and factoring.

The word *factoring* has become almost a generic term which many people apply to both accounts receivable financing and factoring. Factoring, however, is distinctly different; the factor actually *buys* the accounts receivable of its clients—not only at the start of the factoring arrangement, but also on a daily or weekly basis as the receivables are created. Naturally, the factor has the privilege of establishing credit limits on any account sold by the client, but, because factors are credit specialists, they often are more liberal with credit extension than is the client.

On an operational basis, the factored client ships to his customer in any amount up to the limit established by the factor, and each invoice is printed or stamped with a legend instructing the customer to pay the bill directly to the factor. At the time of shipment, the client sends a copy of the invoice to the factor along with shipping evidence such as bills of lading or truck receipts. Upon receipt, the factor posts the invoice and assumes the responsibility of collecting and absorbing any credit losses.

Payment for invoices purchased is made by the factor in one of two ways—maturity factoring or old line factoring.

Maturity Factoring

Under maturity factoring, the factor will pay the client no later than ten days after the maturity date of the invoice. For example, if a client's normal terms to his customer are 2% 10 days, net 30, the factor will remit the entire face value of the invoice—less a factoring fee—on the tenth day following the final net term.

Maturity factoring presupposes that the client has sufficient working capital to carry the amount due from the factor for the term of the invoice, but it also gives the client the comfort of knowing that the factor will pay him regardless of what might happen to his customer. The client is also relieved of virtually all of the costs associated with running a credit department. Because of the assurance of timely payments from the factor and the elimination of any credit losses, he can better plan his cash flow. For those companies that can use factoring, it is often less expensive to factor than to maintain a credit department.

If it is desired, the client may pledge the amount due from the factor to his or her bank and borrow up to a large percentage of the total in the event that funds are needed before the maturity date of his invoices.

Old Line
Factoring

When using old line factoring, the client submits invoices to the factor as in maturity factoring, but the factor extends the privilege to the client of borrowing against the invoices before maturity date. Take, for example, the client who submits invoices for several days up to, say, the fifteenth of the month, and then needs funds to meet payables or payroll. Old line factoring allows the client to borrow against the invoices and pay a nominal rate of interest for the number of days the loan is outstanding up to the maturity date of the invoice. The factor then makes a regular monthly settlement and deducts the amount already loaned against the amount due at maturity.

Factoring got its start hundreds of years ago when exporters sold their goods to overseas factors who not only discounted the bills but actually sold the merchandise. The selling function was discontinued years ago, but factoring as we now know it continues to grow.

Under today's competitive conditions, it would be extremely difficult and expensive to start a true factoring company. Factors need a large staff of credit experts, collection people, posting clerks, computers, and computer people. Because of this, entry into the factoring field should be attempted only by the brave and the strong who not only have the patience to develop business over a period of years, but also have the substantial resources that are necessary to handle sizeable transactions and, possibly, sizeable losses.

Factoring is commonplace in the textiles and carpeting industries and is used extensively in lumbering, chemicals, and toys. It is not commonly used in other industries, primarily due to the notification feature of factoring, which is not acceptable to many borrowers. This reluctance to notify customers that their accounts have been sold to a factor is not entirely logical. It seems to relate to basic instincts not to reveal one's intimate business details to outsiders.

Actually, factoring is just another business device used to make cash flow more predictable. It has the added advantage of relieving the businessman of the time-consuming and arduous task of maintaining a credit department. The time gained in this respect can be put to better and more profitable use in the production of goods and the promotion of sales.

FUNDAMENTALS OF SECURED LENDING

There are four fundamentals of secured lending:

1. The financial responsibility of the borrower;
2. The purpose of the loan;
3. The character of the borrower;
4. The nature of the collateral to be pledged.

Look at these fundamentals and keep them in mind every day your loan is outstanding. If any one of them changes for the worse to any significant degree, your loan may be in trouble. For example, if your borrower gets into financial difficulty, his or her financial responsibility and the purpose of the loan no longer matter and you can only hope that the borrower's character and the value of the collateral will stand up under testing conditions.

When you are confident that your borrower is solvent and the business is profitable, the collateral pledged to you always should be adequate to support your loan. Any problems that may crop up in the ordinary course of business may be adjusted by refunds, credits, substitution of new goods for faulty merchandise, and so forth. However, if your customer falls on hard times, such adjustments are not made so easily, willingly, or promptly. It is only natural, therefore, that there be a deterioration in the value of receivables.

It is important to understand the purpose for which the loan is requested. In almost every instance, revolving loans on collateral are used to free up capital that would otherwise be tied up in receivables or inventory. These are basically short-term loans to be used as working capital, and not for such long-term purposes as purchasing expensive machinery or real estate. Needless to say, receivables and inventory loans should not be used for frivolous purposes, but it is surprising how many times the great improvement in cash flow, created by revolving loans, will make a borrower feel a good deal richer than he or she really is.

The good character of a receivable and/or inventory borrower is a necessity. *You cannot be present whenever a sale is made or inventory is purchased,* and, therefore, you have to trust your borrower to assign to you only sales that are real in every respect and are not subject to any offsets. Because of this element of risk, it is imperative that you carefully check your prospect's integrity *before* entering a loan arrangement, and then constantly police your collateral *and your borrower* during the life of the loan. History is full of examples of otherwise honest men and women who, through desperate circumstances or an overpowering yearning for the "good life," defrauded lenders "for only a little while," and who then realized that they could not extricate themselves from the problems they had created.

CHAPTER 2

Staffing a Commercial Finance Department

At one of the annual seminars conducted by the National Commercial Finance Conference, an association of commercial finance and factoring companies, a panel member extolled the advantages to both borrower and lender of accounts receivable and inventory financing. However, he finished his preliminary remarks by saying, "I must tell you in good faith that in spite of all of these advantages, you can lose your shirt and perhaps your pants too if you have inexperienced people making receivable and inventory loans."

Many banks starting an accounts receivable and inventory department will entrust the running of the department and the supervision of the loans to the newest officer on the lending platform. This is done because of the belief that the filing of notices of liens on the security offered substantially secures the bank at the time of filing and forever more.

Eli Silberman, legal counsel for the National Conference, stated years ago that "a floating lien is not a floating policeman." Already it has been pointed out in this book, and will be emphasized again and again, that the collateral pledged to the lender today is not the same as it was yesterday, and is different from the collateral that will be pledged tomorrow. This is true of both its quantity and quality. In addition to the changes in the volume and values of pledged assets, the lender must continually be alert to the financial health of the borrower. The value of the assets of a going concern will ordinarily be close to what is shown on the borrower's balance sheet. If assets have to be liquidated under crash conditions because of the insolvency or the bankruptcy of the borrower, values can depreciate at an unbelievable rate, frequently with loss to the lender.

For these reasons, the staff of a commercial finance department should be made up of imaginative and dedicated people; the department should never be left to a trainee who will learn mostly from the losses he or she may cause the bank.

If at all possible, the loan officers entrusted with the work should not make unsecured loans as well. The thinking of an unsecured lender does not mix well with secured financing. One who lends on accounts receivable and inventory must always concentrate on the present value of the collateral, and should not try to project what such assets might be worth in the future.

If, because of limited staff or current low volume of accounts receivable and inventory loans, a loan officer must double up in his or her duties, it is preferable that the person most familiar with chattel or mortgage lending be given the responsibility of handling accounts receivable and inventory loans.

In those banks where there is no alternative except for an unsecured loan officer also to handle these revolving loans, the officer must be deeply conscious of the difference between lending against balance sheets with payment to be received at some future date, and the making of loans against security that has constantly changing values. This is not to say that the accounts receivable lending officer has to be entirely rigid in dealing with borrowers. There inevitably will be occasions when it makes sense to give *temporary overadvances*—amounts above established loan formulas. The loan officer should be able to make such loans within his or her own established loan authority or in conjunction with a senior loan officer.

The accounts receivable and inventory lending department should be a profit-making department and should never be used as a dumping ground for bad loans. The department head should have the prerogative to reject substandard loan applications but should be prepared to assist other loan officers in acquiring collateral from any deteriorating accounts and to document properly any troublesome loans.

When loans get to a work-out stage, they either should be left with the loan officer who originated them or, if the bank has the facilities, should be taken over by the work-out department. In either case, the department head should provide guidance whenever required.

NUMBER OF PEOPLE NEEDED

The number of people required to run a department depends more on the number of borrowers and the complexity of the loans than on the number of dollars outstanding. If it were possible to get twenty simple receivable loans of $1 million each, a minimum staff could handle them about as easily as they could handle twenty simple loans of $100,000 each. There is, however, a great scarcity of *simple* receivable loans. On the average, approximately 20 to 25 loans with minimum average balances of $100,000 each can be administered easily by a basic staff consisting of a department head, an examiner, a bookkeeper, and a verification clerk.

If a department is being started from scratch, these people may devote only part of their time to the receivable department, until sufficient volume has been built up to use them on a full-time basis.

LOCATION OF DEPARTMENT

Because lending on the security of accounts receivable and inventory is a very specialized activity, it should be administered from the bank's headquarters by a staff that either is expert in this field at the start or will become so as it gains experience. Receivable and inventory loans should not be handled by branches. Branch managers, of course, will have contact with receivable borrowers in the development of business, in the handling of checking accounts, and in the administration of loans made on machinery and equipment, mortgages, and other collateral. When a borrower requests information about his or her receivable or inventory account, however, the request must be referred to the department head or the staff in the main office. This presupposes that all records and data pertaining to such accounts are kept at the bank's headquarters. Any attempt to have receivable and inventory loans administered in branches will lead to inconsistent, uncertain, and inexpert handling.

This is not intended as any criticism of branch people—they can be fully as competent and as dedicated as anyone in the home office—but this type of financing is best handled at one location, by personnel who completely understand it and who constantly, consistently, and firmly administer and police the ever-changing collateral that supports the bank's loans. Branch managers, of course, should be informed frequently of the collateral and loan positions of receivable and inventory borrowers in order to keep them up to date on the activity of all accounts in their areas.

THE DEPARTMENT HEAD

Qualifications and Line of Authority

The department head should be an officer of the bank who reports directly to the chief lending officer. General qualifications should include an ability to speak easily and confidently to the principal officers of the borrower with firmness but without arrogance or condescension. The borrower's business is every bit as important to him or her as the banker's business is to the bank. In every lending arrangement, therefore, there should be a spirit of cooperation that recognizes the rights and aspirations of both parties.

On the other hand, the department head must give top priority to the bank's best interest, and must maintain firm control over an account. Necessary changes must be made in the dealings with a borrower or in the handling of collateral (permitted by loan agreements between the parties), whether or not these changes are pleasant or agreeable to either the borrower or the lender. A lack of firmness in adhering to sound credit principles is a major reason why loan officers may suddenly realize that a loan has gotten out of hand and that larger than necessary losses will have to be taken by both the lender and the borrower.

In addition to being able to get along with people, the department head should have a good working knowledge of accounting. This will enable the department head to analyze financial statements and to discuss them intelligently with the borrower and, when necessary, with the borrower's accountant. The department head should understand all documents used in the drawing up and administrating of the loan, and the need for all clauses contained in them. The department head, unless he or she is an attorney, should never attempt to write legal documents, but should work closely with the bank's legal counsel in structuring a loan and should always be present when documents are signed.

Finally, the department head should always be alert to and curious about any events that are unusual or that do not bear a proper relationship to each other. For example, if inventory increases but sales do not, what is the reason? Or, if collections slow down, does this relate to faulty merchandise, a relaxation of credit controls, or fictitious invoices?

Responsibilities and Duties

The department head—under the general guidance of the chief lending officer—should have complete responsibility to operate the department as a full-fledged profit center of the bank. This assumes that the manager is made fully aware of all costs that will be charged to the department, such as the cost of funds loaned on the security of receivables and inventory, and the cost of space, salaries, prorated insurance, equipment, and forms.

Specifically, the department head will do the following:

1. Search for accounts receivable and inventory loan business. The search should start with a review of existing loans for which the bank has filed UCC statements (but where documentation or loan supervision is perfunctory or nonexistent), and may also include a review of the bank's unsecured loans. It is possible that some of these latter loans could be increased, to the benefit of all, if secured by the pledge of receivables or inventory. The search should continue using the procedures recommended in Chapter 10;

2. Make initial contacts with prospective accounts receivable and inventory borrowers. This includes evaluating the principals, financial health, and prospects of the interested borrower;

3. Initiate the examination;

4. Review the examination. This includes evaluating the collateral submitted, the accounts receivable turnover (as indicated by sales and collection records), reports of returns and credits, and verification results;

5. Structure the loan and determine—
   a. the percentage of advance to be made against accounts receivable and inventory;
   b. the number of days that receivables will be carried on the bank's records as current;
   c. the extra collateral needed to make the deal comfortable;
   d. the documentation needed to afford the bank the greatest protection possible and still allow the borrower maximum flexibility;
   e. the time and place of filing to conform with UCC regulations;
   f. the scope and frequency of examinations; and
   g. the frequency of verifications;

6. Work with the bank's attorney to determine the documentation needed;

7. Sign on the new account and, with the bank's attorney, ensure that all documents are properly signed and dated and that UCC or other filings are properly made and are not superseded by any other filings;

8. Continually administer the policing of the borrower and of the bank's collateral;

9. Develop meaningful contacts with outside credit and financial organizations such as National Credit Office, Dun & Bradstreet, National Commercial Finance Conference, Robert Morris Associates, bankruptcy and corporate lawyers, and as many CPAs as possible;

10. In the event of liquidation, administer the disposition of the collateral and, with the assistance of the bank's attorney, defend the bank's rights to its collateral against the claims of all others.

Loan Authority

The amount of loan authority given to loan officers ranges from the ridiculously low in some banks to the bank's legal limit in other banks (which in many cases seems dangerously high). It is recommended that loan authority be held to substantially less than the bank's legal limit for the first couple of years; this will give all concerned the opportunity of seeing how things work out for the bank and for the borrower. It must be recognized, however, that one of the great advantages of accounts receivable and inventory financing is its ability to respond to rapidly growing loan requirements. The department head must be prepared to recommend temporary or permanent loan limit increases when it seems propitious and prudent to do so. Increases above the department head's loan authority should be agreed to in writing by the senior loan officer, who should also have a loan limit below the bank's legal limit. When the senior loan officer's limit is reached, loan approvals should come from top bank officers or the board of directors.

ASSISTANT TO THE DEPARTMENT HEAD

During the early stages of the growth of an accounts receivable and inventory lending department, the department head will have to perform many of the department's functions with the part-time assistance of bookkeepers and verification clerks, and possibly with the per diem help of an examiner, as described under Examinations in Chapter Six. As volume grows, however, a very important addition to the staff will be a loan officer who can be assigned part or all of the accounts, who will work with borrowers on a day-to-day basis, and who will review all collateral and credit and collection data submitted to the department.

The qualifications of a loan officer are much the same as for a department head: he or she must have a good understanding of accounting, an ability to analyze financial statements, an ability to get along with people (even under stress), a good credit sense, and an understanding of all the documentation of loans under his or her supervision.

In performing basic duties, a loan officer will do the following:

1. Administer each loan in conformance with the terms and contions included in its documentation;
2. Review and evaluate all collateral submitted, and make prompt adjustments whenever any diminution of value takes place;
3. Work with staff examiners to be sure that examinations are made on a timely basis and that they include all information necessary for proper evaluation of the account;
4. Administer the work of the verification clerk and evaluate the number and quality of the replies;
5. Assist the department head in every phase of the department's work.

CHAPTER 3

Investigation of the Prospective Borrower

TYPES OF BORROWERS

The most desirable accounts receivable and inventory loans are made to manufacturers or wholesalers whose products are staples sold to a large enough group of customers that risk is sufficiently diversified. Each loan application has to stand on its own, however, and all aspects must be examined carefully in order to assure that the collateral offered will protect the bank from loss and will provide the prospective borrower with the requested funds.

The less desirable accounts receivable and inventory loans are to service companies such as advertising agencies, trucking companies (whose receivables may be involved with Interstate Commerce Commission (ICC) regulations), medical or dental companies, and contractors.

Loans on the accounts receivable of contractors should not be made. Such receivables almost always arise from *progress billings*—billings for a part of a total contract. In the event that the contractor fails to complete the contract in full, the billings outsanding at the time of default may not be paid because payment is actually predicated on completion of the entire contract. At best, the receivables are subject to heavy *back charges*—claims against proceeds for a wide variety of reasons—and may be seriously reduced in value.

In every contracting billing, except for those for materials, a portion of the billing is *retainage*—5–15 percent of the bill withheld until the completion of the entire job. Retainages can accumulate at an alarming rate and it is usually against these that the owner applies back charges. Retainages can remain unpaid for many months, and sometimes years, until every item called for in the contract is completed to the entire satisfaction of the owner.

If a bonding company guarantees to the owner that the contract will be completed, the situation of the lender is worsened because the proceeds of the receivables might go first to the bonding company even though the lender had previously made loans against them. In addition, certain statutory liens such as liens placed against collateral by a state agency, landlord's liens, or mechanic's liens, may attain priority over contractual liens. If a loan to a contractor is under consideration it would be advisable to work closely with the bank's attorney.

Finally, no receivable or inventory loans should be made to any company whose average borrowings would be less than $50,000, unless there are important community or public relations reasons for so doing. The revenue from small loans cannot cover the costs of properly supervising the collateral involved.

This does not mean that the bank should not accept the pledges of accounts receivable and inventory collateral from small borrowers; they should, of course, be taken whenever they are available. But loan judgments in these cases should be based on considerations applied to unsecured loans with the collateral taken for whatever it may be worth. The policing of collateral should be limited to a review of monthly lists of aged receivables and, if inventory is involved, to the examination of monthly designations of inventory.

INITIAL CONTACT WITH PROSPECT

Before committing the bank to an extensive investigation of any prospective account, the department head should be contacted to determine whether the prospect in question has any loan potential or whether there should be another form of financing offered. In many instances the department head may justify further investigation or rejection after an initial contact by telephone. In this contact, these questions should be asked:

1. How long has the prospect been in business?
2. What kind of product or service is involved?
3. What is the prospect's tangible net worth at present?
4. What has been the company's history for the past few years, in terms of profits or losses? If there have been losses, what are the reasons for them and what are the chances for a turnaround in the near future?

5. What is the total of accounts receivable and inventory now outstanding?
6. What is the prospect's estimate of funds needed, now and in the near future?
7. What is the purpose of the loan—does the prospect want to relieve creditor pressure, to carry increasing receivables and inventory, or to take available discounts?

Usually these and other subjects may be covered on the telephone well enough to determine whether a personal visit should be made to explore the loan possibility further.

EVALUATION OF PRINCIPALS

The evaluation of principals is one of the most difficult and uncertain tasks that a department head has to perform. There are no specific yardsticks with which to measure people. It must be kept in mind that some of the most affable people, under pressing circumstances, may do everything in their power to put obstacles in the path of the lender if lien rights have to be exerted to the disadvantage of the borrower. Because of this, the interview of the borrower's principals may be one of the most important steps taken before a full-fledged examination of the prospect's business occurs.

Accounts receivable financing is referred to as secured financing, but the security consists of pieces of paper that purport to represent the delivery of goods or services in accordance with a customer's orders. The acceptance of such collateral is largely based on the confidence of the lender in the borrower, and, if any background information indicates larcenous tendencies on the part of the borrower, that confidence no longer exists.

One of the most difficult interviews to conduct is with a prospect who will answer every question put to him but who will not elaborate on his answers in any way, nor volunteer information. The interviewer may be left with the feeling that probably there is more he should know about the borrower or his business if only he had asked the right questions. Sometimes all of the necessary information will come out when inquiries such as the following are made into the principals' backgrounds:

1. What has been their education or experience in the business they are conducting or hope to conduct?
2. What has been their record of success or failure in this or previous

enterprises? If there have been failures, what are the basic reasons for them and may the part played by the principals be corroborated?

3. Is the chief operating officer of the prospect oriented toward sales with only a secondary interest in or knowledge of financial and credit matters? People of this type may sell themselves out of business by building overhead faster than income to handle it. This may be especially true when a borrower is given the flexibility of borrowing on accounts receivable and inventory, which creates borrowing power simultaneous with the shipment of goods.

4. Do the principals appear to have a basic knowledge of financial matters and of the importance of making plans for at least the borrower's near-term requirements?

5. Are the principals employees of a company who have been given the opportunity of buying the company? If so, a judgment has to be made concerning the quality of their management capabilities. Many men who are excellent in their jobs are not necessarily capable of coping with all of the hazards and headaches of running a business.

6. What is the personal financial status of each principal? The principals should be requested to submit a personal financial statement as of a date near or close to the date of the interview; updated statements should be submitted at least on an annual basis.

The bulk of a personal net worth very often will be made up of current value of stocks and bonds, the value of personal residences, boats, cars, and investments in commercial real estate.

Concerning a principal's stocks, the department head should determine if the stocks are listed or unlisted. The value of listed stocks should be checked against current stock price listings. If the stocks are unlisted, inquiries should be made regarding the basis of the values shown on the statement and the readiness with which the stocks can be sold.

Concerning personal fixed assets, the basis of valuation should be explained. In other words, is the valuation that of a professional appraiser, the owner's appraisal of the probable market value, or a representation of the original cost? If it represents the original cost, has proper depreciation been applied since the date of purchase? The bases for the values of investments in other businesses or commercial real estate should also be explained.

Personal financial statements often are poorly and carelessly drawn. Whether or not the lender should insist that a statement be prepared by a CPA is a matter of how important this information is in the overall loan consideration. Every personal financial statement should be signed by the principal on whom it is drawn. It should be indicated to the principal that the statement is an important piece of information on which the bank relies when deciding whether or not to make the loan.

7. What appear to be the general lifestyles of the principals? The interviewer should be able to determine—without invading the privacy of the prospects—whether they have a penchant for big cars, houses, boats, gambling, and the like, or whether there are any drinking problems. If a business is doing well and the principals choose to pay themselves well, it is their privilege so to do. The only time principals' salaries should concern the lender is when expensive ways of living might lead the business into a financial problem, either by drawing off needed working capital or by directing the principals' attention away from their enterprise.

Finally, it is always advisable to draw retail credit reports on at least the chief operating officer of the prospect. Such reports may provide information that was not volunteered and might be the basis for further discussions. Naturally, if a report reveals any dishonest activity, the prospect should be dropped. On the other hand, even after a clean report is received, it does not mean that the lender can relax his or her scrutiny of the borrower's business or the policing of the collateral. History is full of examples of the trusted employee who, after playing it straight for many years, yielded to economic pressures or just the desire for the "good life" and suddenly decided to dip into the till.

EVALUATION OF THE BUSINESS

When evaluating the business of a prospective accounts receivable and inventory borrower, the department head must keep in mind that the size of the loan requested will inevitably be higher than could be loaned prudently on an unsecured basis. In the final analysis, the lender depends more on an ability to dispose of assigned collateral in order to recoup principal and interest, than on the borrower's ability to pay the loan on demand. For this reason, no loan should be made unless the collateral is able to support it fully even after applying all of the liquidation costs outlined in Chapter 9.

There is, however, no rule of secured lending carved in stone. The department head must be given the latitude to make temporary over-advances when a borrower is able to put the funds to such good use as taking advantage of a special buy of goods or capturing discounts that will save more than the cost of the funds. There also may be times when percentages of advance on receivables or inventory may be temporarily increased or when loans may be made on 120-day accounts instead of 90-day accounts. These are judgments to be made by the department head on a selective basis while adhering to the principle that the loan should be kept within a conservative percentage of the pledged collateral.

An easy business to evaluate is one that has shown steady and perhaps rapid growth in recent years, and is simply looking for a larger line of credit in order to handle continuing increases. A business more difficult to evaluate is one that has suffered financial reverses and for which the turn-around time cannot be pinpointed.

An on-the-spot review of current financial statements and agings of accounts receivables and payables may lead to a preliminary opinion concerning the probability of a loan being made, but only in the rarest of instances should a commitment to make a loan be made at the time of the initial visit. The review of material gathered by the department head should take only a day or two and it will guide the examiner in making the initial report. Every new loan request should be handled expeditiously, but enough time should be taken to review carefully the historic and financial data, to be as certain as possible that the contemplated loan will be helpful to the borrower, and that the collateral offered will be adequate security.

One participant in a panel discussion conducted by the National Commercial Finance Conference offered a good example of what may happen when a loan is made too hastily:

> A number of years ago, we got a call from an accountant with a CPA firm we knew in New England. They had a client, then a fledgling syrup manufacturer, which, incidentally, later attained a measure of national prominence. The accountant said that his client required accounts receivable financing, but that we would have to act fast.
>
> I'm sorry to say that we took the bite, and I was up there the next morning with contracts and a pad of assignment schedules.
>
> I recall something about the principal being at home, recovering from some illness. So, I had to go to his house for signatures. My work was otherwise conducted at the office of the CPA where the books were located. While I looked at the books, the accountants had a girl make up the schedule of assignment.
>
> I was back in my office the next morning with a signed contract and the assignment. We actually made an advance right then and there, although, as I recall, it was not a full advance. We wanted to do some checking (after the horse was out of the barn).

Sure enough, we learned very soon from several of the super-market buyers whom we called that the amount we were verifying represented *purchase orders* they had issued, but no such merchandise had been received or expected for a period of time. According to the invoices and receipts, shipments had been made a number of days previous.

There was a great bit of to do the next day. The ailing principal flew down here. He attempted to explain away the discrepancy, but did not quite convince us.

We terminated immediately.

I should note that we collected out the amount we advanced. We were lucky.

This served as a good lesson for me how *not* to do an initial examination, and how *not* to rely on others as to the veracity of the collateral, or the client, or the principal. You, yourself, have to make an independent and thorough examination of the prospect's books and records.

The department head's analysis of a prospective borrower is based on his or her impression of the principals, the history of the business, the industry in which the company operates, the products manufactured and sold, the housekeeping within the plant, and many other factors that contribute to the success (or lack of success) of the business being studied. In addition, a copy of the company's last three annual financial statements (preferably certified) and any available interim statements should be procured, as well as the company's most current agings of accounts receivable and accounts payable.

Statements should be spread, studied, and tested to determine whether ratios seem reasonable in relation to the type of business, its seasonality, and the profits or losses shown. Any apparent distortions, such as overly large accounts receivable, inventory, or accounts or notes payable, should be questioned to determine the reason for them.

The agings of accounts receivable should be reviewed to answer these questions:

1. If the business is seasonal, what are the high and low points of the receivables, and when do they occur? Will there be a seasonal payout of the loan?
2. What are the sizes of accounts? Many small accounts under $100 might be hard to collect. Debtors in certain industries know that the costs of collecting small accounts by mail, telephone, or collection agencies are so high that collection efforts often may be safely ignored, and that eventually the creditor will write off small balances rather than pursue them.

3. Is the concentration of receivables in one or in only a few customers?

4. Are there *contras*—accounts receivable that may be offset against payables? These, of course, are not acceptable as collateral.

5. What are the ages of the accounts? If a large proportion of accounts is over 60 days old, the accounts should be questioned to determine whether: credit has been extended too freely; collection procedures are too lax; accounts are not paying because they are waiting for credits to be issued due to poor quality; invoices are fictitious.

Accounts payable must be reviewed to answer the following questions:

1. Are there any contra situations?
2. What are the ages of the accounts? If there is a large proportion of accounts over 60 days old, how much creditor pressure is there, and how much relief will be afforded by the contemplated loan?
3. Do many payables show only past-due balances open, indicating that these creditors may have stopped shipping until old amounts are reduced or paid in full?
4. Do payables include an amount due to a subsidiary?
5. Are payments for federal and state taxes up to date?

A federal tax lien takes effect the day the notice of lien is filed; anyone who enters into a financing arrangement with a borrower whose assets were subject to a federal tax lien the day after the notice was filed, would be in a junior position. However, if the lender already is financing such a borrower and his financing statement is properly filed, then the federal tax lien will not become effective until 45 days after it is filed. The lender's priority over all loans and all collateral in existence as of the day the notice of federal tax lien is filed, is absolute and will remain. Accordingly, there is no particular problem with respect to chattel mortgages.

With revolving loans such as accounts receivable and inventory, however, both loans and collateral in existence on one day may be replaced by new loans and new collateral on some later day. The lender may continue to make new advances and take new collateral and retain his priority for a period of 45 days if he does not receive notice of the tax lien. After 45 days, the lender's security interest for new advances will be junior to the federal tax lien.

In addition, newly received collateral, whether for new advances or for old advances, will be subject primarily to the tax lien and only secondarily to the lender's lien. This 45 day period is the rule to follow *unless the lender receives actual notice of the tax lien.* Once the lender has received actual notice, all new collateral is subordinate to the lien for payment of federal taxes. State laws sometimes will follow federal law, but there is enough variation among the states to warrant checking out the lien rights of specific states with your attorney. The federal tax lien statutes have been a source of a great deal of confusion, and here again it is advisable to consult a lawyer whenever the possibility of liens is present.

Occasionally, the evaluation of a prospective borrower's business is so straightforward that it is not necessary to request cash flow and balance sheet projections. However, when in doubt, this information may greatly assist in determining whether or not the contemplated loan will be feasible or helpful. It must be kept in mind that projections not only may contain the borrower's best estimates of his business's future activity based on the contemplated loan, but also may reflect some unattainable aspirations. For example, sales projections may be made with optimism, and collections of accounts receivables may show a better turnover than the prospect has enjoyed to date. Cash flows also must take into consideration the possibility of the increased cost of interest, either because the borrower may be paying a higher rate of interest, or because he may be borrowing a larger amount of money than before. If any part of the loan package is put on a term payment basis, the payments should be incorporated within the cash projection.

Along with cash flow projections, it is helpful to have your prospective borrower prepare a balance sheet projection which will show the impact of the new, or possibly larger, debt on the borrower's net worth. Whenever part or all of new borrowings will be used for acquisitions, the submission of balance sheet projections is a necessity.

Not all of the required information may be supplied at the time of the department head's initial visit. If more positive than negative reactions and answers result from the visit, then an initial examination should be made of the prospective borrower's company and its records.

THE INITIAL EXAMINATION

The examination is one of the most important activities related to accounts receivable and inventory lending. An inquisitive, intelligent examiner may uncover many things—both good and bad—that will influence a lending officer in dealing with a prospective or present account.

Before starting an initial examination, the examiner should review the prospective account with the department head, in order to learn some of the prospect's background, including historic and financial data. The examiner should also determine, if possible, the accounts receivable which will be considered as acceptable with regard to: age, type and size; the probable percentage to be advanced against them; the number of days' float to be used; whether there is to be a service charge; whether a custodian will be used; any other items of particular interest that should be investigated.

A successful examiner must have a basic understanding of bookkeeping and accounting, and an ability to relate the figures presented to the general activity observed within the firm. In this regard, it is imperative, early in the examination, that the examiner take a tour of the plant or warehouse to view housekeeping and storage facilities, and get an idea of whether the activity, the accounts receivable, and the inventory that are observed make sense in relation to the company's records.

Exhibit 3, Accounts Receivable Examination Report, is a typical examination form used for both initial and regular examinations. The form is self-explanatory; every item called for should be completed by the examiner in as much detail as possible.

Examination Procedures

In addition to the information called for, the examiner should answer the following questions:

1. Are all remittances keyed to their respective invoices? This is good bookkeeping and will expose any skipped invoices as well as facilitate the aging of accounts.

2. What is the frequency and size of credit memos? A familiar fraudulent practice is to issue a fictitious invoice, obtain funds on it, and then cancel it with a credit memo. This practice is almost impossible to catch through a verification of receivables program if the credit memo is issued within the same month as the invoice.

3. Is there evidence of unusually large invoices being issued? A few years ago a commercial finance company made loans to a soft drink bottler on the security of receivables created by sales to large grocery chains. At that time, the company's average invoice size ranged from $300 to $500, but one day three invoices were submitted (along with

(*Text continues on page 45*)

Metropolitan National Bank

ACCOUNTS RECEIVABLE EXAMINATION REPORT

Client _____ Location _____

Principal _____ Type of Business _____

Advance _____ % S.C. _____ Per Annum   Float _____ Days Minimum Charge $ _____

Terms of Sale: _____

Delinquent Invoices to be Repurchased _____ Days after _____ Date

Assignment Basis: Specific _____ Bulk _____ Subject to 10% Rule _____ _____

Supporting Data Received: (* = Retained by Custodian)

Copies of Invoices _____   Original Checks _____

Evidence of Delivery _____   Remittance Advices _____

Copy of Sales Journal _____   Copy Cash Receipts Journal _____

Monthly Aged Trial Balance _____   Credit Memoranda _____

Monthly Statements _____   Recordak Film _____

Inventory Loan: Warehouse Receipts _____ U.C.C. Lien _____ Advance _____ % Rate _____ %

Loan Value $ _____ at (Date) _____ Collateral Value $ _____ at (Date) _____

Chattel Mortgage: Appraised Value $ _____ at (Date) _____

INDEX TO EXAMINATION REPORT

Date of Report _____ Previous Report Date _____

Date Exam. Performed _____ Time Spent _____ Days

Examiner _____

1. ITEMS REQUIRING IMMEDIATE ATTENTION: _____

_____

_____

_____

_____

_____

EXHIBIT 3—continued

Accounts Receivable Examination Report

35

2. <u>MNB NET INVESTMENT</u>: Date: _____ _____

	Current Exam. Date	Prior Exam. Date

Accounts Receivable (Before Adjustment) $ _____ _____

Inventory _____ _____

Chattel Mortgage or _____ _____ _____

    Total Net Funds Advanced _____ _____

Less: _____ _____ _____

    Total MNB Funds Advanced $ _____ _____

3. <u>CONDITION OF MNB RECEIVABLES</u>:

Current and Not Due $ _____ _____ % _____ _____ %

 1 - 30 Days past due _____ _____ _____ _____

31 - 60 Days past due _____ _____ _____ _____

61 - 90 Days past due _____ _____ _____ _____

91 - Days Past Due and Older _____ _____ _____ _____

Contra _____ _____ _____ _____

10% rule _____ _____ _____ _____

Excess of credit limit _____ _____ _____ _____

Other Ineligible Receivables _____ _____ _____ _____

    Total Ineligible _____ _____ _____ _____

Credit Balances – R _____ _____ _____ _____

    Total Assigned Accounts _____ 100.0 _____ 100.0

Total Eligible Accounts (Incl. Above) _____ _____

Proper Advance at _____ % _____ _____

Actual Loan Balance _____ _____

Net Funds Available or Short (R) _____ _____

Unassigned Accounts:

Government _____ _____

Foreign _____ _____

Affiliated Company _____ _____

Other _____ _____

EXHIBIT 3—continued

Accounts Receivable Examination Report

36

4. <u>RECONCILIATION TO CLIENT GENERAL LEDGER</u>:   Date: _____

	Total Assigned Accounts Receivable	Total Net Funds Advanced
Balance Per MNB Controls (Page 2)	_____	_____
Receivables Not Assigned	_____	xxxxxxxxxxxxxxxxxxxxxxxx
Other Reconciling Items (Explain Fully):		
_____	_____	_____
_____	_____	_____
_____	_____	_____
_____	_____	_____
Balances Per Client General Ledger	_____	_____

5. <u>TEN LARGEST ASSIGNED ACCOUNTS RECEIVABLES</u> (over $1,000.00):

<u>D&B</u>	<u>Name</u>	<u>Total</u>	Current and <u>Not Due</u>	<u>1 – 30</u>	Past Due <u>31 – 60</u>	<u>Over 60</u>
_____	_____	_____	_____	_____	_____	_____
_____	_____	_____	_____	_____	_____	_____
_____	_____	_____	_____	_____	_____	_____
_____	_____	_____	_____	_____	_____	_____
_____	_____	_____	_____	_____	_____	_____
_____	_____	_____	_____	_____	_____	_____
_____	_____	_____	_____	_____	_____	_____
_____	_____	_____	_____	_____	_____	_____
_____	_____	_____	_____	_____	_____	_____
_____	_____	_____	_____	_____	_____	_____
	Totals $ _____	$ _____	$ _____	$ _____	$ _____	$ _____

Percent of Total Accts. Held   _____%

Explain status of all items over 60 days past due (bad credit, dispute, turned over to attorney, etc.) Review correspondence files.

_____

_____

_____

_____

_____

6. <u>ACCOUNTS RECEIVABLE REVIEW</u>:

a. Investigation of Collection Reports:

(1) All items checked to cash receipts book for month of _____

EXHIBIT 3—continued

Accounts Receivable Examination Report

37

(2) Major C/M's, overpayments, shortages, etc. reviewed and investigated for period _____ , including checking of items to books of original entry and customer ledger cards, and investigation of credit or correspondence files.

(3) Attach repurchase letters for last 3 months with notations of present status of each item.

b. Extended Terms Granted:

_____

_____

_____

c. Consignment Accounts or Guaranteed Sales or Return Privileges Noted:

_____

_____

_____

d. Contras Assigned:

Name	Receivable Amount	Payable Amount
_____	$ _____	_____
_____	_____	_____
_____	_____	_____
_____	_____	_____

e. Bad Debts:

Reserve balance as of (Date) _____ $ _____

Charged off in past 12 months _____ $ _____

Estimated losses in present outstandings (List larger accounts) _____

_____

_____

_____

f. Additional Comments on Accounts Receivable: (Attach memo with complete explanation, if necessary)

(1) Are there any skipped invoices on the 10 largest accounts? Yes _____ No _____

Explain _____

(2) Have any of the 10 largest customers made deposits against future billings? Yes _____ No _____

Explain _____

(3) Have any customers submitted notes or post dated checks in payment of account? Yes _____ No _____

List _____

(4) On any of 5 largest accounts has client:

(a) Shipped in excess of amount authorized on purchase order? Yes _____ No _____

(b) Shipped before authorized by purchase order? Yes _____ No _____

Explain _____

(5) Are any bill and hold invoices assigned to us? Yes _____ No _____

Explain _____

EXHIBIT 3—continued

38

Accounts Receivable Examination Report

(6) Total cash sales in past 6 months $ _____

(7) General condition of receivable records _____

(8) Are cash collections being forwarded promptly? _____

(9) Is shipping evidence being forwarded promptly? _____

(10) Who prepared shipping receipts? _____

(11) Does carrier leave supply of signed blank receipts with client? _____

(12) Are credit memoranda being forwarded to account debtors when issued? _____

(13) How often are credit memos prepared? _____

(14) How is assignment shown on receivable records? _____

(15) Did all verification exceptions check out to your satisfaction? Yes _____ No _____

     Explain _____

(16) Bulk receivables test-checked to customer ledgers: By No. _____%   By Amount _____%

(17) Are aged trial balances accurate, reliable and complete? _____

(18) Was summary of all differences sent to Accounts Receivable Dept.? _____

(19) CUSTODIAN ACCOUNTS: Custodian's Name _____

     Does the custodian hold all invoices, shipping documents and other papers required by us? _____
     _____

     What is the physical safeguarding of Custodian's records? _____
     _____

     Invoices and shipping documents examined for period _____

     For what period were sales and collections traced from Custodian's records to our controls? _____
     _____

(20) Other Comments: _____
     _____
     _____
     _____
     _____
     _____
     _____
     _____
     _____
     _____
     _____

7. SALES COMPARISON		Gross Sales	Returns and Allowances	% of Sales
_____ Months Ended _____	$	_____	_____	_____
Same Period Last Year		_____	_____	_____
Increase or Decrease (R)	$	_____ _____%	_____ _____%	
Cash Discounts and % of Collections For Period		$ _____ _____%		
Sales Backlog At _____ :	$	_____ Same Date Last Year $ _____		

EXHIBIT 3—continued

Accounts Receivable Examination Report

39

ACCOUNTS RECEIVABLE CONTROL ANALYSIS FOR LAST 12 MONTHS:

Month	Year	Gross Sales	Returns & Allowances	% To Sales	Accounts Rec. Bal. B.O.M.	Collections	% To Receiv.
TOTALS							

Accounts Receivable Turnover of _____ Days for the _____ Mos. ended _____
(Based on Collections)
_____ Days for the Year ended _____

Any large or unusual C/M's? (List reasons) _____

_____

Any large deductions in cash receipts journal? _____

_____

Were all credit memos for returns & allowances sent to MNB? _____

If not, why? _____

8. INVENTORY REVIEW   Amount as of _____ $ _____

Is Inventory Physical _____ or Estimated (State Basis) _____

Increase of $ _____ or _____ % Since Fiscal Year End (Date) _____

Inventory Turnover of _____ Days for the _____ Mos. ended _____
(Based on cost of sales)
_____ Days for the Year ended _____

Date of most recent physical inventory _____

Your inspection reveals (general condition, possible obsolescence or overstock, etc.)

_____

_____

_____

9. CASH REVIEW

Banks Used _____ Any change since last exam? Yes _____ No _____

Date of General Bank Reconciliation Reviewed _____

Cancelled checks reviewed for month of _____

EXHIBIT 3—continued

Accounts Receivable Examination Report

40

Any checks outstanding over one month? _____ Amounts $ _____

Why outstanding? _____

Any unreleased checks? _____ Amount $ _____ Explain _____

Any large, non-routine checks or large checks payable to "Cash"? Yes _____ No _____

Describe _____

Did you reconcile one month's deposits with funds advanced by MNB _____ Which month? _____ Were differences explain-

ed to your satisfaction? _____

Analysis of exchange account _____

10. <u>ANALYSIS OF LIABILITIES</u>

a. <u>Accounts Payable Aging by Invoice Date:</u>

	Current Exam. Date		Prior Exam. Date	
Current	$ _____	____ %	$ _____	____ %
31 – 60 Days	_____	____	_____	____
61 – 90 Days	_____	____	_____	____
91 – 120 Days	_____	____	_____	____
Over 120 Days	_____	____	_____	____
Book Overdraft	_____	____	_____	____
Totals	$ _____	____	$ _____	____
Special Terms-Balances Due in More Than 30 Days	_____	____	_____	____
Accounts Payable Turnover	_____ Days		_____ Days	

Are any goods purchased on consignment or Trust receipts? _____

_____

_____

Terms of major suppliers _____

_____

b. Ten Largest Accounts Payable (over $1,000.00 only – Show Special Terms if Granted):

Spec. Terms	Name	Total	Current	31-60 Days	61-90 Days	Over 90 Days
_____	_____	$ _____	$ _____	$ _____	$ _____	$ _____
_____	_____	_____	_____	_____	_____	_____
_____	_____	_____	_____	_____	_____	_____
_____	_____	_____	_____	_____	_____	_____
_____	_____	_____	_____	_____	_____	_____
_____	_____	_____	_____	_____	_____	_____
_____	_____	_____	_____	_____	_____	_____
_____	_____	_____	_____	_____	_____	_____
_____	_____	_____	_____	_____	_____	_____
_____	_____	_____	_____	_____	_____	_____
	Totals	$ _____	$ _____	$ _____	$ _____	$ _____

EXHIBIT 3—continued

41

Accounts Receivable Examination Report

Review correspondence files of above accounts with old balances to note if litigation is threatened.

Comment_____

Any unusual deductions taken from accounts payable checks?   Yes_____ No_____

Total amount of unentered bills $_____

Accounts payable control reconciled to general ledger as of _____ Per G L $_____

c. Notes Payable: Date: _____

Secured:

Lender	Collateral	Due in 1 year	Due after 1 year	Total
_____	_____	_____	_____	_____
_____	Accounts Receivable	_____	_____	_____
_____	Inventory	_____	_____	_____
_____	Machinery & Equipment	_____	_____	_____
_____	_____	_____	_____	_____
_____	_____	_____	_____	_____
_____	_____	_____	_____	_____
Total Secured		==========	==========	==========

Unsecured: —   Subordinated

_____	_____	_____	_____	_____
_____	_____	_____	_____	_____
_____	_____	_____	_____	_____
Total Unsecured Subordinated	_____	==========	==========	==========

Unsecured: —   Unsubordinated

_____	_____	_____	_____	_____
_____	_____	_____	_____	_____
_____	_____	_____	_____	_____
Total Unsecured Unsubordinated	_____	==========	==========	==========

Officers Loans:

_____	_____	_____	_____	_____
_____	_____	_____	_____	_____
_____	_____	_____	_____	_____
Total Officers Loans	_____	==========	==========	==========

New notes since last exam? _____

_____
_____
_____
_____
_____
_____
_____

EXHIBIT 3—continued

Accounts Receivable Examination Report

42

d. Taxes:

Type	Accrued as of (Date) _____	Unpaid and Delinquent as of (Date) _____	Last Payment		
			Amount	Date	Check #*
Withholding	$ _____	$ _____	$ _____	_____	_____
Social Security	_____	_____	_____	_____	_____
State Sales or Use	_____	_____	_____	_____	_____
Personal Property	_____	_____	_____	_____	_____
Real Estate	_____	_____	_____	_____	_____
Federal Income	_____	_____	_____	_____	_____
State Income	_____	_____	_____	_____	_____
	_____	_____	_____	_____	_____
	_____	_____	_____	_____	_____
Totals	$ _____	_____			

Were cancelled checks, tax returns, depository receipts, or receipted tax bills checked to substantiate last payment on all of above items? _____

*Also show I.R.S. block # endorsement on checks for withholding and social security taxes.

e. Officers Loans (Receivable)

_____

_____

_____

New Loans or Repayments since last examination: _____

_____

_____

_____

_____

_____

11. FINANCIAL ANALYSIS:

		_____ Mos. Ended		_____ Mos. Ended	
a. Summary of Operations:		_____		_____	
Net Sales	$	_____	100.0%	_____	100.0%
Gross Profit		_____	_____	_____	_____
Operating Profit (Loss – R)		_____	_____	_____	_____
Net Profit (Loss – R) before Taxes		_____	_____	_____	_____
Net Profit (Loss – R) after Taxes		_____	_____	_____	_____
Cash Gain (Loss – R)		_____	_____	_____	_____

EXHIBIT 3—continued

43

Accounts Receivable Examination Report

b. Statement of Working Capital: Date: _____ _____   Increase or Decrease (R)

Current Assets $ _____ _____   _____

Current Liabilities   _____ _____   _____

Working Capital   _____ _____   _____

Fixed Assets (Net)   _____ _____   _____

Other Assets   _____ _____   _____

    Total   _____ _____   _____

Deferred Liabilities   _____ _____   _____

Net Worth per books $ _____ _____   _____

c. Analysis of Tangible Net Worth as of (Date) _____

Capital Stock Per Books _____

Capital Surplus Per Books _____

Earned Surplus Per Books At Beginning _____

Add Or (Deduct): _____

_____

Book Net Worth At End Of Period _____

Add or (Deduct): _____

_____

_____

_____

_____

_____

_____

Tangible Net Worth At End of Period _____

d. Officers Salaries:

Name	Title	Amounts Paid for _____ Months Ended _____	Additional Compensation
_____	_____	_____	_____
_____	_____	_____	_____
_____	_____	_____	_____
_____	_____	_____	_____
_____	_____	_____	_____
_____	_____	_____	_____

12. GENERAL AND COMMENTS:

a. Financial Statements:

General condition of company's books _____

General ledger posted through _____

Company statement obtained as of _____

EXHIBIT 3—continued 44
Accounts Receivable Examination Report

Were major items checked to general ledger? _____

Fiscal Year-end _____ CPA _____ Fully Certified? _____

b. General Activity of Operations Noted: _____

_____

_____

_____

c. Cooperation Received: _____

_____

d. Examiners Comments: _____

_____

_____

_____

_____

_____

_____

_____

Signed _____

New Accounts

Purpose of loan:

1. _____ $ _____

2. _____ _____

3. _____ _____

4. _____ _____

5. _____ _____

Estimated availability:

Acceptable receivables $ _____ x _____% $ _____

Acceptable inventory _____ x _____% _____

Machinery & equipment _____ x _____% _____

Other _____ _____ _____

    TOTAL

Average size of invoice _____

Average number of invoices per month _____

Approximate number of customers _____

Approximate number of checks _____

others) showing sales of $3,000 each—$9,000 in all! It occurred to the account executive who reviewed the invoices that $9,000 worth of soft drinks at wholesale prices might fill a small reservoir. He immediately called the principal for an explanation and insisted on visiting the customers to see this small mountain of bottles. None of the goods were in evidence in any of the three places, and, although the principals made many attempts to explain, nothing made sense. Alertness and immediate action caught this fraud at its inception. Careful liquidation procedures went into effect with no loss to the lender or suppliers.

4. Are there any billings to customers on a progress-billing basis? If, during the period of a contract, the borrower discontinues business either through failure or otherwise, the customer can rightfully say to the borrower that the last invoices submitted will not be paid until the contract is completed in full. At such a time, there could be a number of invoices outstanding against which the lender had already advanced sizeable amounts. The lender, of course, has to determine whether the contracts can be completed (usually impossible under liquidation conditions) or the amount involved ought to be written off.

5. Are there any unusual deductions from customer remittances, unrecorded contras, advertising allowances, or unreported returns? Such items may affect the percent of advance to be made against receivables.

6. Are there any unexplained cash receipts? When a borrower is pledging accounts receivable, virtually his only source of cash should be from the lender. If other deposits are shown, it could mean a duplicate assignment of receivables to another lender, or a conversion of funds.

7. Are there checks made out to cash? This could hide large withdrawals for personal use, or payments to outsiders for services not connected with the business.

8. Are there any withdrawals against any subordinated loan accounts? This is a direct act of default that requires prompt and detailed explanation.

Sometimes—especially when large amounts are involved—loans due to principals, subsidiaries, or affiliates are partially subordinated. This can be a serious mistake and every effort should be made to get the entire indebtedness subordinated with the understanding that any reasonable request for a reduction will be permitted. The definition of reasonable, however, has to be the sole judgment of the lender. If subordinated loans are left outstanding and the company starts to deteriorate, the borrower has the option of withdrawing the unsubordinated balance, which could precipitate a downhill slide with many bad effects on the collectability of collateral.

9. Who prepares shipping receipts? In one case, an alert examiner noticed while working about a client's office that a bookkeeper was writing out and signing shipping receipts. He immediately checked on previously issued receipts and discovered such an obvious similarity that there was no question a fraud was being perpetrated on the current lender.

Another situation encountered occasionally is one in which a truckman has left a pad of receipts (sometimes signed) with an account. This practice opens the door wide for the creation of fraudulent invoices.

Examination reports should include comments by the examiner on any items that need clarification or amplification, as well as the examiner's opinions as to the borrower's financial responsibility, the prospects of the borrower for future progress, and the capabilities of present management.

Search of UCC Filings

Before submitting a report, the examiner should make a search of UCC-1 filings either in person or by using Form UCC-11 to get a record of all prior filings on accounts receivable and inventory. Exhibits 4 and 5 are samples of these UCC forms. Places for filing will vary by state; therefore, the bank's attorney should be consulted in the event there is any doubt as to where the search should be made.

It sometimes happens that a prospect has borrowed from another source on the security of its accounts receivable and inventory, but, after paying the loan in full, has neglected to get a UCC-1 termination statement. The termination copy of the UCC-1 filing should always be secured and filed before filing the bank's UCC-1 notice of liens and before any funds are advanced.

Example of Good Initial Examination

Much of the foregoing has been directed at assisting the bank in ferreting out any larcenous intentions of prospective borrowers, but, in reality, fraud is infrequent and premeditated fraud is extremely rare. However, it is always a possibility, and a good examiner continually should be aware that it can appear in any account on which he is working, no matter how innocent the account appears on the surface. Fraud seems to occur most often when adverse conditions bring pressure to bear on an otherwise honest businessman, who temporarily yields to the temptation to "borrow for only a little while" from his lender.

EXHIBIT 4
UCC-1

47

UNIFORM COMMERCIAL CODE — FINANCING STATEMENT — FORM UCC-1

INSTRUCTIONS
1. PLEASE TYPE this form. Fold only along perforation for mailing.
2. Remove Secured Party and Debtor copies and send other 3 copies with interleaved carbon paper to the filing officer.
3. When filing is to be with more than one office, Form UCC-2 may be placed over this set to avoid double typing.
4. If the space provided for any item(s) on the form is inadequate the item(s) should be continued on additional sheets, preferable 5" x 8" or 8" by 10". Only one copy of such additional sheets need be presented to the filing officer with a set of three copies of the financing statement. Long schedules of collateral, indentures, etc. may be on any size paper that is convenient for the secured party.
5. If collateral is crops or goods which are or are to become fixtures, describe generally the real estate and give name of record owner.
6. When a copy of the security agreement is used as a financing statement, it is requested that it be accompanied by a completed but unsigned set of these forms, without extra fee.
7. At the time of original filing, filing officer should return third copy as an acknowledgement. At a later time, secured party may date and sign Termination Legend and use third copy as a Termination Statement.

This FINANCING STATEMENT is presented to a filing officer for filing pursuant to the Uniform Commercial Code.

1 Debtor(s) (Last Name First) and address(es)	2 Secured Party(ies) and address(es)	3 Maturity date (if any):
		For Filing Officer (Date, Time, Number, and Filing Office)

4 This financing statement covers the following types (or items) of property:

Check ☒ if covered: ☐ Proceeds of Collateral are also covered ☐ Products of Collateral are also covered No. of additional sheets presented:

Filed with: ....

By: ....   By: ....
    Signature(s) of Debtor(s)   Signature(s) of Secured Party(ies)

Filing Officer Copy — Alphabetical   This form of financing statement is approved by the Secretary of State.

STANDARD FORM — UNIFORM COMMERCIAL CODE — FORM UCC-1 Forms may be purchased from Samuel Narcus, Boston, Mass.

EXHIBIT 5

UCC-11

48

Uniform Commercial Code — REQUEST FOR INFORMATION OR COPIES

IMPORTANT - Read instructions on back before filling out form.

REQUEST FOR COPIES OR INFORMATION. Present in DUPLICATE to Filing Officer.

1 Debtor(s) (Last Name First) and Address(es)	Party requesting information or copies: (Name and Address)	For Filing Officer, Date, Time, No. - Filing Office

☐ INFORMATION REQUEST:

Filing officer, please furnish certificate showing whether there is on file as of _____, 19____ at _____ M., any presently effective financing statement naming the above named debtor(s) and any statement of assignment thereof, and if there is, giving the date and hour of filing of each such statement and the name(s) and address(es) of each secured party(ies) therein. Enclosed is uniform fee of $3.00. Filing officer please furnish exact copies of each page of financing statements and statements of assignment listed below, at the rate of $1.00 each, which are on file with your office. Enclosed is $_____ fee for copies requested. In case any of said statements contain more than one page the undersigned agrees to pay the sum of $1.00 for each additional page payable in advance.

Date_____

_____
(Signature of Requesting Party)

☐ COPY REQUEST:

File No.	Date and Hour of Filing	Name(s) and Address(es) of Secured Party(ies) and Assignees, if any

CERTIFICATE: The undersigned filing officer hereby certifies that:

☐ the above listing is a record of all presently effective financing statements and statements of assignment which name the above debtor(s) and which are on file in my office as of _____, 19____ at _____ M.

☐ the attached _____ pages are true and exact copies of all available financing statements or statements of assignment listed in above request.

_____
Date

_____
Signature of Filing Officer

PUBLISHED BY HOBBS & WARREN, INC., BOSTON, MASS. 02101

COPY 1
FORM UCC-11

The following is an example of a good initial examination. It is taken from a panel session on examinations conducted by the National Commercial Finance Conference and relates the experience of an examiner who was investigating a prospective borrower for a large commercial finance company.

I'd like to go on to a specific case history which started out as an initial audit, but interestingly enough, turned out to be an interim audit for a bank which was financing the company at the time.

The company was a tanner of imported hides. As I said, the company, at the time of our examination, was financing with a bank under a receivable and inventory basis.

The company had been in business some fifteen years, and the reputation of the principals checked out extremely well, both with the bank and with the major suppliers.

The company had provided us with financial statements for the last five years, bearing unqualified certifications by their CPA. These statements showed a steady increase in sales to $2.5 million, with modest and steady profits shown during the entire five years.

The year-end December statement (we examined the account in May) showed a substantial increase in inventory which resulted in the company's being unable to repay its seasonal inventory loans with the bank. The principal explained that the large inventory resulted from heavy purchases made at the end of the year, and these purchases were made in anticipation of increasing high prices.

He said that his order position for the coming year was extremely strong and he expected a large volume increase and a good profit because of the good inventory position that he had going into the year. An increased line of credit was required because of the anticipated larger volume, and his bank had expressed an unwillingness to go along with him because of his limited net worth, because of the tight money conditions that existed at the time, and because of his inability to clear up his seasonal inventory borrowing.

All in all, the collateral, the management and the operating history of the company appeared to be acceptable, so we decided to go ahead and make an examination of the account. The examination, initially, appeared to be very routine, with the exception of one thing, and this was the analysis of the accounts receivable controls.

The control indicated that up until the prior year, returns and allowances had averaged about 2-3 percent of sales. However, during the past year there had been a slow but steady increase in this percentage, up to a 12-15 percent rate toward the end of the year, and this rate continued through March, which was the last month it was put in the general ledger.

The general ledger showed total receivables of $400,000 at the end of March. We were given an April aging which showed

$275,000 of receivables. Since it is our normal practice to tie the detailed aging into the general ledger, the examiner listed the invoices for the month of April which totalled $100,000, and the cash collections were listed by him for the month, which totalled $125,000; so that in adding and subtracting the April sales and collections from the $400,000 March ledger figure, we came up with a pro-forma ledger figure of $375,000—$100,000 more than the aging showed.

When the examiner asked the principal about this discrepancy, the principal said that he had issued a large number of credits in April, eliminating old disputed items and other things that should have been cleaned up a long time ago.

The examiner asked to see the credits which totalled $100,000, and a review of these credits determined that these were not old invoices—they were current invoices under three months old.

The examiner naturally went back to the invoices, and he noticed that much of the merchandise had been delivered by hand to customers in the neighborhood, one of whom received a credit for $40,000. Of course, for these hand deliveries there was no delivery evidence and the examiner noticed that the signatures obtained from different truckers were all identical.

Moreover, the company was not able to provide the examiner with evidence for the returned goods for which credit memos had been issued.

With this information in hand, the examiner proceeded to verify by telephone the supposed credits and found that in the larger cases customers refused to verify them, but in many of the smaller ones the customers knew nothing about them, nor about the invoices that were being cancelled.

It should be noted that the verification of the April aging, which was the one we were working from, uncovered nothing because all the questionable receivables had been eliminated by the so-called credits. Going beyond this, the examiner began to take a closer look at other aspects of the business.

In looking at the analysis of the accounts payable control the examiner noticed that purchases had no sensible relationship to the inventories which were shown at the end of the year. The year-end inventories exceeded the purchases for the prior six months, and clearly there had not been the heavy year-end buying that the principal had told us about.

At this point, the principal of the company was not aware of the examiner's suspicions and he granted permission to get in touch with the CPA to obtain a copy of the prior year's receivable verification and inventory work sheets.

The inventory papers were sent to him immediately, but not the receivable verifications. More about this just a little later. Since the particular items of the inventory were identifiable to a specific purchase invoice by lot and item number, the examiner was able to verify the pricing of the individual items in the inventory.

He found that the pricing, in all cases, exceeded the actual costs and in many cases was double that cost.

It was now clear that, rather than the modest profits that had been shown in the company's audited financial statements which were given to the bank and to large suppliers and to us, there had been very substantial losses sustained in the last year and a half. And, it was clear that these losses had been hidden by the inflation of nonexistent sales, profits, receivables and inventories—the whole works.

Moreover, it was apparent that the company had been reporting erroneous collateral to its bank and now, for some reason, was trying to "come clean" by the issuing of $100,000 of credits. There was no indication that any funds had been withdrawn by the principal; in fact, his drawings had been modest.

A meeting was called with the principal and with the CPA. Confronted with the facts, the principal admitted that he had done wrong. Over a year ago the market price for his raw materials, hides imported from overseas, had suddenly taken a drop from $24 per dozen to $6 per dozen in a period of four to five months. Immediately prior to this drop in the market price, in an effort to hedge against prices that had been constantly rising for four years, the principal made purchases at the $24 level to cover his next ten-month needs.

When the market dropped he sustained catastrophic losses and, in an effort to save his business, he saw no alternative other than the one he took. However, he now recognized that he had done wrong to assign nonexistent receivables to his bank and put the phony credits through his books so that the receivables he gave to us, his new prospective lender, would be clean. However, it was clear that he did not intend to tell us about the credits, nor about the inflated inventory, nor about the inflated financial statements if we didn't find something by ourselves.

The CPA stated that he had been the company's accountant since its inception fifteen years ago and that he had a warm relationship with the principal and that he had watched, with great satisfaction, the fine growth of his client's business. He said that in the last year-end audit, he had been present at the physical count, but he turned over the quantity listings to be priced by the principal and he had not checked the pricing himself.

Moreover, he did not circularize the accounts receivable because he had checked with the company's receivable financing bank and they told him they had turned up nothing unusual in their verification efforts.

Fortunately as it turned out, the bank did have enough collateral to come out of its loans. Suppliers, who had made heavy credit available on an extended note basis (as is a practice in this particular trade) did take heavy losses. Had the bank had a field examination program, all this would have been caught much earlier.

In effect, we performed what turned out to be an interim examination for the bank, so I guess you might say that we were the cop that caught the guy trying to leave the bank. Had the examination not been performed, and had the bank acceded to the company's requests for additional loans, this fraud might not have been caught for many months and the result might not have been so fortunate for the bank.

I think this was a classic case of the type of things that the examination is supposed to protect us against—fraud in receivables, fraud in inventories and fraud in the financial statements that were presented to us.

An example such as this shows clearly that the smallest part of an examiner's job is to be sure that numbers add up correctly and that they check with the borrower's (or prospective borrower's) general ledger. An examiner's chief contribution to the protection of his or her employer is in an ability to determine that the numbers on the company's books and on financial statements—certified or not—make sense in relation to the firm's history and the current operation of the company. A good examiner satisfies *himself* that figures shown on a borrower's books are realistic, and confirms, rather than relies upon, statements made by management or the company's accountant.

CHAPTER 4

Putting the Loan on the Books

ACCEPTANCE OR REJECTION OF THE LOAN

When the examiner has completed the report (which can take two days to two weeks depending on the size and complexity of the company and the loan requested), it should be submitted to the department head, along with spread sheets, credit reports, aged lists of receivables and payables, the examiner's comments, and any other data that will assist the department head in making a decision to accept or reject the account.

When studying the information compiled by the department head and the examiner, many factors will be considered in arriving at a decision. Some of these factors are: the capabilities of the management; the acceptability of the product or service in the marketplace; the present financial condition of the prospect and the chances of showing improvement; and the *hard* value of the collateral offered—how much the collateral can deteriorate and still cover the amount of the intended loan.

Every loan that the bank makes—whether secured or unsecured—has to be made with a constructive attitude, and the persons who administrate the loan must do everything possible to contribute to the success of the borrower. On the other hand, the loan officer's paramount consideration should be the safety of the bank's principal. This consideration constantly raises questions: What is the *real* value of the collateral today? How quickly can the loan be liquidated, even under adverse conditions? How much servicing of the loan will be required in relation to the income derived from it?

If, after due deliberation, the decision is made to reject the loan application, notification should be made promptly in order to give the former prospect time to restructure the company's borrowing needs or to make application to another lender.

If, however, the account is found to be acceptable, the prospect should be notified and final agreement should be reached on the following points:

1. The age of accounts that will be considered as acceptable collateral;
2. The percentage to be advanced against the receivables;
3. The term of the loan;
4. If inventory is involved, the kind of inventory that will be accepted as collateral and the percentage of advance which will be made;
5. The rate of interest and any other charges which will be made by the lender;
6. The possible assignment of patents, if any. Patent values will sometimes be worth more than the liquidation values of other assets;
7. The possible pledge of machinery and equipment, tools and dies, etc., as extra collateral;
8. Termination privileges, if any;
9. Any other particulars that should be added to the security agreement, or that are to be made part of a special loan agreement.

When attempting to structure a loan, some or all of these considerations may be challenged by the prospective borrower. In some cases the prospect may be perfectly justified in disagreeing with one or more of the bank's requests; but for the most part, the bank should explain as diplomatically as possible that the lender's function is to loan money on the most secure basis possible and with every intention of getting it back at a profit. The bank does not look for, nor is it usually entitled to, any profits of the business; therefore, the bank should not be expected to take any equity position in the company by making loans which have a high degree of risk. It is not easy—and is frequently impossible—to get the borrower to fully understand the bank's philosophy of lending, but the structuring of a loan can be extremely important to the bank's secured position for the duration of the loan. The key words to keep in mind during negotiations are fairness and firmness; the main object is to insure that the bank's secured position is as fortified as possible with good, valuable, and easily disposable collateral.

When these matters have been finalized, the department head should advise the bank's attorneys of the details of the transactions and consult with them as to the various documents required to properly document the loan.

Incidentally, it is recommended that a change of address form provided by the United States Post Office be included in the documents. In the unhappy event that liquidation must take place in the future, the bank would have the necessary authority on hand to immediately direct the borrower's mail to itself.

PREPARING TO SIGN ON THE NEW ACCOUNT

While documents are being prepared, a date for signing should be set with the principals, the guarantors, and any other signatories needed. During, or just before, the signing process, the bank's examiners should be requested to make a final check on the collateral to update it to the date of closing. For example, if the signing is to take place on the fifteenth of the month and if receivables are to be used as collateral, then the examiner should inspect the last aged list of receivables that has been cross-checked with the prospect's general ledger. To this should be added all sales made since the date of the last aging; care must be taken that sales do not include any unacceptable accounts such as poor credits, sales to affiliates, or contras. From the new total, the examiner should deduct any collections or credit memos.

If inventory is also to be used as collateral, the examiner should go back to the last calculated inventory, add new items bought or produced—at cost—and deduct the cost of goods sold or the cost of raw materials converted to work-in-process or finished goods. The examiner should also make a final check on UCC filings, first determining that no notices of liens have been filed since the last check, and then filing the bank's own UCC statements.

When this is done, the examiner should confirm the filing to the department head and give him or her the computation of the funds available at the agreed percentages on the collateral submitted.

Exhibit 6 is a suggested new account check sheet, which will help the department head to be sure that all items connected with a new account have been handled.

With the use of the recommended documents and procedures, it is not necessary to issue notes for each advance that the bank makes. The

(Text continues on page 59)

EXHIBIT 6

56

New Account Check Sheet

Metropolitan National Bank

NEW ACCOUNT CHECK SHEET

Name: _____   Address: _____

(Check if required)	Requirements	Date Received	By	Remarks
( )	1. Dun Report			
( )	2. Trade References			
( )	3. Bank References			
( )	4. Reports on Individual			
( )	5. Financial Statement			
( )	6. Special List Checked			
( )	7. Cleared with Retail Credit Report			
( )	8. Examination of books completed			

Note: Above requirements to be checked by account executive. Following requirements to be checked by Legal Department and approval to be noted at bottom.

(Check if required)	Requirements	Date Received	By	Remarks
( )	9. Search for prior recordings, filings and liens			
( )	(a) County Recorder of _____			
( )	(b) Secretary of State of _____			
( )	(c) U.S. District Court _____			
( )	(d) Port Authority of _____			
( )	(e) F.A.A.			
( )	(f) Town or City _____			
( )	10. Filing and/or recordation receipt(s)			
( )	(a) U.C.C. (See comments)			
( )	(b) Notice of Intent to Assign Receivables			
( )	(c) Notice of Factor's Lien			
( )	(d) Chattel Mortgage			
( )	(e) Real Estate Mortgage			
( )	(f) Other _____			
	_____			

EXHIBIT 6—continued

New Account Check Sheet

57

New Account Check Sheet — Page Two

(Check if required	Requirements	Date Received	By	Remarks
( ) 11.	Directors resolutions (and waiver of notice, if required) authorizing:			
	(a) Receivable Loan Agreement			
	(b) Inventory Loan Agreement			
	(c) Chattel Loans			
	(d) Real Estate Loans			
	(e) Guaranties			
	(f) Other_____			
( ) 12.	Shareholders resolution or consent and waiver of notice, if required			
( ) 13.	Subordination agreements of			
	(a) _____			
	(b) _____			
	(c) _____			
( ) 14.	Notes stamped or deposited			
( ) 15.	Resolutions of directors: Re #13			
( ) 16.	(a) Collateral assignment of lease and landlord's consent			
	(b) Mortgagee's lien waiver			
( ) 17.	Pledge Agreement (a) Stock Certificates endorsed (or stock power attached) and deposited			
( ) 18.	Custodian Agreement			
	(a) Client Agreement			
	(b) Employee Agreement			
	(c) Employment forms			
( ) 19.	Bailment Agreement			
( ) 20.	Letter of Direction to pay			
	(a) _____			
	(b) _____			
( ) 21.	Release/reassignment by			
	(a) _____			
	(b) _____			

EXHIBIT 6—continued

New Account Check Sheet

58

New Account Check Sheet — Page Three

(Check if required)	Requirements	Date Received	By	Remarks
( )	22. Affidavit as to liens			
( )	23. Option of counsel			
( )	24. Participation			
	(a) Agreement with bank			
	(b) Three party agreement			
	(c) Rate letter			
	(d) Participation certificate			
( )	25. Tax Stamps			
( )	26. Endorsement of Insurance			
( )	27. Assignment of insurance proceeds			
	(a) Inventory, plant, chattels			
	(b) Life			
( )	28. Certificate of title			
( )	29. Deed of real estate			
( )	30. Title Insurance Policy			
( )	31. Bill of Sale			
( )	32. Bulk sale documents			
	(a) Affidavit			
	(b) Notice			
	(c) Filing receipt			
( )	33. Assignment schedule			
( )	34. Designation of inventory			
( )	35. Statement of inventory			
( )	36. Warehouse receipts			
( )	37. Warehouse lease			
( )	38. Consent from company to allow Warehouse Company to disclose total receipts outstanding			
( )	39. Other:_____			
( )	40. _____			

ALL DOCUMENTS RECEIVED, APPROVED AND FILED:

security agreement and/or loan agreement constitute a contract to repay any amount of money that may be outstanding, secured by pledged collateral, in accordance with the terms specified in the agreements. This is one of the major reasons why a loan against receivables and inventory is a truly revolving arrangement: it permits the borrower to obtain new loans by telephone and to make partial repayments by mail, eliminating much negotiation and many visits by principals to the bank.

RATE OF COMPENSATION

The proper supervision of accounts receivable and inventory loans requires considerably more work and attention than the usual unsecured loan; therefore, the rate of interest charged for such loans should compensate for the work done. The three factors in establishing a rate of interest on receivables and inventory loans, in the order of their importance, are: the rate the bank has to pay for its own funds; the amount of work needed to supervise the loan; and the degree of risk involved in the loan.

The second and third elements are related because more work will be required to supervise a highly marginal loan than a loan to a company that is relatively stable. Rates, however, should not be predicated primarily on the degree of risk. No rate is high enough to compensate for the loss of principal in the event of the failure of a marginal company.

For many years an average and fair rate of return on receivable loans was approximately three percentage points above prime. Under the abnormal conditions of the early eighties, with prime interest rates skyrocketing to 20 percent, it has not been easy to charge three over prime. In the first place, such rates approach the usury rates of some states; furthermore, in many instances rates which exceeded 20 percent absorbed all (or more than all) of what the receivables borrower could earn.

This problem has to be dealt with at the time of your initial investigation. If it appears doubtful that your prospect can handle the rate you feel is justified, it is better to reject the account. The time spent and the cost of liquidating collateral, as well as the cost of possible litigation or other legal costs, are almost always more than any income derived from the interest earned.

Rates on receivables and inventory should always be established as floating rates that are tied to the prime rate of interest. This is done in order to protect the bank's gross margin of profit. Some banks and finance companies increase or decrease rates on the first day of the month following any change that has taken place in the prime rate. Changes made within the month sometimes cause a difficult bookkeeping problem, especially if books are kept by hand instead of by some electronic method. Experience shows that, in the long run, losses realized because of deferring increases to the first of a month will be offset by the gains made by deferring decreases to the first of the month.

DATA TO BE SUPPLIED BY THE BORROWER

The lender's records are compiled from data provided by the borrower; therefore it is imperative that the borrower submit complete and accurate details as required, and that such data be constantly verified by the procedures outlined in later chapters.

This does not mean to imply that the average borrower is dishonest and is intent on defrauding the lender. However, changes in accounts receivable and inventory occur daily; if there is not a constant and conscious effort to keep the records straight, discrepancies may creep in which are very difficult to correct when not handled promptly.

The following information is essential to the successful monitoring of an accounts receivable and inventory loan. If this information is not provided promptly and accurately, there is sufficient cause to withhold advances until it is supplied. Continual delay or numerous inaccuracies may be symptoms of default and should prompt the lender to request the borrower to seek financing elsewhere, to ask for payment in full, or to liquidate the collateral by collecting the accounts receivable and to arrange for the sale of inventory.

The forms and procedures recommended here will provide accurate information and are simple to prepare. Many borrowers already will have established a mechanism to provide the necessary data; for those who have not, the bank will be providing a service by helping them establish these records. In any case, forms always should be prepared and procedures maintained in order to establish clear-cut controls over a borrower's accounts receivable. Then, in the event of liquidation, the outstanding balances can be reconstructed easily and accurately, in reconciliation with the borrower's general ledger, from figures compiled or available within the bank.

Schedule of Accounts Receivable Assigned

Exhibit 7 is a sample form for a schedule of accounts receivable assigned. (When the form is printed it may be eleven by seventeen inches with lines one-quarter inch apart to allow room for the handwriting of names and amounts, if that is what the borrower chooses to do.) This form should be submitted to the bank at the time of the establishment of a new accounts receivable account; forms for all existing accounts should be submitted within ten days after the closing of each month. If they are not received within ten days, an inquiry should be made as to when they will be received. The accounts receivable department head should have the prerogative of extending the time of preparation; but if, in the judgment of the department head, undue delays are encountered, new advances should be withheld until the aging is received.

No legal necessity requires assignment of each schedule of accounts receivable—either monthly or daily—because a lien on this collateral, and on inventory, is perfected when accounts receivable and inventory agreements are signed, UCC statements are filed, and cash or other consideration is advanced. The assignment of each schedule is good discipline, however; it is also the best-known method of keeping entirely current on new sales and in reconciliation with the borrower's general ledger and the lender's collateral records.

It is desirable that the aging form be typed with the complete name and address of each customer, as well as aged balances. However, this may be too burdensome a requirement for some borrowers, in which case the forms may be handwritten as long as they are legible. Furthermore, borrowers may show only customers' names on aged schedules as long as a complete listing or card file of the name and addresses is provided to the bank and is updated quarterly.

Every aging schedule received, whether it is an initial schedule or a monthly schedule, should have attached to it a form similar to Exhibit 8, which is called the Assignment of Scheduled Accounts. This warrants that the accounts assigned are all of the accounts owned by the borrower on the date of the assignment. If it is preferred, the suggested wording of this form may be printed on the reverse side of the Schedule of Accounts Receivable Assigned form.

The form should provide a space for the assignor and the name of the person signing it. The name of every person having the authority to sign should be shown on a signature card signed at the time of closing. Any assignment or other collateral form that shows an unauthorized,

EXHIBIT 7

62

Schedule of Accounts Receivable Assigned

Metropolitan National Bank

NAME OF CUSTOMER _____

PAGE_____ OF_____

SCHEDULE OF ACCOUNTS RECEIVABLE ASSIGNED

MONTH ENDING_____

| CUSTOMER'S NAME | DEBIT BALANCES | CRED. BAL. (DO NOT AGE) | ACCOUNTS AGED BY MONTHS | | | | REMARKS |
			THIS MONTH	LAST MONTH	PREV. MONTH	PRIOR	

Please list all Contra Accounts separately on last page and exclude from recap. Assignment form on reverse side must be signed. [See Exhibit 8.]

EXHIBIT 8   63

Assignment of Scheduled Accounts

ASSIGNMENT OF SCHEDULED ACCOUNTS
TO METROPOLITAN NATIONAL BANK

Date _____

The undersigned (hereinafter called "the Borrower") hereby warrants to **METROPOLITAN NATIONAL BANK** (hereinafter called "Bank") that the accounts listed in the schedule of accounts hereto attached or listed on the reverse side hereof constitute all of the outstanding accounts receivable as of _____; that all of said accounts represent undisputed bona fide claims not subject to any setoff, counterclaim or condition of any nature, except as indicated in said schedule; and that said schedule is in all respects complete and accurate.

The Borrower, for value received, and in order further to secure its indebtedness to Bank now existing or hereafter arising, hereby pledges, assigns and transfers to Bank all of the accounts set forth in said schedule, having the total face amount of $ _____, and all the Borrower's right, title and interest in and to all collateral, security, notes, checks, and other commercial paper now or hereafter held by the Borrower for the payment of the accounts hereby assigned, and in and to all property giving rise thereto.

This assignment is made in confirmation, in part or in whole, of previous assignments of Borrower's accounts to Bank, if any, but shall not impair the rights of Bank as to any accounts previously assigned. This assignment is made in furtherance of and subject to the terms of the existing agreement between the Borrower and Bank, which agreement is made a part hereof as if fully set forth herein.

Last assignment, remittance and
credit number covered by this
aging.

_____

A____ R____ C____

By _____

incomplete, or inaccurate signature should be returned to the borrower for correction.

Some prospective borrowers want to assign only part of their accounts because they do not need all of the funds that would become available from the pledging of the total amount of receivables. This practice should be discouraged because of the almost inevitable confusion that will arise in the minds of the borrower's personnel as to whether continuing sales to a particular account should be assigned, and as to whether some collections should be sent to the lender and not others.

If a prospect is adamant on this subject, a compromise can be offered by suggesting that the alphabet be split into two or more parts. For example, the accounts starting with the letters A through L may be assigned, and the balance unassigned. This rarely becomes a big issue when it is explained to a prospect that the assignment of invoices incurs no cost to the borrower because finance charges are related only to the daily loan outstanding.

From the lender's standpoint, it is important that accounts receivable be reconciled with the borrower's general ledger. This may be done more easily when all, rather than part, of the borrower's receivables are assigned. Furthermore, complete assignment is the only way a lender can watch for contras, concentrations, and poor credits, all of which might badly affect the borrower's financial condition. The type of form used for the listing and aging of accounts receivable is not important as long as the accounts are properly assigned using a form similar to Exhibit 7.

Daily List of Accounts Receivable Assigned

Exhibit 9 is a sample form used for daily listing of accounts receivable assigned. This form may be submitted somewhat at the convenience of the borrower. Most accounts receivable customers prefer to make it a daily routine because it is then harder to overlook any day's work, and borrowers soon learn that a receivable may not be used as collateral until it is in the bank's possession. Those borrowers who do not want to make daily assignments should be urged to make them no less than twice each week.

Forms may be provided to the borrower in pads or in snap-out sets (original and duplicate), preferably color coded. The original should be sent to the bank, attached to copies of invoices and proofs of shipment such as bills of lading or customers' signed receipt forms.

These forms should be approximately 8½ by 11 inches and should contain spaces at the top for the date of the assignment, the name of

EXHIBIT 9

Daily List of Accounts Receivable Assigned

65

DAILY LIST OF ACCOUNTS ASSIGNED TO
METROPOLITAN NATIONAL BANK

DATE_____

By ....

ASSIGNMENT NO._____

NAME LIST ALPHABETICALLY	ADDRESS	DATE OF SALE	AMOUNT
		TOTAL	

ASSIGNMENT

Date_____

For value received and to secure its indebtedness to _____ (hereinafter termed _____) now existing or hereafter arising, the undersigned (hereinafter termed the "Borrower") hereby pledges, assigns and transfers to _____ the accounts receivable listed above and all the Borrower's right, title and interest in and to all collateral security, notes, checks and other commercial paper now or hereafter held by the Borrower for the payment thereof and in and to all property given rise thereto, the aforesaid accounts being evidenced in greater detail in delivery receipts, invoices and statements furnished or to be furnished to _____. The Borrower hereby represents and warrants that all of said accounts represent undisputed, bona fide claims not subject to any setoffs, counter-claims or conditions of any nature except as indicated; that all collections received or credits allowed by it upon any and all accounts previously assigned to _____ have been duly, properly and regularly credited to the accounts of the respective debtors on the books or records usually used for such purpose; that all such collections and the amounts of such credits have been properly forwarded to _____ and that none of the said accounts have been sold or assigned to any other party.

This assignment is made in furtherance of and subject to the terms of the existing agreement between the Borrower and _____ which agreement is made part hereof as if fully set forth herein. All the rights and privileges of _____ under the existing agreement shall be cumulative.

_____
NAME OF COMPANY

By _____
AUTHORIZED SIGNATURE

the customer, and the schedule number. The schedule number is extremely important because it serves as a common reference point for the bank and for the borrower whenever referring to any particular day's sales or invoices. The first list of accounts assigned, after the initial total of receivables, should show the number 1, and each list thereafter should be numbered consecutively for as long as the account is on the bank's books.

Vertical columns should provide space for a name, address, date of sale, and the amount of the invoice, and each day's sales should be totalled at the end of this section.

Because of the multitude of invoices created by some borrowers, listing individual transactions may be very time consuming. When this is the case, it is sometimes permissible for a borrower to write across the face of an assignment sheet (or to rubber stamp it) "_____ invoices attached totalling $_____." This total must agree with the total shown on the adding machine tape attached to the invoices which accompany the assignment sheet.

Another variation that is sometimes satisfactory is to accept a copy of the borrower's sales journal, as long as it shows all essential information. In such cases, the sales journal should be attached to an assignment sheet with a regular consecutive number and with the statement on the face of the sheet "per sales journal attached."

When, because of volume, copies of invoices cannot be sent, an employee of the borrower should act as the bank's custodian (the use of custodians is covered at the end of Chapter 6). In such a case, a rubber stamp may be provided to the custodian which reads:

> I certify that I have seen and verified the delivery evidences and invoices giving rise to the accounts assigned, and the credits for return of merchandise.
>
> Custodian_____

Further, the bank's examiner should be instructed to periodically check several days' invoices, on the borrower's premises, against assignment sheets to determine that all invoices are in order.

When a borrower issues invoices on a strictly numerical basis, a different form may be used, such as Exhibit 10. Any break in the numbers should be explained by the borrower.

From time to time a borrower may sell goods to a customer who will accept billing at the time of sale but who does not want the goods for a period of time. This creates a *bill-and-hold* situation—title may not pass until the merchandise is shipped. Invoices arising from these sales

EXHIBIT 10

67

Accounts Assigned to
_____

**ACCOUNTS ASSIGNED TO
METROPOLITAN NATIONAL BANK**

DATE _____

Client _____

ASSIGNMENT NO. _____

INVOICE

NUMBERS		DATES		TOTALS
FROM	TO	FROM	TO	
_____	_____	_____	_____	$ _____
_____	_____	_____	_____	_____
_____	_____	_____	_____	_____
_____	_____	_____	_____	_____
_____	_____	_____	_____	_____
_____	_____	_____	_____	_____
_____	_____	_____	_____	_____
_____	_____	_____	_____	_____

TOTAL _____ $ _____

PER COMPUTER RUN ATTACHED:

_____ _____ _____ _____ $ _____

I hereby certify that I have seen and have verified the delivery evidences and invoices giving rise to the accounts assigned herewith and the credits for returns of merchandise.

CUSTODIAN _____
(If Required)

ASSIGNMENT   Date _____

For value received and to secure its indebtedness to _____ (hereinafter termed _____) now existing or hereafter arising, the undersigned (hereinafter termed the "Borrower") hereby pledges, assigns and transfers to _____ the accounts receivable listed above and all the Borrower's right, title and interest in and to all collateral security, notes, checks and other commercial paper now or hereafter held by the Borrower for the payment thereof and in and to all property given rise thereto, the aforesaid accounts being evidenced in greater detail in delivery receipts, invoices and statements furnished or to be furnished to _____ . The Borrower hereby represents and warrants that all of said accounts represent undisputed, bona fide claims not subject to any setoffs, counter-claims or conditions of any nature except as indicated; that all collections received or credits allowed by it upon any and all accounts previously assigned to _____ have been duly, properly and regularly credited to the accounts of the respective debtors on the books or records usually used for such purpose; that all such collections and the amounts of such credits have been properly forwarded to _____ and that none of the said accounts have been sold or assigned to any other party.

This assignment is made in furtherance of and subject to the terms of the existing agreement between the Borrower and _____ which agreement is made part hereof as if fully set forth herein. All the rights and privileges of _____ under the existing agreement shall be cumulative.

_____   By _____
NAME OF COMPANY   AUTHORIZED SIGNATURE

DO NOT WRITE BELOW THIS LINE

DATE RECEIVED	AUTHORIZED SIGNATURE	SIGNED BY CUSTODIAN	AUDITED	DATE ENTERED	ENTERED BY

are highly questionable collateral. In such cases, a customer should send a letter to the borrower, on the customer's own letterhead, similar to the sample letter in Exhibit 11. The wording of this letter should be checked with your attorney for approval.

Report of
Collections

Exhibit 12 is a sample of a form used to report collections. Except in rare circumstances, customer collections should be remitted to the bank on a daily basis, and in the *same form as received by the borrower,* whether there is one check or many. Checks should be reviewed to see that they match the names and amounts shown on the collection reports, and that check vouchers show the net amount paid, deductions, or any other item affecting the amount. If checks are not received for three days in a row, it should be discussed immediately with the borrower to determine the reason. Diversion of funds is often the first step in fraudulent practices, and a few days' lapse in sending in remittance advices may be an early signal that a problem exists.

The forms themselves should be $8\frac{1}{2}$ x 11 inches with space at the top for the name of the borrower, the date, and the collection report number. Careful numbering is as important for these reports as it is for the daily listing of accounts. The forms may be provided to the borrower in sets of two (original and duplicate), preferably color coded. The original should be sent, along with checks, to the accounts receivable department or to a lockbox controlled by the department; the duplicate should be retained by the borrower. The first report of collections from a new customer should bear the number 1, and subsequent sheets should be numbered consecutively for as long as the account is on the bank's books.

All money columns should be totalled and the form should show a legend at the bottom reading:

> The undersigned represents that the collections listed above include all monies received to date by the Borrower on accounts assigned to _____ Bank since last remittance sheet Number _____ dated _____ .
>   Authorized Signature _____

To save duplicate work, a copy of a borrower's cash receipts journal may be accepted as long as it contains all the information listed above. In such cases, the journal should be sent to the bank, attached to a consecutively numbered remittance sheet which shows totals that agree with the journal.

EXHIBIT 11
Bill and Hold Letter

Gentlemen:

With respect to our Purchase Order #_____, dated
_____ and in the amount of $_____, a copy of
which is attached.

We confirm that title to the merchandise identified in
this purchase order shall pass to us on your invoice
date. Since we do not wish to store the merchandise
on our premises at this time, we authorize you to hold
it for us until we ask you to send it.

We further agree to pay you, your successors and assigns
the invoiced amount according to the terms stated on
your invoice, which are:

regardless of whether or not the merchandise is in your
possession as our bailee at the time payment is due, in
accordance with aforesaid terms.

Very truly yours,

(CUSTOMER)

EXHIBIT 12

70

Report of Collections

REPORT OF COLLECTIONS
TO: METROPOLITAN NATIONAL BANK

Date:_____

By_____

Remittance No._____

Assignment Page or Date of Invoice	Debtor's Name List Alphabetically	Date Credited Customer	Amount of Invoice	√	Amount of Remittance	Deduction	Over Payment
TOTALS							

The undersigned hereby represents that the collections listed above include all monies received to date by the Borrower on accounts assigned to Metropolitan National Bank since last remittance sheet no._____, dated _____.

Authorized Signature_____

The "assignment page or date of invoice" column is not generally used, although the information is helpful in cases of large payments or large deductions. The deduction column may be used to record discounts and small allowances, but it is suggested that any deductions over $25, or any deductions more than 10% of a check, should be shown with proper explanation on the form for credits and returns described later in this book. However, businesses which receive cash from their customers should be allowed to deposit the cash in their own accounts.

A borrower should not be permitted to deposit noncash collections to the company's accounts. They should be sent to the bank in the same form as received by the borrower. The review of account debtors' checks by the receivable department is an important control function which should not be released. However, some businesses (such as fuel oil dealers, department stores, and other retail enterprises) receive cash from their customers. This procedure has to be allowed, and such collections should be listed separately at the bottom of a remittance sheet, under the heading of cash collections. The cash should be deposited in the borrower's local bank, but a check must be sent to the accounts receivable department on the same day and in the same amount.

Memo of Returns and Credits

Borrowers should be required to submit a consecutively numbered memo of returns and credits form (Exhibit 13) at the end of each week, whether or not any returns and credits were made during the week. When no credits have been given, the form may simply be marked "no credits issued since report number _____ dated _____ ." The number and date of the report should refer to the previous form submitted to the bank.

Spaces should be provided at the top for consecutive numbering, the date of the report, and instructions to the borrower regarding the submission of the report. The form should be 8½ x 11 inches in size, and of a distinctive color so that it will not be confused with other forms. Money columns should be totalled and copies of credit memos should be attached to the form.

All credits should be reviewed carefully by the department head to determine their size, nature, and frequency. For example, if credits appear too large and frequent for the borrower's type of business, learn more about them by talking with the borrower's principal. A frequent review of invoices, remittances, and credits may tell a lot about a borrower's business, and it makes it easier to spot any irregularities.

EXHIBIT 13   72

Memo of Returns and Credits

MEMO OF RETURNS AND CREDITS
TO
METROPOLITAN NATIONAL BANK

Sheet No. _____

_____ 19_____

This report MUST be made immediately upon the receipt of any returns, whether or not the right of your customers to make the returns is disputed by you. In the event no returns are received, then this report MUST be make weekly stating no returns were received during the preceding week.

In addition, this report should be used to advise us of any other credits claimed for any reason whatsoever, whether or not the claim is disputed by you.

Also, this form should be used to report to us any charges or credits actually made to customers' accounts and not already reported on "Daily List of Accounts Assigned" or on "Collection Reports" such as bad debts written off, contra'd accounts, etc.

Posted By	Added By

Name of Account	Address	Amount of Credit		Applies Against Invoice		
				Invoice #	Date	Amount

We herewith advise you that the above _____ returns, are all of the returns, claims, allowances and credits which we have this day received or allowed on accounts previously assigned to you. Our last memo of returns and credits sent to you was number _____ dated _____ 19____.

Firm Name_____ By _____ Title _____

*Requests for
Loans*

One of the outstanding features of accounts receivable and inventory financing is its great flexibility. Borrowing power is created each day by the assignment of new sales and by the refund of the borrower's equity in customer collections which are turned in. This is like providing the borrower with a pipeline to the treasury. Collateral in the hands of the lender forms a basis for instant loans to the borrower (up to the percentage as shown in loan agreements) without continual negotiations.

Occasionally, requests will be received from borrowers to keep their accounts up to full availability by automatically depositing into their accounts whatever funds are due to them. This request seems to come about because of the fear that the lender might willfully hold back loans to which the borrower is entitled.

In making such a request, the borrower is within his or her rights, but the practice should be discouraged for several reasons. Such a practice could result in funds accumulating in the borrower's bank account, with interest, therefore, being paid on money not in use. Furthermore, unnecessarily frequent borrowings add to the cost of handling for both the bank and the borrower. Another point against this practice is that excess cash in the bank could lead the borrower into spending money for goods or services not vital to the business. Finally, the creation of availability provides the bank with an extra margin of safety.

Generally, requests for loans will be made by telephone on the exact day that the funds are needed. Occasionally, borrowers may want funds deposited into their accounts on specific future dates—such as payroll periods—in which case a Request for Loan form (Exhibit 14) is convenient. The form may be approximately check size and of a distinctive color which will immediately identify it as a request form. When it is received, it may be filed in a chronological "tickler" file as a reminder to make the transfer of funds on the day specified.

Accounts receivable and inventory borrowers may easily determine the amount of funds available to them by using established formulas, and, after computing the availability of these funds, they may instruct the bank to deposit a certain amount to their accounts, either at once or on some future date.

*Report and
Designation of
Inventory*

Inventory is very difficult collateral to control with respect to quantity, quality, and value; therefore, great care should be taken to develop a system of reporting that will be as accurate and as frequent as possible.

Exhibit 15, entitled Report and Designation of Inventory, may be

EXHIBIT 14

74

Request for Loan

REQUEST FOR LOAN

Date _____

PLEASE

☐ DEPOSIT TO OUR ACCOUNT

☐ MAIL US

Check for the SUM of $ _____

on _____ _____
       DAY   DATE

ACCOUNT # _____

To: **METROPOLITAN NATIONAL BANK**

FINANCIAL PLACE

RECEIVABLE CITY, USA

COMPANY

BY

EXHIBIT 15

Report and Designation of Inventory

75

**REPORT AND DESIGNATION OF INVENTORY
TO: METROPOLITAN NATIONAL BANK**

_____

(Date Prepared)

In accordance with the Security Agreement between us dated _____ and any amendments thereto,

Client: _____

Address: _____

designates and makes subject to your security interest our entire inventory of goods generally described as follows:

and all such merchandise hereafter acquired.

The undersigned represents that:

1) Inventory locations other than client's address shown above are named below.
2) Inventory designated is owned free and clear other than your lien.
3) After-acquired merchandise will be owned by us free and clear.
4) Merchandise consigned to us is not included in this designation.
5) Inventory is insured for at least the amount designated below.
6) Your firm is named as Loss Payee.
7) If on a monthly reporting form, a copy of report to insurance company is attached.
8) Inventory value designated is not in excess of its price.
9) The value of our last physical inventory count taken on (date) _____
was $_____. This inventory (was) (was not) certified.

SCHEDULE OF INVENTORY COMPUTATION

Other locations: _____   Client: _____

_____   By: _____

used both for the initial designation of inventory made by a new account and for all subsequent reportings. If inventory is stored in several locations, a form should be used for each location and an additional form should be provided to summarize the total.

Before loans are made on inventory collateral, in-depth discussions should be held with the borrower's management and accountant to ascertain the best way to report additions to and deletions from inventory. This will be discussed more fully in Chapter 6, in the section titled Inventory as Collateral, but following are some factors to be considered when establishing the amount of detail to be provided and the frequency of the report.

If the inventory is manufactured, there are a number of questions which must be answered in order to ensure its value as collateral:

1. Does the raw material have a resale value in the condition in which it is purchased?

2. Is there a public source of information giving frequent listings that show the changes that take place in such values? An example is the section on commodity prices listed in the *Wall Street Journal.*

3. What records are maintained by the borrower to show the conversion of raw material to work-in-process to finished goods?

4. Are such records substantially accurate?

5. Does raw material consist of component parts purchased by the manufacturer? Do such parts have a resale value in the condition in which they are purchased?

6. Does work-in-process inventory have any resale value at any stage of its manufacture? Most work-in-process has little or no collateral value, although there may be exceptions such as leather, precious metals, precious gems, alcoholic beverages during an aging process, and certain petroleum products.

7. Do finished goods have a ready market with wide distribution, or is there a small market because the goods are a specialty item? Who might likely buyers be?

8. Is any part of the inventory on consignment to the borrower?

9. Is it advisable to employ an expert to appraise the inventory at the beginning and on a periodic basis?

10. If the borrower rents his or her premises, how long is the lease, what is the rent, and what are the insurance costs? Related to this is the question of whether a Landlord's Waiver and Consent, as shown in Exhibit 16, may be secured, which will permit the

EXHIBIT 16   77
Landlord's Waiver and Consent

Metropolitan National Bank

LANDLORD'S WAIVER AND CONSENT

WHEREAS, the Undersigned is the owner and lessor of premises located at _____

_____ and

_____

(hereinafter called "Borrower"), is the lessee of such premises; and

WHEREAS, Metropolitan National Bank (hereinafter called "Bank") is considering entering into financing arrangements with Borrower under which Borrower will grant to Bank a security interest in property used by Borrower in the conduct of its business and which are or may from time to time hereafter be located at such premises. (All such property and the records relating thereto shall be hereafter called "Collateral".)

NOW, THEREFORE, to induce Bank to enter into said financing arrangements with Borrower, the Undersigned hereby irrevocably agrees and consents to refrain from taking any action to bar, restrain or otherwise prevent Bank from entering said premises for the purpose of inspecting or taking possession of its Collateral.

The Undersigned further irrevocably agrees and consents that Bank may occupy said premises for the purpose of maintaining possession of its Collateral and preparing for and conducting a sale of the same whether private or public. (With limitation, this shall include the finishing of work in process.)

In the event that Bank enters into occupation of the subject premises for the purposes set forth above, it shall be liable for only reasonable use and occupation charges for all such use and occupation after the first _____ days.

This instrument is executed and delivered to Bank on this_____ day of_____, 19_____, and intended to take effect as a sealed instrument.

BY: _____

BY: _____

bank or its nominee (such as an auctioneer) to enter the premises, do whatever is necessary to get the inventory ready for sale, and then to sell it. A landlord's waiver may be very important if a loan is being liquidated and space is needed to store goods until they can be sold and delivered. It usually entails some negotiating with the landlord at the time the original loan agreement is being prepared. Payment of back rent, if any, and the cost of occupying the area required for the period of time needed to dispose of inventory, are issues to be decided at this time.

11. Should a professional warehouse company such as NYTCO Services, Inc., or Lawrence Systems, Inc., be used to control the in-and-out movement of goods?

12. Is the inventory kept in sufficient depth as to quantity, styles, sizes, and colors, so as to be attractive to buyers in the event of liquidation? A reasonable depth of inventory is important, as auctioneers cannot afford to spend much time on small quantities. For example, truckloads usually may be sold more easily than just a few cases of goods, and the larger quantities generally will bring higher unit prices than small lots.

13. How many items are there to inventory? Sometimes inventories may include hundreds, or even thousands, of items. If this is the case, the problems of keeping track of them may be formidable, and should they ever have to be sold at auction, the cost of assembling, tagging, and pricing may be monumental.

14. Can inventory be easily counted and checked as to quantity and quality?

15. Is the inventory seasonal, and if so, how drastically would the price have to be reduced if it had to be sold in the off season?

16. Do the goods have a style factor, as in women's clothes, hats, or shoes, where values may drop to the vanishing point after the season is over? Where style goods are involved, it is imperative that loans be paid out at the end of the season or before.

17. What portion of the inventory, if any, may be considered to be slow-moving or obsolete?

18. Can a strong third-party guarantor be secured for any loans made on inventory?

19. Can a buy-back agreement, or a *put,* be arranged with one or more suppliers? In such an agreement, the suppliers will promise to buy back their goods at the borrower's cost (frequently less a restocking charge); this will be done at the lender's request or at a specified time, such as at the end of a season. Many suppliers

are willing to do this rather than have a flood of their goods put on the market at greatly discounted prices.

If the inventory is owned by a wholesaler, then the same questions outlined above, starting with number 7, have to be considered.

The creation of inventory through a manufacturing process must be supported by manufacturing records that are satisfactory to the lender. The purchase of raw materials or component parts may be substantiated by copies of purchase orders. The deduction of goods from inventory may be shown on a 'cost of goods sold' basis, the formula for which should be a matter of complete agreement between the borrower and lender.

Ideally, additions to and deductions from inventory should be reported on a daily basis, but this frequently is impossible because of the number of items and the constant fluctuations of the collateral. As a compromise, it may be necessary to back off to weekly, monthly, or even quarterly reporting, but with the full realization that great changes may take place between reporting periods. This may create a very real risk for the lender. If infrequent reporting is necessary, the lender's department head or examiner should spot-check collateral as often as possible in order to avoid surprises when reports are received.

Insurance

A business's insurance requirements may change substantially in a very short time and for a number of reasons. For example, an old line of merchandise may be phased out, but insurance coverage continues only because no one has cancelled the policy. On the other hand, whenever new products are taken on or manufactured, someone has to remember to talk to the insurance agent. Furthermore, in inflationary periods when the cost of goods purchased or manufactured has increased substantially, the insurance coverage should be increased to keep up. Whenever loans are made on inventory, the department head should be sure that coverage is adequate to protect the bank and the borrower to at least the full extent of the loan.

There are many types of insurance coverage that a borrower may purchase, but, from a lender's viewpoint, there are a few that are considered very important. One of these is full coverage of inventory value, regardless of its type or quantity, with proper loss payee clauses to protect the lender. If inventory fluctuates, either because of the growth of the business or for seasonal needs, a reporting form policy frequently gives better coverage than policies written for specific amounts. A reporting form policy requires the insured to report inventory changes to the insurance company on an agreed schedule. This automatically provides increased coverage for net additions to inventory or decreased coverage for net decreases with a resulting fluctuation in the cost of the insurance.

Security agreements between the parties should contain a clause permitting the lender to order insurance at the expense of the borrower if the lender feels that coverage provided by the borrower is inadequate.

Business interruption insurance is another important type of coverage, and will reimburse a company for its operating expenses, and sometimes its profits, for the period of time the company is out of business because of a catastrophe.

If the borrower is a closely held corporation with only a few key owners, life insurance for the benefit of the business on at least the major principals is a desirable form of coverage. The loss of an important executive may hurt a business badly and sometimes may lead to liquidation. Funds from life insurance, however, may buy time until a replacement can be found or until necessary adjustments can be made in the responsibilities of the remaining executive staff. Term policies may be used which will cover the expected period of the loan.

Finally, accounts receivable insurance is the type of insurance which will pay a company up to the full value of its accounts receivable in the event that such records are destroyed and cannot be reconstructed. This kind of insurance is inexpensive but may be of great value to both borrower and lender.

Whether or not the three latter types of insurance should be purchased is a matter of their relative importance to the lender and their expense to the borrower. They are desirable to have but ordinarily are not made a condition of the loan. Adequate insurance coverage on inventory is a requirement, however, and no loan should be made without it.

The bank should get the original or a copy of all insurance policies covering assets used as security for loans. Each policy should have a rider attached, clearly noting that the bank is named as loss payee as its interest may appear. Without it, the bank may not be able to share in insurance proceeds. The rider also should state the number of days' notice to be given to the lender before the policy can be cancelled for any reason.

It is preferable that the bank keep the original policy in its files to guarantee that no changes are made in the insurance coverage without the bank's prior knowledge. This presupposes that the bank will study each policy to determine: that it contains a description of the collateral sufficient to properly identify it; that the period of time covers the expected period of the loan; or that the policy may be easily renewed to give this coverage.

It is not always possible to get possession of the original policy, but the bank should insist on a copy with the rider attached. When it is received, a "tickler" file should be set up for about 30 days before the expiration date, so that the department head can be sure the borrower renews and, if necessary, increases coverage.

INITIATING THE FIRST ADVANCE

When the new borrower has provided the bank with all the data and forms required to initiate the first advance, and after all documents have been signed and all filings made, the department head should arrange to get the loan started. Arrangements must first be made to effect the initial advance on collateral. The department head should set up a "tickler" file for the return of the termination statement copy of the UCC form from the city hall or state house. After the copy has been received, the time and date of filing (as shown on the termination copy) should be posted on the secured party copy, and all copies then should be filed with other documents in the legal file.

A line of credit should be set up, for internal use only, on each type of loan; this will serve as a checkpoint for the department head. The borrower does not necessarily have to know what the limit is, but when it is reached, the department head may want to review the loan to determine if the limit should be raised or lowered. Limits should be flexible and should change with the financial condition of the borrower and the quality of collateral submitted.

Also at this time, the department head should arrange to secure all risk coverage on any inventory or fixed asset pledged to the bank, with the bank named as loss payee. Finally, the department head should set up verification procedures as outlined in Chapter 6.

FINANCING OF SALES TO THE FEDERAL GOVERNMENT

Occasionally the accounts receivable of a prospective borrower will arise partly or entirely from sales made to, or services performed for, the federal government.

Prior to 1940, the government would not recognize the assignment of amounts due from it to third parties, and, as a result, many potential suppliers were unable to do government business because the financing of such receivables was unacceptable to many lenders.

In 1940, however, the Assignment of Claims Act was passed by Congress permitting the assignment of claims against the government to third parties. The routine to be followed, while rigid, is simple; if instructions are followed, collections of accounts may be no more difficult than with ordinary trade receivables.

A copy of the regulations pertaining to the Assignment of Claims (Sub Part. 1-30.7) may be secured from the Procurement Division of the General Services Administration in Washington, D.C., or in any of the General Services Administration regional offices. The main points of the regulations are as follows:

1. The contract must provide for payments amounting to $1,000 or more in the aggregate;
2. Payments must be assigned to a bank, trust company, or other financing institution, including any federal lending agency;
3. The contract may not forbid assignment;
4. The contract must not be assigned to more than one party and must not be reassigned unless it is expressly permitted by the contract;
5. The assignee shall file a written notice of the assignment with the contracting officer or the head of his or her department or agency, and the disbursing officer (if any), and also shall notify the surety or sureties upon the bond or bonds (if any) in connection with the assigned contract.

The regulations suggest the form of a Notice of Assignment and of the Acknowledgement of the Notice.

When proper notices have been filed, government checks will be mailed directly to the lender. It is recommended that separate ledgers be kept for each contract assigned and that payments be keyed to applicable invoices. If payments are less than called for, the borrower should be contacted for an explanation.

Other than following prescribed regulations to secure good assignment and prompt payment, the lender may view government contracts as any other contract. If a contract calls for progress payments, the lender should be as sure as possible that the borrower can complete the contract. Otherwise, the last invoices may not be paid even though the lender has made advances against them. Be sure that a profit can be realized at the price negotiated. It is difficult to get any relief if costs of supplying the government exceed original estimates.

The lender should be sure that the terms of the contract coincide with the production and wage schedules. One unfortunate contractor who won a contract to supply dairy products to a military installation, after spending a large amount of money for new equipment, found that deliveries were to be made only as called for by the installation. The products—mostly ice cream and milk—were called for in satisfactory volumes only when the weather was hot. The spasmodic and uncertain flow of business caused by a relatively cool summer season resulted in such a loss of revenue that the contractor's business failed.

In another instance, a contractor got caught in a rising market for the raw materials he needed, and, because of many delays by the government in calling for his goods, the prices he eventually paid made it impossible for him to complete the contract successfully.

If any bonding company is involved, the lender must recognize, in the event the contractor is unable to complete his contract, that the bonding company may have first claim on the proceeds of any receivables outstanding at the time of his failure to complete.

The absence of any credit problems when selling to the government, and the comfort of having payments come directly to the lender, makes the financing of government contractors attractive. Government contracts are not always free from troubles, however, and should be checked carefully by the borrower to be sure that they can be handled profitably.

PREPARING TO CLOSE THE LOAN

When all conditions of the loan have been agreed upon, and all required data have been provided by the borrower, the legal documents necessary to bring the transaction to reality may be prepared. Loan officers can help keep legal fees down if they themselves prepare standard forms where only variables need to be filled in. It is recommended, however, that the bank's attorney review all documents to be sure that they adequately cover the new loan situation. Any special loan agreements should be prepared only by legal counsel.

CHAPTER 5

Loan Documentation

Proper documentation, proper assignment of collateral, and proper filing of notices of lien are fundamental to any loan arrangement using accounts receivable and inventory as security for the loan. This book will not attempt to deal with the legal matters related to accounts receivable and inventory lending. Specialized legal skills are required in the structuring and documentation of a loan in accord with the intents of the lender and the borrower, and in conformance with the laws of the state in which the transaction is consummated.

A lender on revolving collateral must always stay alert; the lender must be in a position to move quickly to take possession of the bank's collateral, and to start prompt liquidation if it appears that the pledged assets will deteriorate if not disposed of promptly. Keeping this in mind, loan and security agreements should be structured so as to recognize the volatility of collateral (due to its widely differing values within short periods of time), and so as to provide default clauses which cover as many of the lender's risks as possible. Lender's rights should be made effective immediately, subject to applicable provisions of law, and not geared to any period—however short—before which the lender cannot act on them.

Every legal document for every type of loan, secured or unsecured, is important, but because of the constantly changing values of accounts receivable and inventory collateral, special expertise is required to protect the lender under all possible circumstances.

If a borrower runs into financial difficulties that may lead to non-payment of bills, in whole or in part, attorneys for unsecured creditors will examine every document carefully for any loopholes that might yield some recovery. Documents that are not properly constructed and executed may lead to embarrassment, lawsuits, and losses. The attorneys selected to construct and execute these documents, therefore, should be experienced in secured lending and specifically experienced in the structuring of accounts receivable and inventory loan agreements.

STANDARDIZED FORMS

There are many legal documents constructed for many special purposes, but the forms discussed on the following pages may be standardized and preprinted, especially when used for loan agreements that are not too complex, and when used for private companies whose stock is closely held.

Accounts Financing Security Agreement

The title of the Accounts Financing Security Agreement form (Exhibit 17) varies to some degree, but it is the form of agreement used in connection with loans secured by accounts receivable, and it clearly states terms and conditions of the loan and the rights of borrower and lender.

Much of the form contains definitions of terms used and specific warranties of the borrower regarding legal incorporation, title to the assets pledged, adherence to local, state, and federal laws, and the obligations of each party to the other in the event of default.

The variables representing matters of negotiation between the parties, for which open spaces are left in an accounts receivable or an accounts financing security agreement, include those in the following list. There is no representation made here that all of the listed variables need to be used or that the list is complete. Each loan situation is different, and the specifics to be incorporated in any agreement will be decided by the borrower, the lender, and their respective attorneys:

1. The rate of advance to be made against acceptable accounts receivable—acceptable receivables to be defined by the lender;

2. When a refund of the reserve held against receivables will be made. For example, if a loan of 80 percent is to be made against receivables up to 90 days old, when will the 20 percent reserve and collections from unacceptable accounts be refunded to the borrower?

3. The number of days for the clearance of checks (if any) that will be used—in other words, the number of days the bank requires to convert a check into collected funds, and whether clearance days will consist of consecutive days or business days. If a three-business-day clear-

(*Text continues on page 90*)

EXHIBIT 17   86

Accounts Financing Security Agreement

ACCOUNTS FINANCING SECURITY AGREEMENT

1. LIEN AND SECURITY INTEREST

_____,

whose chief place of business is located at _____,
                                            Number   Street

_____
            City   County   State

hereinafter called "Borrower", for valuable consideration, receipt whereof is hereby acknowledged, hereby grants to _____
_____, hereinafter called "_____", a continuing general lien and security interest in all accounts receivable, instruments, chattel paper,
general intangibles and contract rights (hereinafter collectively called "Accounts"; the obligors thereon being sometimes referred to as "account debtor" or
"account debtors"), now or hereafter owned or acquired by Borrower, however the same shall arise or be acquired, and all proceeds and collections thereof,
all guaranties and other security therefor, all right, title and interest of Borrower in the merchandise which gave rise thereto, including the right of
stoppage in transit, all returned, rejected, rerouted or repossessed goods, the sale or lease of which shall have given rise to any account or any such
instruments or chattel paper (all, including the Accounts, hereinafter collectively called the "Collateral"), in the proceeds thereof and in all of Borrower's books and records relating to the Collateral. The lien and security interest of _____ (or, in those states in which the Uniform Commercial Code
has not become effective, the lien of _____ arising by the assignment to _____ of accounts receivable) is to secure the payment and performance of
all liabilities and obligations of Borrower to _____ of every kind and description, direct, absolute or contingent, due or to become due, whether now
existing or hereafter arising hereunder or under any other agreement, document or instrument heretofore, now or hereafter executed and delivered
by Borrower to _____ or under any oral agreement between Borrower and_____ or by operation of law, whether or not evidenced by any
written agreement, document or instrument, including obligations to perform acts and refrain from taking action as well as obligations to pay money,
including, without limitation, those arising under:

(all hereinafter called "Obligations").

2. WARRANTIES

Borrower hereby represents and warrants to_____, and covenants, as follows:

a. All books, records and documents relating to the Accounts are and will be genuine and in all respects what they purport to be; the amount
of the Account shown on the books and records of Borrower represented as owing or to be owing at maturity by each account debtor is and
will be the correct amount actually owing or to be owing by such account debtor at maturity; each debtor liable upon the Accounts has and
will have capacity to contract; Borrower has no knowledge of any fact which would impair the validity or collectibility of any of the Accounts.

b. If Borrower is a corporation, it is duly organized and existing under the laws of the state of its incorporation, as set out above and is duly
qualified and in good standing in every other state in which the nature of its business requires such qualification.

c. The execution, delivery and performance hereof are not in contravention of law or of any indenture, agreement or undertaking to which
Borrower is a party or by which it is bound and, if Borrower is a corporation, the same are within Borrower's corporate powers, have been
duly authorized and are not in contravention of its charter, by-laws, or other incorporation papers.

d. At the time of assignment, each account receivable represents and will represent an undisputed, bona fide sale and delivery of goods or services
rendered, or both, (or in the case of a contract right, represents and will represent an undisputed, bona fide agreement) and is not and will
not be subject to any setoff, contra-claim, discount or condition of any nature, except as specified in writing on or before the delivery to _____
of schedules of assignment of accounts receivable; Borrower is, or, at the time of the assignment, will be the lawful owner of each Account
and has unqualified right to assign and grant liens and security interests to_____ therein; Borrower will, with respect to each Account, deliver
to_____such papers as_____may require, including, without limitation, the original delivery or other receipts and duplicate invoices.

e. Borrower keeps and will continue to keep all of its books and records concerning accounts receivable and contract rights and all of its other
books and records at its chief place of business, unless written notice to the contrary is given by Borrower to_____.

f. In addition to those shown in Paragraph 1. hereof, Borrower has places of business only at the following locations:

_____

_____

_____

g. All information furnished by Borrower to _____ concerning Collateral and proceeds thereof, its financial condition or otherwise, is and will
be complete, accurate and correct in all material respects at the time the same is furnished.

h. Borrower has fully complied and will fully comply hereafter with the requirements of all applicable laws, federal, state and local, and all
reserves provided upon Borrower's books and records are now and will be maintained hereafter in sufficient amounts to fully reflect all
liabilities which have accrued or may hereafter accrue.

i. The Collateral and all goods giving rise thereto are and, for so long as any of Borrower's Obligations remain unpaid, will remain free of
any liens, charges, security interests, encumbrances and adverse claims, except for the benefit of _____

j. All covenants, representations and warranties contained in this Agreement shall be true and correct at the time of the execution of this
Agreement and shall be deemed continuing.

3. LOANS

a. _____ agrees, during the continuance of this Agreement, to make loans and advances to Borrower, payable on demand, against those Accounts

which _____ in its sole discretion considers eligible for borrowing, as follows: up to _____% of the face value of each Account shall be

paid upon the acceptance thereof by _____; the remainder, being not less than _____% of said face value, shall be held by _____ as a
reserve to secure the collection and payment of such Account and to secure the payment and performance of all Obligations. It is _____ intention, in the absence of any default in the Obligations, to refund the amounts held as such reserve to Borrower to the extent that the Accounts,
in respect of which such amounts are held, have been collected. The aggregate amount of Borrower's indebtedness and obligations to _____
incurred pursuant to this Agreement, from time to time, shall be referred to hereinafter as "Borrower's Receivables Loan Balance." If Bor-

EXHIBIT 17—continued   87

Accounts Financing Security Agreement

rower's Receivables Loan Balance shall at any time exceed _____% of the aggregate face value of said accepted Accounts, _____ may, but need not, require Borrower, upon demand, to pay such excess to _____or may require Borrower to immediately deliver such additional security to _____ as may be satisfactory to _____.

b. To evidence such loans, Borrower shall, at _____ request, execute and deliver to   promissory notes payable to _____ on demand, which said notes shall be in the amount of any portion or portions of Borrower's Receivables Loan Balance as at the time of _____ request, up to the full extent thereof. Said notes shall provide for the payment to_____of interest at the rate provided in Paragraph 3. (d) and shall be upon forms acceptable to _____. The execution and delivery of such notes shall not constitute payment, satisfaction or release of any Obligation.

c. Checks received by _____ shall not constitute payment, but credit therefor, when earned, shall, solely for the purpose of computing interest earned by _____, be given as of the third calendar day after receipt, to allow for clearance.

d. Until all Obligations of Borrower to _____ are fully paid, Borrower will pay, monthly, as interest, _____ percent per _____ computed on the daily Borrower's Receivables Loan Balance, from the date accrued until the date paid.

e. Borrower agrees to pay interest in an amount not less than $_____ per (month) (year), irrespective of the amount of the daily Borrower's Receivables Loan Balance.

f. _____ shall give Borrower, each month, an extract or a statement of Borrower's account, prepared from _____ records, which will conclusively be deemed correct and accepted by Borrower, unless Borrower gives _____ a written statement of exceptions within thirty (30) days after receipt of such extract or statement.

4. RETURNED GOODS; INSTRUMENTS

a. Borrower will physically segregate all rejected, rerouted, repossessed or returned goods sold or delivered in respect of any Account, will immediately notify _____ thereof, will receive such merchandise in trust for _____ and will hold the same for such disposition as _____ may direct, or, at _____ option, will promptly refund all advances, loans and extensions made on such Accounts, and will post written notice that they are subject to _____ lien and security interest.

b. Borrower will deliver to _____, endorsed to _____, all instruments, chattel paper, guarantees or other documents immediately when received by Borrower as evidence or in payment of, or as security for, any of the Accounts, and will immediately transfer to_____all security received for any of the Accounts.

5. REPORTS; INSPECTION OF RECORDS; FURTHER ASSURANCE

Borrower represents and agrees:

a. At all time to allow _____, by or through any of its officers, agents, employees, attorneys and accountants, to possess, remove to the premises of _____ or any agent of _____ for so long as _____ may desire, to make full use thereof in aid of _____ rights under this agreement, and to examine, audit and make extracts and copies from Borrower's books and all other records, and, for said purposes or to aid _____ in the enforcement of any of its rights under this Agreement, to enter, to remain upon and, without cost to _____, to use the premises of Borrower or wherever the same may be found as often and for as long as _____ may desire.

b. To furnish _____an aged accounts receivable trial balance in such form and as often as _____ requires.

c. To furnish to _____, promptly upon request, Borrower's monthly statements of account with its customers. Borrower agrees that _____ may from time to time verify the validity, amount and any other matters relating to the Accounts by means of mail, telephone or otherwise, in the name of Borrower, _____ or such other name as _____may choose.

d. To do all things required by _____ in its sole judgment, in order more completely to vest in and assure to _____ its rights hereunder. The Accounts shall be assigned to _____ by written or printed instruments (hereinafter called "Schedules") in form acceptable to _____, executed in such quantities as _____ may require, but the lien and security interest of _____ hereunder shall not be limited in any way to or by the inclusion of Accounts within such Schedules and to the extent the terms and provisions hereof shall conflict with said Schedules this Agreement shall be controlling; in the event the Uniform Commercial Code applies to any of the Accounts, Borrower need not furnish Schedules relating thereto unless _____ shall so request; but Borrower's failure to execute and deliver such Schedules shall not limit the security interest granted to _____ hereinunder.

e. To furnish to _____ within sixty (60) days from the end of its fiscal year, financial statements (including balance sheet, profit and loss figures and accountant's comments) for that year and, at _____ request, will furnish to _____ financial statements for each month by the fifteenth day of the following month. All such annual financial statements shall be prepared by certified public accountants acceptable to _____

f. Borrower will promptly notify _____ in writing of any change of its officers, directors and key employees, change of location of its principal offices, change of location of any of its assets (except the shipment, temporary storage or use in its manufacturing processes of inventory in the ordinary and normal course of Borrower's business), change of Borrower's name, death of any co-partner (if Borrower is a partnership), any sale or purchase out of the regular course of Borrower's business and any other material change in the business or financial affairs of Borrower.

6. NOTICE OF ASSIGNMENT; COLLECTION; EXPENSES

a. Borrower agrees that it will, upon the request of _____ and in such form and at such times as _____ shall request, give notice of the assignment of or the granting of a security interest in all or any of the Accounts to the account debtors and that _____ may itself give such notice at any time and from time to time in _____ or Borrower's name, without notice to Borrower, requiring such account debtors to pay the account directly to _____.

b. Borrower irrevocably appoints _____ its true and lawful attorney, with power of substitution, in the name of Borrower or in the name of _____ or otherwise, for the use and benefit of _____, but at the cost and expense of Borrower, without notice to Borrower or any of its representatives or successors, to repair, alter or supply goods, if any, necessary to fulfill in whole or in part the purchase order of any account debtor from which any Collateral has arisen; to demand, collect, receipt for and give renewals, extensions, discharges and releases of any Collateral; to institute and to prosecute legal and equitable proceedings to realize upon the Collateral; to settle, compromise, compound or adjust claims in respect of any Collateral or any legal proceedings brought in respect thereof; and generally to sell in whole or in part for cash, credit or property to others or to itself at any public or private sale, assign, make any agreement with respect to or otherwise deal with any of the Collateral as fully and completely as though _____ were the absolute owner thereof for all purposes. Borrower shall have no power to make any allowance or credit to any account debtor without _____ written consent.

c. Borrower also hereby irrevocably appoints _____ its true and lawful attorney, with power of substitution, to take control in any manner of any cash or non-cash items of payment or proceeds thereof; to endorse the name of Borrower upon any notes, acceptances, checks, drafts, money orders, bills of lading, freight bills, chattel paper or other evidences of payment or Collateral that may come into _____ possession; to sign Borrower's name on any invoices relating to any Accounts, on drafts against account debtors and notices to account debtors; to sign Borrower's name on any Proof of Claim in Bankruptcy against account debtors; to sign Borrower's name on any Notice of Lien, Claim of Mechanic's Lien or Assignment or Satisfaction of Mechanic's Lien; and to do all other acts and things necessary, in _____ sole judgment, to carry out this Agreement. At any time or times when Borrower is in default hereunder, _____ shall have the right to enter upon Borrower's premises and to receive and open all mail directed to Borrower; _____ shall turn over to Borrower all of such mail not relating to Collateral. In the event of default, _____ shall have the right, in the name of Borrower, to notify the Post Office authorities to change the address for the delivery of mail addressed to Borrower to such address as _____ may designate. All checks and other forms of remittance received as provided herein by Borrower shall be endorsed: "Pay to the order of _____" or in such other manner as _____ may designate. Borrower's signature or name may be inserted by _____ in longhand, in typewriting or by rubber stamp. Every such endorsement, however signed or made, shall be deemed to be the valid endorsement of Borrower.

d. Borrower shall have the privilege of collecting the Accounts for the account of and in trust for _____. Such privilege may be revoked by

EXHIBIT 17—continued 88

Accounts Financing Security Agreement

_____ at its option, at any time by: i) giving notification of its assignment of, or lien and security interest in the Accounts to the account debtors, and no notice thereof to Borrower shall be required, or ii) giving notice of such revocation to Borrower. All moneys, checks, notes, drafts, other things of value and items of payment together with any and all relating vouchers, identifications, communications or other data received from account debtors collected or received by Borrower (or by any receiver, trustee, or successor in interest of Borrower, or by any person acting on behalf of Borrower) in reference to the Accounts shall belong to _____ and shall be immediately transmitted by Borrower to _____ at its office (or, if directed by _____, deposited in _____ account in a bank designated by _____) in the original form in which the same are received and endorsed by Borrower. Borrower shall have no right and agrees not to commingle with its own funds or to use, divert or withhold any of the proceeds of any collections. Borrower hereby divests itself of all dominion over the Accounts and the proceeds thereof and collections received thereon. Borrower shall make entries on its books and records in form satisfactory to _____ disclosing the absolute and unconditional assignment of Accounts to _____ and shall keep a separate account on its record books of all collections received thereon. Borrower further agrees to advise _____ immediately of any claims or disputes arising with respect to any Account and of any occurrence that may in any way impair or affect any of the Accounts or tend to reduce the value thereof. Should any suit or proceeding be instituted by or against _____ or Borrower upon any of the Collateral or for the collection or enforcement of any Account, Borrower shall, without expense to _____, make available such of its officers, employees, agents, books, records and files as _____ may deem necessary to make proper proof in Court.

e. _____ shall be entitled to recover from Borrower all damages sustained by _____ by reason of any misrepresentation, breach of warranty or breach of convenant of Borrower herein, expressed or implied, whether caused by the acts or defaults of Borrower, account debtors or others; and also all reasonable attorneys' fees, court costs, court reporter expenses, long distance telephone charges, telegram costs, collection expenses, accountants' fees, supervisory fees, expenses of attorneys, agents, officers, auditors, collectors, clerks and investigators for travel, lodging and food costs, traveling expenses, disbursements, and all other expenses which may be incurred by _____ in enforcing payment of any Account or of Borrower's Obligations in attempting to enforce payment, in realizing upon any Collateral, whether against any debtor, Borrower, Borrower's guarantors or others, in supervising the records and proper management and disposition of the collection of Accounts, in prosecuting or defending any proceeding arising from the efforts of _____ to recover any money or other thing of value or otherwise to enforce or protect any of _____ rights hereunder.

f. Borrower agrees that, as to any insurance it now or hereafter may maintain covering risks of damage to or loss or destruction of its books and records, each such policy of insurance shall contain a loss payable clause in a form satisfactory to _____ naming _____ as payee and providing that all proceeds payable thereunder shall be payable in any event to _____, unless written consent to the contrary is obtained from _____; such proceeds shall be applied to Borrower's Receivables Loan Balance. Each such insurer shall agree that it will give _____ thirty (30) days written notice before any such policy shall be altered or cancelled and that no act or default of Borrower or any other person shall affect the right of _____ to recover thereunder in case of such damage, loss or destruction. Certified copies of such policies shall be delivered to _____ upon demand.

7. FINANCING STATEMENTS AND NOTICES OF ASSIGNMENT

a. At the request of _____, Borrower will join with _____ in executing one or more Financing Statements and/or Notices Of Assignment of Accounts Receivable pursuant to any applicable law, in form satisfactory to _____.

b. Without the written consent of _____, Borrower will not allow any Financing Statement or Notice Of Assignment of Accounts Receivable covering any Collateral or proceeds thereof to be on file in any public office. •

8. EVENTS OF DEFAULT; ACCELERATION

All Obligations shall, notwithstanding any time or credit allowed by any instrument evidencing a liability, become immediately due and payable without notice or demand upon the occurrence of any of the following events of default:

a. Borrower shall fail to make any payment or to perform any Obligation promptly when due;

b. Any warranty, representation, or statement made or furnished to _____ by or in behalf of Borrower shall have been false in any material respect when made or furnished;

c. Any event shall arise which results in the acceleration of the maturity of the indebtedness of Borrower to others under any indenture, agreement or undertaking;

d. There shall occur any loss, theft, damage, destruction, sale or encumbrance to or of any of the Collateral, or any levy, seizure or attachment thereof or thereon shall be made;

e. Any of the following shall occur: dissolution, termination of existence, insolvency, business failure, appointment of a receiver for any part of the property of, assignment for the benefit of creditors by, or the commencement of any proceeding under any bankruptcy or insolvency law by or against Borrower or any guarantor or surety for Borrower, entry of a court order which enjoins, restrains or in any way prevents Borrower from conducting all or any part of its business affairs in the ordinary course, failure to pay any federal, state or local tax or other debt of Borrower unless the same is being contested in good faith, termination of guaranty by any guarantor of Borrower's indebtedness to _____, whether under this Agreement or otherwise; it being expressly agreed that upon the happening of any event described herein, Borrower and each of Borrower's guarantors and sureties hereunder having or acquiring knowledge thereof shall immediately give written notice of said event or fact to _____;

f. _____ shall determine, at any time or times hereafter, that it is insecure with respect to the performance by Borrower of all or any part of the Obligations;

g. Borrower recognizes that, in the event it violates any of the warranties, covenants, terms and conditions of this agreement, no remedy at law will provide adequate relief to _____ and Borrower hereby agrees that _____ shall be entitled to temporary and permanent injunctive relief in case of any such breach without the necessity of proving actual damages.

9. RIGHTS AND REMEDIES

Upon the occurrence of any such event of default, and at any time thereafter, _____ shall have the rights and remedies of a secured party under the _____ Uniform Commercial Code and under any and all other laws in addition to the rights and remedies provided herein or in any other instrument or paper executed by Borrower. All rights, powers and remedies hereunder or in any other instrument provided are cumulative and none is exclusive.

10. ONE GENERAL OBLIGATION; CROSS COLLATERAL

All loans and advances by _____ to Borrower under this Agreement and under all other agreements constitute one loan, and all indebtedness and obligations of Borrower to _____ under this and under all other agreements, present and future, (including, without limitation, the documents listed in Paragraph 1 hereof) consititute one general Obligation secured by collateral and security held and to be held by _____ hereunder and by virtue of all other agreements between Borrower and _____ now and hereafter existing. It is distinctly understood and agreed that all of the rights of _____ contained in this Agreement shall likewise apply insofar as applicable to any modification of or supplement to this Agreement and to any other agreements, present and future, between _____ and Borrower.

11. APPLICATION OF PAYMENTS

All payments made by or in behalf of and all credits due Borrower may be applied and reapplied in whole or in part to any of Borrower's Obligations to the extent and in the manner that _____ may see fit.

EXHIBIT 17—continued

89

Accounts Financing Security Agreement

12. TERMINATION

This Agreement, on acceptance by _____, shall continue in effect for _____ year(s) from the date hereof and from year to year thereafter unless terminated as to future transactions by the giving of notice by registered mail by either party to the other, not less than thirty (30) days prior to any anniversary hereof. Borrower, at such termination date, shall make payment in full of all Obligations, whether evidenced by installment notes or otherwise, and whether or not all or any part of such Obligations are otherwise then due and payable by Borrower to _____. _____may terminate upon immediate notice at any time in the event Borrower commits any act of default enumerated in Paragraph 8. hereof. No termination of this Agreement shall in any way affect or impair any right of _____ arising prior thereto or by reason thereof, nor shall any such termination relieve Borrower or any of the guarantors of any obligation to _____ under this Agreement or otherwise until all of said obligations are fully paid and performed, nor shall any such termination affect any right or remedy of _____ arising from any such obligation, and all agreements, warranties and representations of Borrower shall survive termination.

13. BENEFITS OF THIS AGREEMENT

This Security Agreement shall be binding and inure to the benefit of the parties hereto and their respective heirs, successors, representatives and assigns.

14. GOVERNING LAW; SUBMISSION TO JURISDICTION

The validity, interpretation, enforcement and effect of this Security Agreement shall be governed by the laws of the State of _____.

Borrower hereby consents to the jurisdiction of all courts in said State and hereby appoints _____,

whose address is _____,

as Borrower's agent for service of process in said State.

15. SEPARABILITY

In the event that any provision hereof be deemed to be invalid by reason of the operation of any law or by reason of the interpretation placed thereon by any court, this Agreement shall be construed as not containing such provision and the invalidity of such provision shall not affect the validity of any provision hereof and any and all other provisions hereof which are otherwise lawful and valid shall remain in full force and effect.

16. NOTICES AND PAYMENTS

Any notice, payment or refund required hereunder or by reason of the application of any law shall be deemed to have been given by either party hereto when the same shall have been deposited in the United States mail, postage prepaid, at least five (5) calendar days prior to the action proposed thereby (except that notice of termination shall be given in the manner set forth in Paragraph 12. hereof), addressed:

    a. If to Borrower, at the address of Borrower specified in Paragraph 1. hereof, or to the latest address of Borrower of which _____ shall have received notice from Borrower;

    b. If to _____, at _____

17. ATTORNEYS' FEES

If, at any time or times hereafter, _____ employs counsel for advice or other representation with respect to any Collateral or this Agreement or any other agreement, document or instrument heretofore, now or hereafter executed by Borrower and delivered to _____, or to commence, defend or intervene, file a petition, complaint, answer, motion or other pleadings, or to take any other action in or with respect to any suit or proceeding relating to this Agreement or any other agreement, instrument or document heretofore, now or hereafter executed by Borrower and delivered to _____, or to protect, collect, lease, sell, take possession of, or liquidate any of such Collateral, or to attempt to enforce any security interest or lien in any Collateral, or to represent _____ in any litigation with respect to the affairs of Borrower or in any way relating to any of the Collateral, or to enforce any rights of _____ or Obligations of Borrower, liabilities of Account Debtors, or any other person, firm, or corporation which may be obligated to _____ by virtue of this Agreement or any other agreement, document or instrument heretofore. now or hereafter delivered to _____ by or for the benefit of Borrower; then, in any of such events, all of the reasonable attorneys' fees arising from such services, and any expenses, costs and charges relating thereto, shall constitute additional Obligations of Borrower, secured by the Collateral, payable on demand.

18. WAIVERS

    a. Borrower hereby waives any and all causes of action and claims which it may ever have against _____ as a result of any possession, collection or sale by _____ of any Collateral in the event of a default by Borrower, notwithstanding the effect of such possession, collection or sale upon the business of Borrower, and Borrower waives all rights of redemption, if any, it may have.

    b. The failure at any time or times hereafter to require strict performance by Borrower of any of the provisions, warranties, terms and conditions contained in this Agreement or any other agreement, document or instrument now or hereafter executed by Borrower and delivered to _____, shall not waive, affect or diminish any right of _____ hereafter to demand strict compliance and performance therewith and with respect to any other provisions, warranties, terms and conditions contained in such agreements, documents and instruments, and any waiver of any default shall not waive or affect any other default, whether prior or subsequent thereto, and whether of the same or of a different type. None of the warranties, conditions, provisions and terms contained in this Agreement or any other agreement, document or instrument now or hereafter executed by Borrower and delivered to _____ shall be deemed to have been waived by any act or knowledge of _____, its agents, officers or employees, but only by an instrument in writing, signed by an officer of _____ and directed to Borrower specifying such waiver.

    c. Borrower waives any and all notice or demand which Borrower might be entitled to receive with respect to this Agreement by virtue of any applicable statute or law, and waives demand, protest, notice of protest, notice of default or dishonor, notice of payments and nonpayments, or of any default, release, compromise, settlement, extension, or renewal of all commercial paper, accounts, contract rights, instruments, chattel paper, guaranties, and otherwise, at any time held by _____ on which Borrower may in any way be liable, notice of nonpayment at maturity of any and all accounts, instruments or chattel paper, notice of any action taken by _____ unless expressly required by this Agreement and hereby ratifies and confirms whatever _____ may do pursuant to this Agreement and agrees that _____ shall not be liable for any acts of commission or omission or for any errors of judgment or mistakes of fact or law.

19. EFFECTIVE DATE

This Agreement, which has been signed and delivered to _____ on the day and year first above written, shall not become effective until accepted by _____ under the signature of its duly authorized officers at its address set forth herein in Paragraph 16.

_____

              Borrower

Accepted at:_____,

this _____ day of _____ 19_____

BY:_____

                                          _____

TITLE:_____

                                          BY:_____

ATTEST:_____

                  Secretary

        (affix corporate seal here)

                                            TITLE:_____

ance period is used, a check received in the bank on Thursday would not be considered cleared until the opening of business on Tuesday;

4. The rate of interest to be charged;

5. How the rate will be computed. For instance, the rate could be an agreed number of points over the current prime rate, or a flat interest rate based on the daily or weekly average balance;

6. The minimum charge to be made, if any. A minimum charge is frequently used when a small loan is involved because the cost of policing and handling a small loan is often higher than the interest income derived;

7. The kind of reports, and the frequency with which they are to be submitted to the lender;

8. The *right of set off*, if this is to be exercised. This is the right given the bank in security agreements to set off any cash balances in any of the borrower's bank accounts against any debt due to the bank;

9. The service charge to be made, if any. Some banks will offer a borrower a favorable interest rate, but will add a flat charge per month representing their computed cost of handling. This will be done most frequently when the circumstances of the borrower or the special requirements of the loan add significantly to the bank's administrative expenses.

Almost without exception, a bank can work comfortably within the usuary statutes of the state in which the borrower has his or her place of business; but care should be taken to be sure that any minimum charge or service charge, plus rate of interest, does not violate the maximum interest allowed by the state. For the purpose of determining whether the lender is staying within the maximum, the state may include all charges such as clearance days, accounting fees, auditing fees, and check charges. The total of all charges added to the stated interest rate must be no more than the maximum allowed.

Some states that have usury statutes will have different maximum rates depending on whether loans are being made to a proprietorship, a partnership, or a corporation.

Attempts to circumvent usury statutes almost always are struck down by the courts, and the penalties for violation may be severe—even to the point of the loss of both principal and interest. A September 1975 ruling by a civil court judge in New York points up the importance of staying well within the maximum rates allowed by the state. In this case, a major New York City bank was found to be charging usurious rates when audit, legal, and other fees were added to the stated interest rate. Appeals to this ruling have been made, but as of this writing a final decision has not been rendered. Even if the bank should win, the time and expense spent, and the notoriety gained, are a very high price to pay for coming too close to maximum rates allowed. Although in this case the decision of the court was handed down in connection with consumer loans, it carries a warning that commercial lenders should heed;

10. The rights and time of termination by either party. It is recommended that security agreements be written for a minimum of one year, and that a penalty be invoked if the agreement is cancelled by the borrower prior to any anniversary date. The only exception to this is when a borrower is located in a state with usury laws, and the minimum charge plus interest earned up to the date of cancellation would exceed the maximum earnings allowed by the state. The minimum charge may be based on a flat sum agreed to by the parties, or on an average month's earnings, such as the average for the previous six months multiplied by the number of months from the date of cancellation up to the next anniversary date;

11. The name of the state the laws of which will apply to the agreements. For purposes of clarity and because it is generally appropriate, the applicable state law should be the law of the place where the lender conducts business. Generally, the entire transaction will be carried on in that state and no problems will arise. However, problems may present themselves, as in the case of tangible collateral (inventory or equipment) located on the borrower's premises in another state. In such cases, although the parties have agreed that the law of the lender's state shall apply to all aspects of the transaction, a particular part of the transaction might run afoul of provisions of law in the state where the collateral is located. Even though these provisions are valid and enforceable in the lender's state, the courts of the state where the collateral is located may refuse to apply the law of the state which the parties have agreed is applicable. To insure against this, even though all agreements should set forth that the law of the lender's state shall apply so far as the perfection of security interests are concerned, the lender should still comply with the provisions of the Uniform Commercial Code of the state where the collateral is located.

Other Legal Forms

Other legal forms which may be needed for proper documentation are:

1. A certificate of the secretary/clerk of the borrower's corporation relating to minutes of a meeting of shareholders, shown in Exhibit 18. This document pertains to the approval of the loan agreement by share-

EXHIBIT 18 92

Certificate of Secretary/Clerk Relating to Minutes
of a Meeting of the Shareholders

Certificate Of Secretary/Clerk Relating To Minutes
Of A Meeting Of The Shareholders
Of

_____

I, _____ do hereby certify that I am the duly elected and

acting _____ Secretary of _____,

a corporation organized and existing under and by virtue of the laws of the State of _____;
that I am the keeper of the corporate records and the seal of said corporation; that the following is a full,
true and correct copy of the minutes of an (annual) (special) meeting of the Shareholders of said cor-

poration, held at _____, State of _____ _____ on the _____ day of

_____, 19___; that the meeting was duly convened in accordance with the by-laws of
the corporation and in accordance with all applicable laws; that there was a quorum present at such
meeting; that the following resolutions were duly unanimously adopted at said meeting; and that the
same have not in any way been modified, or rescinded, but are in full force and effect:

RESOLVED, that either the President, any Vice President, any Assistant Vice President, the

Secretary, any Assistant Secretary, the Treasurer, any Assistant Treasurer, _____,

_____ or _____, and each of them, is hereby authorized,
directed and empowered from time to time to make, execute and deliver, either jointly or severally,
for and on behalf of and in the name of this corporation, agreements with _____
_____ a corporation (hereinafter called "_____") providing for various financing arrangements with , including but not limited to the borrowing of monies by the corporation and the
pledging of any or all of its assets as security therefor or otherwise, the sale of any or all of its accounts
receivable, evidences of debt and contract rights, and the sale of any or all other assets pursuant to any
sale and lease-back financing arrangement (all of the foregoing are hereinafter in these minutes sometimes referred to collectively as "financing arrangements") and containing such other provisions as such
officer, officers, employees or agents as aforesaid may in his or their sole discretion deem advisable,
necessary or expedient in the premises; and

BE IT FURTHER RESOLVED, that the President, any Vice President, any Assistant Vice

President, the Treasurer, any Assistant Treasurer, the Secretary, any Assistant Secretary, _____

_____, _____ or _____, and each of them, is hereby
authorized, directed and empowered, either jointly or severally, for and on behalf of and in the name of
the corporation: (a) to borrow from _____ such amount or amounts of money as may be made available to this corporation by _____ at this time or any other time while this resolution shall be in effect
as hereinafter provided; (b) to extend or renew any loan or loans or any installment of principal or
interest thereof, or any indebtedness owing to _____; and (c) to enter into such financing arrangements
at this time or at any other time while this resolution shall be in effect as herein provided as they, or any
of them may see fit; and

BE IT FURTHER RESOLVED, that such loans, financing arrangements, extensions or renewals
be made for such time and payable in such installments and at such rates of discount or interest (which
may be deducted from or added to said loan or loans) and upon such terms as such officer, employee or
agent, or any of them, may see fit; and

BE IT FURTHER RESOLVED, that such loan or loans, before deduction of such discount or
after adding such interest, are hereby acknowledged and declared to be the principal of such indebtedness then owing; and

BE IT FURTHER RESOLVED, that the President, any Vice President, any Assistant Vice

President, the Treasurer, any Assistant Treasurer, the Secretary, any Assistant Secretary, or _____

_____, _____, or _____, and each of them, for and in behalf of
and in the name of the corporation, is hereby authorized, directed and empowered to make, execute and
deliver, from time to time, the note or notes of the corporation (including confession of judgment clauses
therein), evidencing said loan or loans, extensions or renewals, and to sell, transfer, lease, assign, grant
security interests in, mortgage or pledge (and to include therein a waiver of equity of redemption in or
to any real or personal property) any or all of the property and assets of the corporation, real, personal,
or mixed, tangible or intangible, as security or otherwise, including but not limited to inventories of raw

EXHIBIT 18—continued   93

Certificate of Secretary/Clerk Relating to Minutes
of a Meeting of the Shareholders

material, work in process and finished goods, equipment, fixtures, supplies, rights, privileges, franchises, certificates of public convenience and necessity, good will of the corporation, customer's lists, routes, trademarks, trade-names, copyrights, music rights, distribution rights, exhibition rights, contract rights, processes, formulae, patents, patent applications, patent-rights, licenses, inventions, and all of the rents, issues and profits of said property, accounts receivable, conditional sales or title retaining contracts, leases, guaranties, agreements, purchase orders, chattels, intangible rights, chattel mortgages, real estate, real estate mortgages, trust deeds, land contracts, agreements for warranty deed or for purchase of real estate, certificates of beneficial interest in or to trusts or land trusts, contracts, notes, drafts, trade acceptances, liens, obligations, `evidences of indebtedness, judgments, warehouse receipts, bills of lading, trust receipts, and choses in action; and

BE IT FURTHER RESOLVED, that any of said officers, employees or agents as aforesaid, and each of them, is further authorized, directed and empowered, either jointly or severally, for and in behalf of and in the name of the corporation, to make, amend, assign, execute, acknowledge and deliver to _____ any and all other instruments, papers and documents which may be required or requested by _____ to effectuate the purpose and intent hereof or to further secure _____ from time to time or otherwise, including, but not limited to, Loan Agreements, Security Agreements, Financing Statements, Schedules and Assignments of Accounts Receivable in form provided by and used by _____ (all of the terms of which are hereby expressly incorporated herein by reference), assignments of purchase orders, Notices of Factor's Lien, statements designating goods subject to Factor's Lien or other instruments required, necessary or requested to effectuate liens under Factor's Lien, Chattel Mortgage, Conditional Sale or Sales Statutes, Uniform Commercial Code or any other applicable law, demands, liens and agreements, notices of intent to finance accounts receivable, affidavits of mortgagor, and any and all other instruments or forms required under the laws of any state, or of the United States or any of its agencies, and to sign the name of said corporation upon and to endorse over to the order of _____ any and all checks, notes, drafts, money orders or acceptances payable to the order of or endorsed over to the corporation; and

BE IT FURTHER RESOLVED, that any one of said officers, employees, or agents as aforesaid, may from time to time, make, execute, deliver or give to _____ any direction for the payment, disposition of or receipt for any funds, instruments, securities or property, real or personal, belonging to the corporation, or designate persons so to do; and

BE IT FURTHER RESOLVED, that in order to induce _____ to make certain financing arrangements with one or more of this corporation's subsidiaries and/or affiliates, _____ being unwilling to extend credit or to render such assistance unless this corporation shall enter into a guaranty agreement with _____ substantially in the form of the draft of said agreement submitted to this meeting, and in view of the inter-corporate or business relations between this corporation and the said subsidiaries and/or affiliates, it is deemed to be to the direct interests and advantage of this corporation that it enter into said agreement, any of said officers, employees or agents, and each of them, is further authorized and directed, either jointly or severally, to make, execute on behalf of and in the name of this corporation and deliver to _____ an agreement with _____, substantially in the form submitted to this meeting, and to do and perform all such acts and things deemed by any such officer, employee or agent necessary, convenient or proper to carry out or modify any such guaranty agreement; and

BE IT FURTHER RESOLVED, that the acts and doings of said officers, employees or agents so designated, or any of them, shall at all times receive full faith and credit without the necessity of inquiry by _____ or other persons relying upon the same as to any of the circumstances attending the same, or to the application of any monies loaned pursuant hereto, and that the acts and doings of said officers, employees or agents so designated, or any of them in respect to the subject matter hereof, and all of the prior acts and doings of the officers, employees or agents of the corporation with _____, and all agreements, written or oral, and any and all instruments of any and every kind, nature, or description whatsoever heretofore executed and delivered by the corporation to _____, are hereby fully ratified, approved, adopted and confirmed, and declared to be and represent binding obligations of the corporation in accordance with the respective terms and provisions thereof, and that said officers, employees or agents, or any of them, are hereby authorized, empowered and directed to do any and all acts and things as they or any of them may deem necessary or proper in order to fully carry out and perform the terms and provisions of said instruments hereinbefore more particularly described; and

BE IT FURTHER RESOLVED, that the authorizations herein set forth shall remain in full force and effect until written notice of their modification or discontinuance shall be given to and actually received by _____ at its offices in _____, but no such modification or discontinuance shall affect the validity of the acts of any person, authorized to so act by these resolutions, performed prior to the receipt of such notice by Heller.

BE IT FURTHER RESOLVED, that the _____ Secretary of the corporation is hereby authorized to furnish to _____ a copy of these resolutions and to certify and affix the corporate seal thereunto.

IN WITNESS WHEREOF, I have hereunto subscribed my name as _____

Secretary and have caused the corporate seal of this corporation to be hereto affixed this _____

day of _____, A.D. 19____.

Corporate Seal.

_____
Secretary as aforesaid

holders. Shareholders' votes are sometimes difficult to get when shares are widely or publicly held, but if the loan involves all or substantially all of the company's assets, it would be necessary to get them. The law of the state in which the borrower is located should be checked in this regard;

2. The certificate of the secretary/clerk relating to minutes of a meeting of the Board of Directors, shown in Exhibit 19;

3. The guaranty (personal), shown in Exhibit 20. This usually is secured from the principals of closely held companies and their spouses. It is very rarely given by the principals of companies whose shares are widely or publicly held. The personal guaranties of spouses cannot always be secured, but it is comforting to get them whenever possible. This obviates the possibility of the transfer of any assets from one spouse to the other, thereby making those assets unavailable;

4. The guaranty by corporation, shown in Exhibit 21. This often may be obtained from the parent, subsidiary, or affiliate of the borrower, and should be supported by votes of their boards of directors;

5. Subordination and stand-by agreement, Exhibit 22. This covers loans due to a principal or to a parent, subsidiary, or affiliated company. Company subordinations should be supported by a vote of the appropriate board of directors;

6. The Custodian Agreement, Exhibit 23. This may be used when the volume of invoices is so large that it is impractical for the borrower to provide copies to the lender. This is discussed in detail in Chapter 6;

7. The Participation Agreement, Exhibit 24. This is used when a bank or banks or other financial institutions share the loan. This agreement is made only between the "lead" lender and the participant, and unless there is some specific action that the participant may take which would directly affect the borrower, it need not be shown to the borrower. There is no implication here that the existence of a participation agreement should be hidden from the borrower; in fact, it is recommended that such disclosure be made. The details of the agreement covering arrangements between the participants do not necessarily have to be made known to any third party;

8. The Certification of Corporate Resolutions, Exhibit 25. This is the certificate by the borrower's corporate Secretary of appropriate corporate action permitting the lender to endorse, by rubber stamp or otherwise, any checks received from the borrower, whether issued by a third party or the borrower; and to apply the checks to the borrower's loan balance;

(*Text continues on page 111*)

EXHIBIT 19   95

Certificate of Secretary/Clerk Relating to Minutes
of a Meeting of the Board of Directors

Certificate Of Secretary/Clerk Relating To Minutes
Of A Meeting Of The Board Of Directors
Of

_____

I, _____ do hereby certify that I am the duly elected and

acting _____ Secretary of _____,

a corporation organized and existing under and by virtue of the laws of the State of _____;
that I am the keeper of the corporate records and the seal of said corporation; that the following is a full,
true and correct copy of the minutes of an (annual) (special) meeting of the Board of Directors of said

corporation, held at _____, State of _____ on the _____ day of

_____, 19____; that the meeting was duly convened in accordance with the by-laws of
the corporation and in accordance with all applicable laws; that there was a quorum present at such
meeting; that the following resolutions were duly unanimously adopted at said meeting; and that the
same have not in any way been modified, or rescinded, but are in full force and effect:

RESOLVED, that either the President, any Vice President, any Assistant Vice President, the

Secretary, any Assistant Secretary, the Treasurer, any Assistant Treasurer, _____,

_____ or _____, and each of them, is hereby authorized,
directed and empowered from time to time to make, execute and deliver, either jointly or severally,
for and on behalf of and in the name of this corporation, agreements with _____
_____. a corporation (hereinafter called "_____") providing for various financing arrangements with _____, including but not limited to the borrowing of monies by the corporation and the
pledging of any or all of its assets as security therefor or otherwise, the sale of any or all of its accounts
receivable, evidences of debt and contract rights, and the sale of any or all other assets pursuant to any
sale and lease-back financing arrangement (all of the foregoing are hereinafter in these minutes sometimes referred to collectively as "financing arrangements") and containing such other provisions as such
officer, officers, employees or agents as aforesaid may in his or their sole discretion deem advisable,
necessary or expedient in the premises; and

BE IT FURTHER RESOLVED, that the President, any Vice President, any Assistant Vice

President, the Treasurer, any Assistant Treasurer, the Secretary, any Assistant Secretary, _____

_____, _____ or _____, and each of them, is hereby
authorized, directed and empowered, either jointly or severally, for and on behalf of and in the name of
the corporation: (a) to borrow from _____ such amount or amounts of money as may be made available to this corporation by _____ at this time or any other time while this resolution shall be in effect
as hereinafter provided; (b) to extend or renew any loan or loans or any installment of principal or
interest thereof, or any indebtedness owing to _____; and (c) to enter into such financing arrangements
at this time or at any other time while this resolution shall be in effect as herein provided as they, or any
of them may see fit; and

BE IT FURTHER RESOLVED, that such loans, financing arrangements, extensions or renewals
be made for such time and payable in such installments and at such rates of discount or interest (which
may be deducted from or added to said loan or loans) and upon such terms as such officer, employee or
agent, or any of them, may see fit; and

BE IT FURTHER RESOLVED, that such loan or loans, before deduction of such discount or
after adding such interest, are hereby acknowledged and declared to be the principal of such indebtedness then owing; and

BE IT FURTHER RESOLVED, that the President, any Vice President, any Assistant Vice

President, the Treasurer, any Assistant Treasurer, the Secretary, any Assistant Secretary, or _____

_____, _____ or _____, and each of them, for and in behalf of
and in the name of the corporation, is hereby authorized, directed and empowered to make, execute and
deliver, from time to time, the note or notes of the corporation (including confession of judgment clauses
therein), evidencing said loan or loans, extensions or renewals, and to sell, transfer, lease, assign, grant
security interests in, mortgage or pledge (and to include therein a waiver of equity of redemption in or
to any real or personal property) any or all of the property and assets of the corporation, real, personal,
or mixed, tangible or intangible, as security or otherwise, including but not limited to inventories of raw

EXHIBIT 19—continued   96

Certificate of Secretary/Clerk Relating to Minutes
of a Meeting of the Board of Directors

material, work in process and finished goods, equipment, fixtures, supplies, rights, privileges, franchises, certificates of public convenience and necessity, good will of the corporation, customer's lists, routes, trademarks, trade-names, copyrights, music rights, distribution rights, exhibition rights, contract rights, processes, formulae, patents, patent applications, patent-rights, licenses, inventions, and all of the rents, issues and profits of said property, accounts receivable, conditional sales or title retaining contracts, leases, guaranties, agreements, purchase orders, chattels, intangible rights, chattel mortgages, real estate, real estate mortgages, trust deeds, land contracts, agreements for warranty deed or for purchase of real estate, certificates of beneficial interest in or to trusts or land trusts, contracts, notes, drafts, trade acceptances, liens, obligations, evidences of indebtedness, judgments, warehouse receipts, bills of lading, trust receipts, and choses in action; and

BE IT FURTHER RESOLVED, that any of said officers, employees or agents as aforesaid, and each of them, is further authorized, directed and empowered, either jointly or severally, for and in behalf of and in the name of the corporation, to make, amend, assign, execute, acknowledge and deliver to _____ any and all other instruments, papers and documents which may be required or requested by _____ to effectuate the purpose and intent hereof or to further secure _____ from time to time or otherwise, including, but not limited to, Loan Agreements, Security Agreements, Financing Statements, Schedules and Assignments of Accounts Receivable in form provided by and used by _____ (all of the terms of which are hereby expressly incorporated herein by reference), assignments of purchase orders, Notices of Factor's Lien, statements designating goods subject to Factor's Lien or other instruments required, necessary or requested to effectuate liens under Factor's Lien, Chattel Mortgage, Conditional Sale or Sales Statutes, Uniform Commercial Code or any other applicable law, demands, liens and agreements, notices of intent to finance accounts receivable, affidavits of mortgagor, and any and all other instruments or forms required under the laws of any state, or of the United States or any of its agencies, and to sign the name of said corporation upon and to endorse over to the order of _____ any and all checks, notes, drafts, money orders or acceptances payable to the order of or endorsed over to the corporation; and

BE IT FURTHER RESOLVED, that any one of said officers, employees, or agents as aforesaid, may from time to time, make, execute, deliver or give to _____ any direction for the payment, disposition of or receipt for any funds, instruments, securities or property, real or personal, belonging to the corporation, or designate persons so to do; and

BE IT FURTHER RESOLVED, that in order to induce _____ to make certain financing arrangements with one or more of this corporation's subsidiaries and/or affiliates, _____ being unwilling to extend credit or to render such assistance unless this corporation shall enter into a guaranty agreement with _____ substantially in the form of the draft of said agreement submitted to this meeting, and in view of the inter-corporate or business relations between this corporation and the said subsidiaries and/or affiliates, it is deemed to be to the direct interests and advantage of this corporation that it enter into said agreement, any of said officers, employees or agents, and each of them, is further authorized and directed, either jointly or severally, to make, execute on behalf of and in the name of this corporation and deliver to _____ an agreement with _____, substantially in the form submitted to this meeting, and to do and perform all such acts and things deemed by any such officer, employee or agent necessary, convenient or proper to carry out or modify any such guaranty agreement; and

BE IT FURTHER RESOLVED, that the acts and doings of said officers, employees or agents so designated, or any of them, shall at all times receive full faith and credit without the necessity of inquiry by _____ or other persons relying upon the same as to any of the circumstances attending the same, or to the application of any monies loaned pursuant hereto, and that the acts and doings of said officers, employees or agents so designated, or any of them in respect to the subject matter hereof, and all of the prior acts and doings of the officers, employees or agents of the corporation with _____, and all agreements, written or oral, and any and all instruments of any and every kind, nature, or description whatsoever heretofore executed and delivered by the corporation to _____, are hereby fully ratified, approved, adopted and confirmed, and declared to be and represent binding obligations of the corporation in accordance with the respective terms and provisions thereof, and that said officers, employees or agents, or any of them, are hereby authorized, empowered and directed to do any and all acts and things as they or any of them may deem necessary or proper in order to fully carry out and perform the terms and provisions of said instruments hereinbefore more particularly described; and

BE IT FURTHER RESOLVED, that the authorizations herein set forth shall remain in full force and effect until written notice of their modification or discontinuance shall be given to and actually received by _____ at its offices in _____, but no such modification or discontinuance shall affect the validity of the acts of any person, authorized to so act by these resolutions, performed prior to the receipt of such notice by _____.

BE IT FURTHER RESOLVED, that the _____ Secretary of the corporation is hereby authorized to furnish to _____ a copy of these resolutions and to certify and affix the corporate seal thereunto.

IN WITNESS WHEREOF, I have hereunto subscribed my name as _____

Secretary and have caused the corporate seal of this corporation to be hereto affixed this _____

day of _____, A.D. 19____.

Corporate Seal.   _____
                                                 Secretary as aforesaid

EXHIBIT 20   97
Guaranty (Personal)

Guaranty

TO: METROPOLITAN NATIONAL BANK

Date _____, 19____

Gentlemen:

To induce you to purchase or otherwise acquire from _____
(hereinafter called "Debtor") accounts receivable, conditional sale or lease agreements, chattel mortgages, drafts, notes, bills, acceptances, trust receipts, contracts or other obligations or choses-in-action (herein collectively called "receivables"), or to advance moneys or extend credit to the Debtor thereon, or to factor the sales or finance the accounts of the Debtor (either according to any present or future existing agreement or according to any changes in any such agreement or on any other terms and arrangements from time to time agreed upon with the Debtor, hereby consenting to and waiving notice of any and all such agreements, terms and arrangements and changes thereof) or to otherwise directly or indirectly advance money to or give or extend faith and credit to the Debtor, or otherwise assist the Debtor in financing its business or sales, (without obligating you to do any of the foregoing, we, the undersigned, for value received, do hereby jointly and severally unconditionally guarantee to you and your assigns the prompt payment in full at maturity and all times thereafter (waiving notice of non-payment) of any and all indebtedness, obligations and liabilities of every kind or nature (both principal and interest) now or at any time hereafter owing to you by the Debtor, and of any and all receivables heretofore and hereafter acquired by you from said Debtor or in respect of which the Debtor has or may become in any way liable, and the prompt, full and faithful performance and discharge by the Debtor of each and every the terms, conditions, agreements, representations, warranties, guaranties and provisions on the part of the Debtor contained in any such agreement or arrangement or in any modification or addenda thereto or substitution thereof, or contained in any schedule or other instrument heretofore or hereafter given by or on behalf of said Debtor in connection with the sale or assignment of any such receivables to you, or contained in any other agreements, undertakings or obligations of the Debtor with or to you, of any kind or nature, and we also hereby jointly and severally agree on demand to reimburse you and your assigns for all expenses, collection charges, court costs and attorney's fees incurred in endeavoring to collect or enforce any of the foregoing against the Debtor and/or undersigned or any other person or concern liable thereon; for all of which, with interest at the highest lawful contract rate after due until paid, we hereby jointly and severally agree to be directly, unconditionally and primarily liable jointly and severally with the Debtor, and agree that the same may be recovered in the same or separate actions brought to recover the principal indebtedness.

Notice of acceptance of this guaranty, the giving or extension of credit to the Debtor, the purchase or acquisition of receivables, or the advancement of money or credit thereon, and presentment, demand, notices of default, non-payment or partial payments and protest, notice of protest and all other notices or formalities to which the Debtor might otherwise be entitled, prosecution of collection or remedies against the Debtor or against the makers, endorsers, or other person liable on any such receivables or against any security or collateral thereto appertaining, are hereby waived. The undersigned also waive notice of and consents to the granting of indulgence or extension of time payment, the taking and releasing of security in respect of any said receivables, agreements, obligations, indebtedness or liabilities so guaranteed hereunder, or your accepting partial payments thereon or your settling, compromising or compounding any of the same in such manner and at such times as you may deem advisable, without in any way impairing or affecting our liability for the full amount thereof; and you shall not be required to prosecute collection, enforcement or other remedies against the Debtor or against any person liable on any said receivables, agreements, obligations, indebtedness or liabilities so guaranteed, or to enforce or resort to any security, liens, collateral or other rights or remedies thereto appertaining, before calling on us for payment; nor shall our liability in any way be released or affected by reason of any failure or delay on your part so to do.

This guaranty is absolute, unconditional and continuing and payment of the sums for which the undersigned become liable shall be made to you at your office from time to time on demand as the same become or are declared due, notwithstanding that you hold reserves, credits, collateral or security against which you may be entitled to resort for payment, and one or more and successive or concurrent actions may be brought hereon against the undersigned jointly and severally, either in the same action in which the Debtor is sued or in separate actions, as often as deemed advisable. We expressly waive and bar ourselves from any right to set-off, recoup or counterclaim any claim or demand against said Debtor, or against any other person or concern liable on said receivables, and, as further security to you, any and all debts or liabilities now or hereafter owing to us by the Debtor or by such other person or concern are hereby subordinated to your claims and are hereby assigned to you.

Each guarantor shall continue liable hereunder until you actually receive written notice from him by registered mail terminating the same as to him; but the giving of such notice shall not terminate this guaranty as to any other guarantor, nor relieve the one giving such notice from liability as to any debt, undertaking or liability incurred or undertaken prior to such time. The death of any of the guarantors shall not terminate this guaranty as to his estate or as to the surviving guarantors, but the same shall continue in full force and effect until notice of termination is given and received as hereinbefore provided and all of said indebtedness, liabilities or obligations created or assumed are fully paid.

In case bankruptcy or insolvency proceedings, or proceedings for reorganization, or for the appointment of a receiver, trustee or custodian for the Debtor or over its property or any substantial portion thereof, be instituted by or against the Debtor, or if the Debtor becomes insolvent or makes an assignment for the benefit of creditors or attempts to effect a composition with creditors, or encumber or dispose of all or a substantial portion of its property, or if the Debtor defaults in the payment or repurchase of any of such receivables or indebtedness as the same falls due, or fails promptly to make good any default in respect of any undertaking, then the liability of the undersigned hereunder shall at your option and without notice become immediately fixed and be enforceable for the full amount thereof, whether then due or not, the same as though all said receivables, debts and liabilities had become past due.

This guaranty shall inure to the benefit of yourself, your successors and assigns. It shall be binding jointly and severally on the undersigned, their heirs, representatives and assigns, regardless of the number of persons signing as guarantors or the turn or order of their signing.

This instrument shall be governed as to validity, interpretation, effect and in all other respects by the laws and decisions of the States of _____, unless this instrument is delivered to your office in the City of _____ , _____, in which event the laws and decisions of the State of _____ shall govern.

_____ (SEAL)

_____ (SEAL)

EXHIBIT 21   98

Guaranty by Corporation

Guaranty by Corporation

TO: METROPOLITAN NATIONAL BANK

Date _____, 19____

Gentlemen:

_____, a corporation organized under the laws of the state of _____ (herein called "Debtor") is (a) engaged in business as a corporate affiliate of the undersigned, or (b) engaged in selling, marketing, using, or otherwise dealing in merchandise, supplies, products, equipment or other articles supplied to it by the undersigned, or (c) _____

Because of our inter-corporate or business relations, it will be to our direct interest and advantage to assist the Debtor to procure funds, credit or other financial assistance from you in order to further its business and sales.

Accordingly, in order to induce you to purchase or otherwise acquire from the Debtor accounts receivable, conditional sale or lease agreements, chattel mortgages, drafts, notes, bills, acceptances, trust receipts, contracts or other obligations or choses-in-action (herein collectively called "receivables"), or to advance moneys or extend credit to the Debtor thereon, or to factor the sales or finance the accounts of the Debtor (either according to any present or future existing agreement or according to any changes in any such agreement or on any other terms and arrangements from time to time agreed upon with the Debtor, hereby consenting to and waiving notice of any and all such agreements, terms and arrangements and changes thereof) or to otherwise directly or indirectly advance money to or give or extend faith and credit to the Debtor, or otherwise assist the Debtor in financing its business or sales, (without obligating you to do any of the foregoing, we, the undersigned, for value received, do hereby unconditionally guarantee to you and your assigns the prompt payment in full at maturity and all times thereafter (waiving notice of non-payment) of any and all indebtedness, obligations and liabilities of every kind or nature (both principal and interest) now or at any time hereafter owing to you by the Debtor, and of any and all receivables heretofore or hereafter acquired by you from said Debtor or in respect of which the Debtor has or may become in any way liable, and the prompt, full and faithful performance and discharge by the Debtor of each and every the terms, conditions, agreements, representations, warranties, guaranties and provisions on the part of the Debtor contained in any such agreement or arrangement or in any modification or addenda thereto or substitution thereof, or contained in any schedule or other instrument heretofore or hereafter given by or on behalf of said Debtor in connection with the sale or assignment of any such receivables to you, or contained in any other agreements, undertakings or obligations of the Debtor with or to you, of any kind or nature, and we also hereby agree on demand to reimburse you and your assigns for all expenses, collection charges, court costs and attorneys' fees incurred in endeavoring to collect or enforce any of the foregoing against the Debtor and/or undersigned or any other person or concern liable thereon; for all of which, with interest at the highest lawful contract rate after due until paid, we hereby agree to be directly, unconditionally and primarily liable jointly and severally with the Debtor, and agree that the same may be recovered in the same or separate actions brought to recover the principal indebtedness.

Notice of acceptance of this guaranty, the giving or extension of credit to the Debtor, the purchase or acquisition of receivables, or the advancement of money or credit thereon, and presentment, demand, notices of default, non-payment or partial payments and protest, notice of protest and all other notices or formalities to which the Debtor might otherwise be entitled, prosecution of collection or remedies against the Debtor or against the makers, endorsers, or other person liable on any such receivables or against any security or collateral thereto appertaining, are hereby waived. The undersigned also waives notice of any consents to the granting of indulgence or extension of time payment, the taking and releasing of security in respect of any said receivables, agreements, obligations, indebtedness or liabilities so guaranteed hereunder, or your accepting partial payments thereon or your settling, compromising or compounding any of the same in such manner and at such time as you may deem advisable, without in any way impairing or affecting our liability for the full amount thereof; and you shall not be required to prosecute collection, enforcement or other remedies against the Debtor or against any person liable on any said receivables, agreements, obligations, indebtedness or liabilities so guaranteed, or to enforce or resort to any security, liens, collateral or other rights or remedies thereto appertaining, before calling on us for payment; nor shall our liability in any way be released or affected by reason of any failure or delay on your part so to do.

This guaranty is absolute, unconditional and continuing and payment of the sums for which the undersigned become liable shall be made to you at your office from time to time on demand as the same become or are declared due, notwithstanding that you hold reserves, credits, collateral or security against which you may be entitled to resort for payment, and one or more and successive or concurrent actions may be brought hereon against the undersigned, either in the same action in which the Debtor is sued or in separate actions, as often as deemed advisable. We expressly waive and bar ourselves from any right to set-off, recoup or counter-claim any claim or demand against said Debtor, or against any other person or concern liable on said receivables, and, as further security to you, any and all debts or liabilities now or hereafter owing to us by the Debtor or by such other person or concern are hereby subordinated to your claims and are hereby assigned to you

We shall continue liable hereunder until you actually receive written notice from us by registered mail terminating the same; but the giving of such notice shall not terminate this guaranty or relieve us from liability as to any debt, undertaking or liability incurred or undertaken prior to such time.

In case bankruptcy or insolvency proceedings, or proceedings for reorganization, or for the appointment of a receiver, trustee or custodian for us or the Debtor or over our or its property or any substantial portion thereof, be instituted by or against either us or the Debtor, or if we or the Debtor become insolvent or make an assignment for the benefit of creditors, or attempt to effect a composition with creditors, or encumber or dispose of all or a substantial portion of our or its property, or if we or the Debtor default in the payment or repurchase of any of such receivables or indebtedness as the same falls due, or fail promptly to make good any default in respect of any undertaking, then the liability of the undersigned hereunder shall at your option and without notice become immediately fixed and be enforcible for the full amount thereof, whether then due or not, the same as though all said receivables, debts and liabilities had become past due.

This guaranty shall inure to the benefit of yourself, your successors and assigns. It shall be binding on the undersigned, its successors and assigns, and shall continue in full force and effect until notice of termination is given and received as hereinbefore provided and all of said indebtedness, liabilities or obligations created or assumed are fully paid.

This instrument shall be governed as to validity, interpretation, effect and in all other respects by the laws and decisions of the State of _____, unless this instrument is delivered to your office in the City of _____, _____, in which event the laws and decisions of the State of _____ shall govern.

ATTEST: _____

_____ By _____
        Secretary   *President*

(AFFIX CORPORATE SEAL HERE)

EXHIBIT 21—continued

Guaranty by Corporation

99

RESOLUTION

WHEREAS, _____ (a corporation organized under the laws

of the State of _____), herein called the "Debtor," is engaged (a) in business as a corporate affiliate of this corporation or (b) in the business of selling, marketing, using or otherwise dealing in merchandise, supplies,

equipment, products or other articles supplied to it by this corporation; or (c) _____

_____ and

WHEREAS, said Debtor is desirous of obtaining funds, credit or other financial assistance from _____ _____ (a Delaware corporation), herein referred to as "_____," and said_____ is unwilling to extend credit or to render such assistance to the Debtor unless this corporation shall enter into a guaranty agreement with _____ substantially in the form of the draft of said agreement submitted to this meeting; and

WHEREAS, in view of the premises aforesaid and because of the inter-corporate or business relations between this corporation and said Debtor it is deemed to be to the direct interests and advantage of this corporation that it enter into said agreement with_____:

RESOLVED, that the President, any Vice-President, Secretary, Treasurer or other officer or any agent of this corporation, or any one or more of them, be and they are hereby authorized, empowered and directed to enter into and execute on behalf of the corporation an agreement with _____ substantially in the form of a draft of said agreement submitted to the meeting, and to do and perform all such acts and things deemed by any such officer or agent necessary, convenient or proper to carry out or modify any such agreement, hereby ratifying, approving and confirming all that any said officers or agents have done or may do or cause to be done in the premises.

I, _____, do hereby certify that I am the Secretary of _____,

a corporation organized and existing under and by virtue of the laws of the State of _____, having its principal

place of business in the City of _____, State of _____; that I am the keeper of the corporate records and the seal of said corporation; that the foregoing resolution is a true and correct copy of a resolution duly adopted and ratified at a special meeting of the Board of Directors of said corporation duly convened and held in accordance with its by-laws and the laws of

said State at the office of said corporation in the City of _____, State of _____, on the _____

day of _____, 19____, as taken and transcribed by me from the minutes of said meeting and compared by me with the original of said resolution recorded in said minutes and that the same has not in any way been modified, repealed or rescinded but is in full force and effect; that the within agreement is the agreement referred to in said resolution and was duly executed pursuant thereto.

I do further certify that the within agreement is the agreement referred to in said resolution and was duly executed and delivered pursuant thereto; also, that the following are the officers of said corporation, namely:

President _____

Vice-President _____

Secretary _____

Treasurer _____

WITNESS my hand and the seal of said corporation this _____ day of _____, 19____

_____
(Secretary of said Corporation)

(AFFIX CORPORATE SEAL HERE)

EXHIBIT 22   100
Subordination and Stand-by Agreement

Subordination And Stand-by Agreement

TO: METROPOLITAN NATIONAL BANK

The undersigned (sometimes hereinafter referred to as "we" or "us") are financially interested in _____

_____ , a _____corporation, referred to as the "Company." The Company as now appears on the books is indebted to the undersigned as follows:

To induce you to discount or purchase from the Company deferred payment paper, accounts receivable, notes, conditional sales contracts, chattel mortgages, customer obligations, or other receivables (herein called "Receivables"), at any time offered to you by the Company, or to lend or advance monies or otherwise extend faith or credit to the Company, and to better secure you in respect thereof and in consideration of the premises and the sum of One Dollar ($1.00) to us in hand paid, receipt whereof is hereby acknowledged, we agree to and do hereby subordinate the aforesaid indebtedness owing by the Company to the undersigned (as well as any and all other indebtedness which said Company may now or at any time hereafter owe to the undersigned, together with all collateral and security, if any, for the payment of any such indebtedness aforesaid) to any and all debts, demands, claims, liabilities or causes of action for which the Company may now or at any time hereafter in any way be liable to you; and we further covenant and agree with you that the Company shall not pay, and we will not accept payment of or assert or seek to enforce against the Company, any indebtedness now or hereafter owing by the Company to the undersigned or any collateral or security thereto appertaining, unless and until you have been paid in full any and all such debts, claims, liabilities, demands or causes of action now or hereafter owing to you by the Company; and as further security for the undertakings of the undersigned in that behalf, the undersigned hereby subrogate you to any and all such indebtedness now or hereafter owing by the Company to the undersigned and to any and all collateral or security therefor, and covenant and agree to assign, endorse and deliver to and deposit with you any and all notes or other obligations or instruments evidencing any such indebtedness and all collateral and security thereto appertaining, hereby irrevocably authorizing you to collect, receive, enforce and accept any and all sums or distributions of any kind that may become due, payable or distributable on or in respect of such indebtedness, either principal or interest, or such collateral or security, whether paid directly or indirectly by the Company, or paid or distributed in any bankruptcy, receivership, reorganization or dissolution proceedings or otherwise; hereby irrevocably authorizing you in your discretion to make and present claims therefor in any such proceedings either in your name or ours; and in case any such sums or distributions come into our hands, we agree to promptly turn the same over to you. The undersigned represent and warrant to you that the undersigned have not assigned or transferred any of said indebtedness or any interest therein or any such collateral or security to any other person and that they will make no other assignment or transfer thereof, and that any notes or written obligations taken to evidence said indebtedness or any renewal notes or written obligations will be endorsed with a proper notice of this agreement.

In further consideration hereof, the undersigned hereby postpone in your favor any and all claims of every kind and description that the undersigned may now or hereafter have against the Company to the payment to you of any and all debts, claims, demands or causes of action of every character and description that you may now or hereafter have against the Company, whether arising hereunder or in any other manner. The undersigned waive notice of acceptance hereof, notice of the creation of any indebtedness or liability of the Company to you, the giving or extension of credit to the company, or the taking or releasing of security for the payment thereof, and waive presentment, demand, protest, notice of protest or default and all other notices to which the undersigned might otherwise be entitled.

This agreement shall be continuing irrevocable and binding on the undersigned (jointly and severally, if there be two or more persons who sign the same) and their respective heirs, personal representatives and assigns, and shall inure to the benefit of yourselves, your successors and assigns. The death of any one of the undersigned (if there be more than one party signatory hereto) shall not affect this agreement as to any other of the undersigned. If there be only one person who has signed this agreement, the words "undersigned," "we" and "us" shall be deemed to mean that one person.

IN WITNESS WHEREOF, the undersigned have set their hands and seals this _____

day of _____ 19____.

_____ (SEAL)   _____ (SEAL)

_____ (SEAL)   _____ (SEAL)

_____ (SEAL)   _____ (SEAL)

THE ABOVE NAMED COMPANY assents to the foregoing and agrees in all respects to be bound thereby and to keep, observe and perform the several matters and things therein intended of it to be done, and particularly agrees not to make any payment contrary to the foregoing.

_____

By _____

EXHIBIT 23   101
Custodian Agreement

METROPOLITAN NATIONAL BANK
FINANCIAL PLACE
RECEIVABLE CITY, USA

Custodian Agreement

Re: CUSTODIAL AGENT

Dear

This will confirm our agreement for you to act as our Custodial Agent in connection with certain financing arrangements we have entered into with

(Borrower).

1. Your duties as our Agent will commence immediately, and will be without any salary from us. Your entire compensation is to be paid by your employer.

2. With respect to our inventory lien, if any, you are to forward to us periodically a report in such form and at such times as requested by us showing the value of all inventory, the cost or selling price of all such inventory received and sold or released in each such period.   You will arrange with Borrower to obtain such information and examine such evidence of receipts and deliveries in form satisfactory to you so that you can verify, and have complete confidence in the figures you report to us.   If such is not the case, you are to notify us immediately.

3. As sales are made, you are to furnish us with assignments of all sales, including those under conditional sale contracts, if any, on forms supplied to you by us entitled "List of Accounts Assigned."   Each conditional sale contract is to be assigned to us separately on a form suitable to us, and is to be sent by you to us with the aforesaid "List of Accounts."   You are also to furnish us with a "Memo of Returns and Credits", on a form supplied by us, immediately upon receipt of any returns or the issuance of any credits.   At the end of each month, you are to furnish us with an aging of all accounts or a list of delinquent accounts as defined by us, whichever may be required by us.

4. You are also to retain custody of invoices and delivery receipts, or to send them to us as instructed by us, so that you can sign on each assignment of the "List of Accounts" the following statement:

   "I hereby certify that I have seen and have verified the delivery evidences and invoices giving rise to the accounts assigned herewith and the credits for returns of merchandise."

   _____
   Signature of Custodial Agent

5. You have no authority or power, expressed or implied, to bind us in any way, or to incur any debt, obligation, or liability to anyone for us in our behalf.   Your duties shall continue so long as your services are satisfactory to us or are required by us, but we shall have the right to terminate your duties anytime we deem advisable and you shall have the same right.

EXHIBIT 23—continued

Custodian Agreement

102

-2-

6. You recognize that we are imposing special trust and confidence in you as our Agent, and so long as you continue in such capacity you agree that you will give us your complete and undivided loyalty and fidelity in connection therewith. Contemporaneously herewith, you agree to fill out and execute an application for a fidelity bond to be issued to our company covering your duties as aforesaid.

7. The above mentioned duties and responsibilities shall remain in full force and effect unless modified by us in writing or until your duties as Custodial Agent are terminated.

Please indicate your acceptance of the foregoing terms and conditions of your duties as our Agent by signing the enclosed copy of this letter where indicated and returning it to us:

Very truly yours,

METROPOLITAN NATIONAL BANK

ACCEPTED AND AGREED TO

_____

_____

The undersigned hereby consents to the performance of
as Custodial Agent on the terms and conditions outlined above, and we agree that said Agent shall be under your exclusive control and direction in the performance of his (her) duties as your Custodial Agent, and that we shall not require or demand any service of said Agent at such time or in such manner as to interfere with or affect his (her) faithful and prompt performance of his (her) duties as your Agent.

The undersigned agrees to furnish or maintain, rent-free and without cost to Metropolitan National Bank (Bank) or the Agent, a suitable and adequate safe space at its said office and the office furniture, files, ledger cards, charge and credit slips, and the trays therefor and equipment for the use of such Agent. The undersigned agrees to furnish also free light, heat and access to its premises during the usual business hours and at such times as may be reasonably necessary or convenient to carry on the bank's operations. The undersigned further agrees that the Agent may occupy such space and use such office furniture, files, ledger cards, charge and credit slips, and the trays therefor and equipment rent-free until all accounts assigned to the bank by the undersigned shall be fully discharged and performed.

_____

By_____

Title_____

Date_____

EXHIBIT 24   103
Participation Agreement

METROPOLITAN NATIONAL BANK
Financial Place
Receivable City, USA

PARTICIPATION AGREEMENT

Re: Accounts Financing Security Agreement dated
                , 19 , between Metropolitan National
     Bank (Bank) and   ("Borrower")

Gentlemen:

This letter confirms the agreement between

        ("Participant") and Bank for the participation of the Participant

in Bank's present and future financing of Borrower, pursuant to the provisions

of the Accounts Financing Security Agreement between Borrower and Bank

dated   , 19 .

Bank is simultaneously herewith delivering to the Participant copies of

the above Accounts Financing Security Agreement and related Inventory Security

Agreement, (the "Documents"). Any other documents and agreements relating to

Bank's financing arrangements with Borrower are available for Participant's

inspection at Bank's office and copies will be furnished to Participant upon

request.

Bank and Participant agree that Participant shall participate in all loans

and advances now outstanding or hereafter made by Bank to Borrower pursuant to

the Documents, on the following terms and conditions:

EXHIBIT 24—continued
Participation Agreement
104

-2-

1. Participant hereby agrees to participate in all loans and advances now outstanding or hereafter made by Bank to Borrower, pursuant to the Documents to the extent of an undivided   (%) percent of the aggregate principal loan balance thereof from time to time outstanding (the "Balance") provided the Participant's participating share hereunder shall not exceed $ except in Participant's discretion.

2. Participant's participating share hereunder shall constitute an undivided interest to the extent of Participant's participation in the balance and Participant shall have a corresponding undivided interest in all rights, collateral and guarantees granted to Bank pursuant to the Documents.

3. Borrower's account with Bank and all transactions with Borrower relating to the Documents shall be administered by Bank and conducted solely in Bank's name and Bank shall have the sole right to perform and enforce the terms and provisions of, and to exercise all rights and remedies relating to the Documents. Bank will notify Participant at least weekly of the status of the Borrower's account. Participant will then promptly make payments to Bank to the extent required to maintain its participating share in the Balance at   % thereof. If Participant's participating share in the Balance exceeds   % at any time, Bank will accompany its weekly status report with a remittance of excess. Participant's portion of all interest to be earned under the Documents shall be computed at the rate of   (%) percent per annum on the amount of Participant's participating share in the Balance. If the prime rate of interest charged by Participant to its prime commercial borrowers for short term loans (presently   % per annum) is increased, the interest payable to Participant on its participating share hereunder shall be increased by the amount of such increase in the prime rate effective the first day of the month following such increase. If such prime rate is decreased,

EXHIBIT 24—continued

Participation Agreement

105

-3-

the interest payable to Participant on its participating share hereunder shall

be decreased by the amount of such decrease in the prime rate effective as of

the first day of the month following such decrease provided that in no event

shall the interest rate payable to Participant be less than   (%)

percent per annum. Bank will promptly remit Participant's portion of such in-

terest to Participant out of the interest actually earned and collected by Bank

from the Borrower.

4. Bank may, in its discretion and without the consent of Participant,

amend or modify the Documents or enter into additional agreements with Borrower,

but Bank will give Participant reasonably prompt notice of any such eventuali-

ties. Bank will service the Borrower's account in accordance with its usual

practices in the ordinary course of business, and Bank will not be liable to

the Participant except for Bank's own bad faith or willful misconduct. Bank

makes no express or implied warranties with respect to the financial condition

of Borrower or of the obligors on accounts assigned by it or with respect to the

legality, validity, genuineness, subsistence, enforceability, priority or value

of the Documents or of any of the collateral or guarantees received or to be

received by Bank, or of Bank's security interest therein. Participant shall be

entitled to examine Bank's books and records relating to Borrower's account during

normal business hours and make copies thereof.

5. If Borrower defaults under any of the Documents, and Bank takes action

to realize upon the collateral held as security for Borrower's indebtedness and

obligations to Bank or to enforce its rights against Borrower or any guarantor

thereof, or if Bank exercises its rights pursuant to the Accounts Financing

Security Agreement to terminate as to future transactions, then the transactions

with the Borrower shall be immediately deemed to be in liquidation. Thereafter,

EXHIBIT 24—continued

Participation Agreement

106

-4-

collections and all monies received or held by Bank or Participant in connection with the Documents and the proceeds from the sale, collection or other disposition of collateral and any guarantees securing the indebtedness and obligations of Borrower to Bank shall be applied as follows:

(a) First, to the costs and expenses (including attorneys' fees) incurred in effecting or attempting to effect any recovery of such monies or in enforcing or attempting to enforce any right or remedy under the Documents in retaking, protecting, preserving or disposing of any collateral, but exclduing any expenses of ordinary overhead or clerical or executive hire of any party hereto. In the event such costs, fees and expenses are not collected from the Borrower, any guarantors thereof, or recovered out of the proceeds of liquidation, any deficiency will be shared by Bank and Participant, pari passu, in the ratio that each of their participating shares then bears to the Balance;

(b) Next, to accrued interest owing on the Balance which shall be shared by Participant and Bank, pari passu, in the ratio that the aggregate accrued interest payable to Participant and the aggregate accrued interest owing by Borrower which is to be retained by Bank, respectively, then bears to the aggregate accrued interest owing by Borrower on the Balance; and

(c) Next, to the principal amount outstanding of Participant's and Bank's respective participating shares in the Balance, pari passu, in the ratio that each of their participating shares then bears to the Balance.

6. Nothing herein contained shall confer upon any of the parties hereto any interest in, or subject any of the parties hereto to any liability for, the assets or liabilities of any of the other parties hereto, except only as to the transactions referred to herein. Bank does not assume any liability to Participant for

EXHIBIT 24—continued

Participation Agreement

107

-5-

the repayment of its participation, except to the extent that Participant shall

be entitled to receive payments in accordance with Paragraphs 3 and 5 hereof out

of amounts received by Bank from Borrower or from realization on the collateral.

7. The following shall be considered and treated as costs and expenses of

collection to be payable under the provisions of Paragraph 5(a) hereof:

(a) Any monies paid by Bank in defending, settling or satisfying

any claim, action or demand asserted by any receiver, trustee in bankruptcy or

reorganization, assignee, creditor, stockholder or other person in connection

with Borrower or the Documents or any transaction or collateral related thereto,

on any theory of preference, fraudulent conveyance, subordination, usury, ultra

vires, invalidity or similar theory;

(b) Any monies paid by Bank in satisfying any prior lien asserted

with respect to the collateral, including any expenses, costs and attorneys' fees

which may be incurred in connection with any of the foregoing; and

(c) Any monies advanced by Bank to or for the account of Borrower

to the extent necessary in connection with the effectuation of an orderly liquida-

tion of the Balance or the collateral therefor, and in which Participant does not

participate.

8. Participant may terminate its participation in the Balance following

at least 90 days' prior written notice to Bank. If Participant terminates its

participation pursuant to the foregoing, Bank shall, on or before the effective

date of such termination, either pay to Participant the amount of its entire

participating share in the Balance, together with accrued interest thereon, or

exercise its right to terminate the above Accounts Financing Security Agreement

with respect to future transactions with the Borrower. If Bank elects to termin-

ate as to future transactions with Borrower, as provided in the above Accounts

EXHIBIT 24—continued
Participation Agreement

108

-6-

Financing Security Agreement, Bank will give Participant a copy of the notice of termination and the transactions with Borrower shall thereafter be deemed in liquidation, and this Participation Agreement will terminate with respect to future transactions thereunder on the termination date specified in such notice.

9. If Participant realizes any proceeds or monies from Borrower, or holds or attaches any deposits or credits of Borrower, and the amount so realized, held or attached exceeds monies owing to the Participant on any indebtedness of Borrower other than the Balance, then such excess funds shall be divided and applied pursuant to Paragraph 5 above, provided that Participant may legally hold such funds for division hereunder.

10. This instrument shall be governed by the laws of shall not be amended except by a writing signed by both Bank and Participant and shall inure to the benefit of and be binding upon their respective successors and assigns. All notices shall be in writing and mailed to each of Bank and Participant at the above-noted addresses. Participant shall not, without the consent of Bank, sell, pledge, assign or otherwise transfer any of its rights under this instrument, otner than in connection with the sale of all or substantially all of the assets of Participant; and Bank shall not, without the consent if Participant, sell, pledge, assign or otherwise transfer any of its rights in connection with the Balance other than (i) in connection with a sale of all or substantially all of the assets of Bank, or (ii) a sale, assignment or transfer made in connection with liquidation of collateral for the Bank loans.

EXHIBIT 24—continued

Participation Agreement

109

-7-

If the foregoing correctly sets forth our understanding with respect to your participation in the Balance, please indicate your acceptance and approval thereof by executing and returning the attached counterpart of this letter where indicated together with your initial participaing share of $

Very truly yours,

METROPOLITAN NATIONAL BANK

By_____

ACCEPTED AND AGREED TO:

By_____
                              Title

Date_____

EXHIBIT 25   110
Certification of Corporate Resolutions

(For Bank)

CERTIFICATION OF CORPORATE RESOLUTIONS

* The undersigned, Clerk or Secretary of...

* a corporation duly organized and existing under the laws of the State of..(hereafter called "this

corporation"), DOES HEREBY CERTIFY to the _____ that at meetings of the Board of Directors and

* of the Stockholders of this corporation, duly and properly called and held on the...................day of.........................., 19........,

pursuant to law and the by-laws of this corporation, and at which Board of Directors' meeting all of the directors were present

throughout and voted, and at which Stockholders' meeting all of the stock entitled to vote was represented throughout and

voted in person or by valid proxy, the following resolutions were unanimously adopted by each respective body:

RESOLVED, that in order to facilitate the handling of any matters between this corporation and _____

_____ , its successors and assigns (herein called "_____") said _____ or any one of its officers or agents or

any of the officers or agents of this corporation be and each is hereby authorized to endorse from time to time, in writing or by rubber stamp

or by any other method, any and all checks, drafts or other instruments for the payment of money, payable or purporting to be payable to,

or purporting to be, in whole or in part the property of this corporation, for deposit of said items to the credit of _____ in any bank account

of _____ and the _____ and any other bank or depository is hereby authorized and directed to receive and accept such

items for such deposit to the credit of _____ when tendered to the bank by or for _____ without further inquiry and without responsibility

as to the validity or sufficiency of the endorsement of this corporation thereon, and neither said bank nor any other bank or depository shall

be under any liability to this corporation for the disposition which _____ may or shall make of such items or of any proceeds which at any time

stand to the credit of _____; hereby ratifying, confirming and approving anything heretofore done in the premises.

RESOLVED, that the Clerk or Secretary or any other officer of this corporation be and each is hereby authorized to certify to _____

and/or to any bank under the seal of this corporation or not and with like effect in either case, any or all of the resolutions adopted at this

and other and future meetings, and also to certify the names, offices and positions of the present and future officers and others authorized

to sign and act for this corporation.

RESOLVED, that any resolutions and any authority conferred thereby and any statement as to the officers or other authorized persons,

as may be so certified to _____ or any bank, may be conclusively relied upon by them as continuing in full force and effect until they actually

receive official written notice by registered mail as to any revocation or modification of the certified resolutions, or of any authority, or of

any change of officers or of others authorized.

I FURTHER CERTIFY that there is no provision in the Charter or By-laws of this corporation limiting the power of the

Board of Directors or of the Stockholders to pass the foregoing resolutions and that the same are in conformity with the pro-

visions of said Charter and By-laws and are now in full force and effect.

* IN WITNESS WHEREOF, I hereunto set my hand and the seal of this corporation this...day of

* ....19........

Confirmed:

* ....Title................... .... { Corporation
(Other Officer)   (Clerk or Secretary)   { Seal

9. Assignment forms, already shown in Exhibit 8, to be attached to accounts receivable schedules—initial, daily, or monthly schedules;

10. Inventory Loan Security Agreement, Exhibit 26. Much of the wording in this agreement is the same as or similar to the wording in the accounts receivable agreement, particularly in the "boiler plate" referring to the representations and warranties of the borrower, the events of default, and the rights of both parties. It is recommended, however, when loans are to be made on either or both receivables and inventory, that a separate inventory agreement be signed. There is no legal necessity for having two agreements rather than one, but from a practical and public relations standpoint, there may be some advantages to having separate agreements. Separate agreements look less formidable than the bulk required for one agreement. A separate agreement is geared specifically to inventory loans and may provide places for such details as:

1. A careful description of the inventory pledged;
2. The listing of locations where inventory is stored;
3. The definitions of values used, such as cost or market, sales price, or latest listed commodity prices;
4. The percentage of advance to be made against values of inventory, as agreed to by borrower and lender;
5. The type and amount of insurance to be carried;
6. The right of the lender to take possession of inventory under specified circumstances.
7. The interest rate to be charged. This is usually the same as on an accounts receivable loan, but might be different if the handling and supervision of inventory records, or the checking of collateral, creates excessive costs for the lender;
8. The termination privileges of both parties. These should be the same as they appear in the accounts receivable security agreement.

SPECIAL LOAN AGREEMENT

General Terms   When the terms of a prospective loan are even slightly more complex than can be handled by a standard preprinted accounts receivable and/ or inventory loan agreement form, it is advisable to have a special loan agreement drawn which will spell out all of the terms and conditions relevant to the transaction in question. For example, a loan agreement

(*Text continues on page 118*)

EXHIBIT 26   112

Inventory Loan Security Agreement

INVENTORY LOAN SECURITY AGREEMENT

1. LIEN AND SECURITY INTEREST

. . . . ,

whose chief place of business is located at . . . . ,

. . . . ,
          City   **County**   **State**

hereinafter called "Borrower," for valuable consideration, receipt whereof is hereby acknowledged, hereby grants to _____, hereinafter called "_____," a continuing general lien and security interest in all of its inventory, goods, merchandise, materials, raw materials, goods in process, finished goods, packaging and shipping materials and other tangible personal property now owned or hereafter acquired and held for sale or lease or furnished or to be furnished under contracts of service or consumed in Borrower's business (hereinafter collectively called "Inventory"), and in all accounts receivable, contract rights, instruments, documents and chattel paper arising from the sale of Inventory, and all proceeds, products and collections of and in all books and records of Borrower pertaining to all of the foregoing. Without limitation, the term Inventory includes

The continuing general lien and security interest granted hereby is to secure payment and performance of the liabilities and obligations of Borrower to _____ hereunder and also any and all other liabilities and obligations of Borrower to _____ of every kind and description, direct or indirect, absolute or contingent, due or to become due, and whether now existing or hereafter arising, regardless of how they arise or by what agreement or instrument, including obligations to perform acts and refrain from taking action as well as obligations to pay money (all hereinafter called "Obligations").

2. WARRANTIES

Borrower hereby represents and warrants to _____, and covenants, as follows:

    a. All books, records and documents relating to Inventory are and will be genuine and in all respects what they purport to be.

    b. All of the Inventory now owned or hereafter acquired by Borrower is and will be of good and merchantable quality and free from defects and Borrower is and will be the owner of such Inventory free from any lien, security interest or encumbrance, except in favor of _____; that none of the Inventory is or will be stored with a bailee (hereinafter called "Warehouseman") without the written consent of _____, and, in such event, Borrower will immediately cause Warehouseman to issue and deliver to _____, should _____ so require, warehouse receipts or other documents in _____ name and in form acceptable to _____, evidencing the storage of such Inventory; that Borrower warrants and will defend the Inventory against all claims and demands of any persons at any time; and that Borrower has good, legal and absolute right and power to pledge and grant liens and security interests in the same to _____.

    c. That it keeps and will continue to keep all its books and records concerning Inventory, contracts relating thereto and proceeds thereof and all of its other books and records at its chief place of business, unless written notice to the contrary is given by Borrower to _____.

    d. All Inventory presently owned and which will be hereafter acquired by Borrower is and will be kept only at the following locations:

. . . .

. . . .

. . . .

. . . . ,

unless _____ shall otherwise consent in writing.

EXHIBIT 26—continued 113

Inventory Loan Security Agreement

e. All information furnished to _____ concerning Inventory, contracts relating thereto and proceeds thereof, its financial condition or otherwise, is and will be complete, accurate and correct in all material respects at the time the same is furnished.

f. All covenants, representations and warranties contained in this Agreement shall be true and correct at the time of the execution of this Agreement and shall be deemed continuing.

3. LOANS

a. _____ agrees, during the continuance of this Agreement, to make loans and advances to Borrower, payable on demand, of up to the following percentages of value of the following categories of Borrower's Inventory:

For the purposes hereof, "value" shall mean cost or market price, whichever is lower.

The aggregate amount of Borrower's indebtedness and obligations to _____ incurred pursuant to this Agreement, from time to time, shall be referred to hereinafter as "Borrower's Inventory Loan Balance." Borrower's Inventory Loan Balance shall at no time exceed the aggregate amount of the percentages of value of Borrower's Inventory set forth in Paragraph 3.a., unless _____ shall elect to make advances in excess of said amount. Only Inventory acceptable to _____ and subject to _____ perfected lien or security interest shall be considered in determining compliance herewith. If at any time _____ shall be of the opinion that Borrower's Inventory Loan Balance exceeds the aggregate of the aforesaid percentages of value, that the Inventory is not of the value represented by Borrower or that _____ is not adequately secured, Borrower will, promptly upon demand, repay to _____ such amount of Borrower's Inventory Loan Balance as will, in _____ sole judgment, place _____ in an adequately secured position.

b. To evidence such loans, Borrower, at _____ request, shall execute and deliver to _____ promissory notes payable to _____ on demand, which said notes shall be in the amount of any portion or portions of Borrower's Inventory Loan Balance as at the time of _____ request, up to the full extent thereof, evidencing Borrower's Obligations. Said notes shall provide for the payment to _____ of interest at the rate provided for in Paragraph 3.c. and shall be upon forms acceptable to _____. The execution and delivery of such notes shall not constitute payment, satisfaction or release of any Obligation; and _____ lien and security interest shall not be limited in any way thereby or by _____ failure to request such notes.

c. Until all Obligations of Borrower to _____ are fully paid, Borrower will pay, monthly, as interest, ... percent per .... computed on the daily Borrower's Inventory Loan Balance, from the date accrued until the date paid. The amount of such interest shall be computed as a charge against Borrower as of the close of business on the last day of each calendar month.

d. _____ shall give Borrower, each month, an extract or a statement of Borrower's account, prepared from _____ records, which will conclusively be deemed correct and accepted by Borrower, unless Borrower gives _____ a written statement of exceptions within thirty (30) days after receipt of such extract or statement.

e. Borrower's Inventory Loan Balance shall be charged with all damages sustained by _____ by reason of any misrepresentation, breach of warranty or breach of covenant of Borrower herein, expressed or implied, whether caused by the acts or defaults of Borrower or others; and also all attorneys' fees, court costs, collection expenses, accountants' fees, traveling expenses, disbursements, and all other expenses which may be incurred by _____ in enforcing its lien and security interest in any Inventory, contracts relating thereto or proceeds thereof or of Borrower's Inventory Loan Balance, whether against Borrower, Borrower's guarantors, a receiver or trustee in bankruptcy, or others; or in supervising the records and proper management and disposition of the Inventory and all accounts receivable, contract rights, instruments, documents and chattel paper arising from the sale of Inventory, and all proceeds, products and collections of all of the foregoing; or in prosecuting or defending any proceeding arising from the efforts of _____ to recover any money or other thing of value or otherwise to enforce or protect any of _____ rights under this Agreement. In case of any failure of Borrower to keep the Inventory and the proceeds thereof free from all liens, charges, encumbrances, security interests and adverse claims, or if _____ shall deem it otherwise necessary or desirable, then _____ may, but need not, pay, contest or settle the same, or any judgment based thereon, or otherwise take any action to terminate, discharge or prevent the same, and charge Borrower's Inventory Loan Balance for any and all sums paid or advanced by _____ for any such purposes.

EXHIBIT 26—continued 114

Inventory Loan Security Agreement

4. REPORTS; INSPECTION OF RECORDS; FURTHER ASSURANCE

Borrower represents and agrees:

    a. At all times, to allow _____, by or through any of its officers, agents, employees, attorneys and accountants, to possess, remove to the premises of _____ or any agent of _____ for so long as _____ may desire, to make full use in aid of _____ rights under this Agreement, and to examine, audit and make extracts and copies from Borrower's books and all other records, and, for said purposes, or to aid _____ in the enforcement of any of its rights under this Agreement, to enter, to remain upon and, without cost to _____, to use the premises of Borrower or wherever such books and records may be found, as often and for as long as _____ may desire.

    b. To report, in form satisfactory to _____, such information as _____ may request regarding Inventory; such reports shall be for such periods, shall reflect Borrower's records as at such times and shall be rendered with such frequency as _____ may designate.

    c. To notify _____, immediately, of any event causing loss or depreciation in the value of Inventory and the amount of such loss or depreciation.

    d. To execute and deliver to _____ all instruments, documents and evidences deemed by _____ to be necessary or desirable to perfect the lien and security interest granted to _____ hereby in accordance with any applicable law, or otherwise, and to carry out the intent and purpose of this Agreement. Wherever any Inventory is located upon leased premises, Borrower shall, at _____ request, cause the owner and lessor of such premises to execute and deliver to _____ consents and subordinations of lien in form acceptable to _____.

5. INSURANCE; RECORDS; INSPECTION

    a. Borrower agrees that, as to any insurance it now or hereafter may maintain covering risks of damage to or loss or destruction of its books and records, each such policy of insurance shall contain a loss payable clause in form satisfactory to _____ naming _____ as payee and providing that all proceeds payable thereunder shall be payable, in any event, to _____, unless written consent to the contrary is obtained from _____. Borrower, at all times, shall have and maintain insurance with respect to all Inventory, to the fullest extent of the insurable value thereof, against risks of fire, theft, sprinklers and such other risks as _____ may require, in such form, for such periods and written by such insurers as may be satisfactory to _____, such insurance to bear endorsements, in form acceptable to _____, designating _____ as loss payee. Borrower shall deliver to _____ promptly as rendered true copies of all monthly reports made to insurance companies under any reporting forms of insurance policies. Originals of all such policies shall be delivered to and held by _____ for so long as any of the Obligations are unpaid or unperformed. _____ may act as agent for Borrower in making, adjusting, settling, instituting suit upon and prosecuting claims regarding, obtaining and cancelling such insurance and in endorsing and collecting any drafts and other forms of payment. Except as to business record insurance, should Borrower fail to maintain such insurance, _____ may, but need not, obtain the same and charge the cost thereof to Borrower's Inventory Loan Balance. The proceeds of any such insurance shall be applied in reduction of Borrower's Inventory Loan Balance.

    b. Borrower shall keep correct current stock, cost and sales records of its Inventory, accurately and sufficiently itemizing and describing the kinds, type and quantities of Inventory and the cost and selling prices thereof, all of which records shall be continuously available to _____ for inspection; and _____ shall at all reasonable times have access to and the right to inspect and draw off data from any of Borrower's other books and records for the purpose of checking and verifying all such statements, stock, cost and sales records.

    c. Borrower shall at all reasonable times and from time to time allow _____, by or through any of its officers, agents, attorneys or accountants, to examine or inspect the Inventory wherever located and, for such purposes, to enter upon Borrower's premises or wherever any of the Inventory may be found.

6. BORROWER'S USE OF INVENTORY

Until default, Borrower may use the Inventory in any lawful manner not inconsistent with this Agreement or with the terms or conditions of any policy of insurance thereon, may use and consume any raw materials or supplies, the use and consumption of which is necessary in order to carry on Borrower's business, and may also sell the Inventory in the ordinary course of business, but Borrower shall make no sale which would cause Borrower's Inventory Loan Balance to exceed the percentages of value of Borrower's Inventory subject to _____ lien and security interest as specified in Paragraph 3 (a). A sale in the ordinary course of business does not include a transfer in partial or total satisfaction of a debt owing by Borrower to someone other than _____.

7. FINANCING STATEMENTS AND NOTICES OF FACTOR'S LIEN

    a. At the request of _____, Borrower will join with _____ in executing one or more Financing Statements, Notices of Factor's Lien or such other notices as _____ may require, in form satisfactory to _____.

EXHIBIT 26—continued   115

Inventory Loan Security Agreement

8. EVENTS OF DEFAULT; ACCELERATION

All Obligations shall, notwithstanding any time or credit allowed by any instrument evidencing a liability, become immediately due and payable without notice or demand upon the occurrence of any of the following events of default;

a. Borrower shall fail to pay or to perform any Obligation promptly when due; or shall fail to keep or observe any warranty or covenant of Borrower contained in this or any other Agreement, whether now or hereafter existing, between Borrower and _____ ;

b. Any representation or statement made or furnished to _____ by or in behalf of Borrower shall have been false in any material respect when made or furnished;

c. Any default in any other agreement, whether now or hereafter existing, between Borrower and _____;

d. There shall occur any loss, theft, damage, destruction, sale or encumbrance to or of any of the Inventory, or any levy, seizure or attachment thereof or thereon shall be made;

e. _____ shall determine, at any time or times hereafter, that it is insecure with respect to the performance by Borrower of all or any part of the Obligations;

f. Borrower recognizes that, in the event it violates any of the warranties, covenants, terms and conditions of this Agreement, no remedy at law will provide adequate relief to _____ and Borrower hereby agrees that _____ shall be entitled to temporary and permanent injunctive relief in case of any such breach without the necessity of proving actual damages.

9. RIGHTS AND REMEDIES

Upon the occurrence of any such event of default, and at any times thereafter, _____ shall have the right:

a. To take possession of Inventory without judicial process and to enter any premises without hindrance and without the consent of Borrower where any Inventory may be located, for the purpose of taking possession of the Inventory; however, should _____ seek to take possession of any or all of the Inventory by court process, Borrower hereby irrevocably waives any bonds and any surety or security relating thereto required by any statute, court rule or otherwise as an incident to such possession, and waives any demand for possession prior to the commencement of any suit or action to recover possession thereof and waives the right to trial by jury with respect thereto and in any other action in which _____ is a party.

b. To sell or to otherwise dispose of all or any Inventory in its then condition, or after any further manufacturing or processing thereof, at public or private sale or sales, with or without notice, demand or advertisement, in lots or in bulk, for cash or on credit, all as _____ in its sole discretion may deem advisable; such sales may be adjourned from time to time with or without notice. If any Inventory is in process or otherwise unfinished, _____ may, but need not, complete the manufacturing or processing thereof, utilizing without charge Borrower's plant, machinery, equipment and processes, and any expenses incurred in connection therewith shall be charged to Borrower's Inventory Loan Balance. _____ shall have the right to conduct such sales on Borrower's premises or elsewhere and shall have the right to use Borrower's premises without charge for such sales for such time or times as _____ may see fit. _____ is hereby granted a lien and security interest in and the right to use, without charge, Borrower's labels, patents, copyrights, music rights, rights of use of any name, trade secrets, trade names, trade marks and advertising matter, or any property of a similar nature, in completing the manufacturing, advertising for sale and selling any Inventory, and Borrower's rights under all licenses and all franchise agreements shall inure to _____ benefit. _____ reserves the right to purchase any Inventory at any such sale. The proceeds realized from the sale of any Inventory shall be applied first to the costs, expenses and reasonable attorneys' fees incurred by _____ for collection and for acquisition, completion, protection, removal, storage, sale and delivery of Borrower's Inventory, second to the principal of Borrower's Obligations and third to interest due upon any of Borrower's Obligations. The surplus, if any, shall be paid to Borrower; or, if any deficiency shall arise, Borrower shall remain liable to _____ therefor.

c. _____ shall not be liable or responsible in any way for the safeguarding of any of said Inventory, for any loss or damage thereto, for any diminution in the value thereof, or for any act or default of any carrier, warehouseman, forwarding agency or other person whomsoever, but the same shall be at all times at Borrower's risk.

d. _____ shall have whatever further rights and remedies as may be provided by any applicable law and all rights, powers and remedies provided under this Agreement and in any other instrument or agreement between _____ and Borrower are cumulative and none is exclusive.

e. The failure or delay of _____ to exercise any right, power, or remedy shall not operate as a waiver thereof, but all rights, powers and remedies shall continue in full force and effect until all of Borrower's Obligations are fully paid and performed.

EXHIBIT 26—continued

Inventory Loan Security Agreement

116

10. ONE GENERAL OBLIGATION; CROSS COLLATERAL

All loans and advances by _____ to Borrower under this Agreement and under all other agreements constitute one loan, and all indebtedness and obligations of Borrower to _____ under this and under all other agreements, present and future, constitute one general Obligation secured by collateral and security held and to be held by _____ hereunder and by virtue of all other agreements between Borrower and   now and hereafter existing. It is distinctly understood and agreed that all of the rights of _____ contained in this Agreement shall likewise apply insofar as applicable to any modification of or supplement to this Agreement and to any other agreements, present and future, between _____ and Borrower.

11. APPLICATION OF PAYMENTS

All payments made by or in behalf of and all credits due to Borrower may be applied and reapplied in whole or in part to any of Borrower's Obligations to the extent and in the manner that _____ may see fit.

12. TERMINATION

This Agreement, on acceptance by _____, shall continue in effect for . . . . year(s) from the date hereof and from year to year thereafter unless terminated as to future transactions by the giving of notice by registered mail by either party to the other, not less than thirty (30) days prior to any anniversary hereof. Borrower, at such termination date, shall make payment in full of all indebtedness and obligations due hereunder, whether evidenced by installment notes or otherwise, and whether or not all or any part of such indebtedness and obligations are otherwise then due and payable by Borrower to _____. _____ may terminate upon immediate notice at any time in the event Borrower commits any act of default enumerated in Paragraph 8. hereof. No termination of this Agreement shall in any way affect or impair any right of _____ arising prior thereto or by reason thereof, nor shall any such termination relieve Borrower or any of the guarantors of any Obligation to _____ until all of the Obligations are fully paid and performed, nor shall any such termination affect any right or remedy of _____ arising from any Obligation, and all agreements, warranties and representations of Borrower shall survive termination.

13. BENEFITS OF THIS AGREEMENT

This Security Agreement shall be binding upon and inure to the benefit of the parties hereto and their respective heirs, successors, representatives and assigns.

14. GOVERNING LAW; SUBMISSION TO JURISDICTION

The validity, interpretation and effect of this Security Agreement shall be governed by the laws of the State of . . . .

Borrower hereby consents to the jurisdiction of all courts in said State and hereby appoints . . . .

whose address is . . . . , as Borrower's agent for service of process in said State.

15. SEPARABILITY

In the event that any provision hereof be deemed to be invalid by reason of the operation of any law or by reason of the interpretation placed thereon by any court, this Agreement shall be construed as not containing such provision, the invalidity of such provision shall not affect the validity of any other provision hereof and all other provisions hereof which are otherwise lawful and valid shall remain in full force and effect.

16. NOTICES AND PAYMENTS

Any notice required hereunder or by reason of the application of any law shall be deemed to have been given by either party hereto when the same shall have been deposited in the United States mail, postage prepaid, at least five (5) calendar days prior to the action proposed thereby (except that notice of termination shall be given in the manner set forth in Paragraph 12. hereof), addressed:

    a. If to Borrower, at the address of Borrower specified in Paragraph 1. hereof, or to the latest address of Borrower of which _____ shall have received notice from Borrower;

    b. If to _____, at . . . .

17. WAIVERS

    a. Borrower hereby waives any and all causes of action and claims which it may ever have against _____ as a result of any possession, use, collection or sale of any assets of Borrower by _____, and Borrower waives all rights of redemption, if any, it may have.

EXHIBIT 26—continued

117

Inventory Loan Security Agreement

b. The failure at any time or times hereafter to require strict performance by Borrower of any of the provisions, warranties, terms and conditions contained in this Agreement or any other agreement, document or instrument now or hereafter executed by Borrower and delivered to _____, shall not waive, affect or diminish any right of _____ hereafter to demand strict compliance and performance therewith and with respect to any other provisions, warranties, terms and conditions contained in such agreements, documents and instruments. Any waiver of any default shall not waive or affect any other default, whether prior or subsequent thereto, and whether of the same or of a different type. None of the warranties, conditions, provisions and terms contained in this Agreement or any other agreement, document or instrument now or hereafter executed by Borrower and delivered to _____ shall be deemed to have been waived by any act or knowledge of _____, its agents, officers or employees, but only by an instrument in writing, signed by an officer of _____ and directed to Borrower, specifying such waiver.

c. Borrower waives any and all notices or demands which Borrower might be entitled to receive with respect to this Agreement by virtue of any applicable statute or law, and waives demand, protest, notice of protest, notice of default or dishonor, notice of payments and nonpayments, or of any default, release, compromise, settlement, extension, or renewal of all commercial paper, accounts, contract rights, instruments, chattel paper, guaranties, and otherwise, at any time held by _____ on which Borrower may in any way be liable, notice of nonpayment at maturity of any and all accounts, instruments or chattel paper, notice of any action taken by _____ unless expressly required by this Agreement. Borrower hereby ratifies and confirms whatever _____ may do pursuant to this Agreement and agrees that _____ shall not be liable for any acts of commission or omission or for any errors of judgment or mistakes of fact or of law.

18. EFFECTIVE DATE

This Agreement, which has been signed and delivered to _____ on the day and year first above written, shall not become effective until accepted by _____ under the signature of its duly authorized officers at its address set forth in Paragraph 16.

Accepted at _____,

_____
Borrower

this _____ day of _____, 19__.

BY: _____

TITLE: _____

_____

ATTEST: _____
Secretary

BY: _____

TITLE: _____

(Affix corporate seal here.)

may contain some, all, or more than, the following general conditions:

1. A certified public accountant, satisfactory to the lender, will be used to prepare all financial statements required by the lender.
2. Loan limits may be set as to dollar amounts for the total loan to be made, and as to specific amounts on each type of collateral.
3. The sum of the percentage of advance to be made for each class of collateral will not exceed the total dollar amount to be loaned specified in the agreement.
4. All types of collateral are collateral for all loans and no releases will be given of any collateral until all debts are paid in full, including attorneys' fees and all other charges agreed to by the borrower.
5. The attorney for the borrower will give a written opinion to the effect that the borrower has the complete legal right to make this and all other agreements relating to the initial loans and loans to be made in the future. Furthermore, the opinion should state that the borrower has clear and unencumbered title to the assets to be pledged for loans.
6. The borrower will secure corporate guaranties from a parent, subsidiary, or affiliate corporation as named in the agreement.
7. The borrower will secure personal guaranties as required by the lender. In the case of both personal and corporate guaranties, the agreement may contain limitations as to the amount of each guaranty.
8. Any amounts due from the borrower to officers, a parent company, a subsidiary, or an affiliate will be subordinated to the lender, and no offsetting amount due to a parent, subsidiary, or affiliate can be created.
9. Whenever appropriate, each of these actions will be supported by a vote of the directors and shareholders.

Negative Covenants

The following are preceded by a statement to the effect that none of the acts referred will be done, nor will the conditions specified be permitted to exist, without the written approval of the lender.

1. No dividends will be paid while the borrower is in debt to the lender.
2. The borrower will not permit any liens to be placed on any assets. However, if liens are recorded without the borrower's consent, the agreement may specify that such liens must be removed within a

certain number of days or else it will be considered to be an event of default.

3. No mergers, acquisitions, or consolidations will be made while in debt to the lender.

4. No expenditures for fixed assets will be made, within a stated period, which exceed a certain amount.

5. No organizing of any other company for any purpose will be undertaken by the borrower.

6. No loans will be made to officers, stockholders, a parent company, a subsidiary, or an affiliate.

7. Salaries and bonuses will be (1) limited to those presently paid, (2) reduced to certain amounts, or (3) increased by no more than certain amounts.

Affirmative Covenants

The following clauses assert that the borrower will provide or maintain certain things, and that failure so to do will result in default on which the bank may act to protect its interest.

1. The borrower agrees to maintain working capital at no less than a specified level. Working capital often is affected at an early point when a company is deteriorating. By being able to move quickly on this act of default, the bank may save valuable time in protecting its interest. The method of calculating working capital should be recited in this clause. The lender may wish to delete certain items from current assets, such as loans due from officers and prepaid expenses, before determining the borrower's working capital position.

2. Tangible net worth will be no less than a certain amount. A definition of tangible net worth should be included here.

3. All federal and state taxes will be paid when due.

4. All debts will be paid within terms. This covenant often has to be modified depending on the borrower's cash, plus borrowing power, as they exist at the time of the signing.

5. Insurance of specific kinds and in amounts satisfactory to the lender will be carried, and all policies on pledged collateral will show the lender as loss payee as his interests may appear.

6. If, in the judgment of the lender, insurance coverage is inadequate to cover the value of pledged collateral, the lender may order insurance and charge the cost to the borrower's loan account.

7. The payment of legal fees in connection with the preparation of security documents will be the responsibility of the borrower.
8. The payment of legal fees for the enforcement of any agreement will be borne by the borrower.
9. The borrower will advise the lender immediately of any lien placed against assets in excess of a certain amount, or of any suit, the claim of which exceeds a certain amount.
10. The lender, if a bank, has the right to set off at any time. The right to set off would also apply to any amount of the loan shared by a participating bank or finance company. The right to apply *any* bank balance will have to be defined; it is doubtful that any special funds, such as escrowed funds or pension funds, can be set off against secured loan balances.

Events of Default   Many loan agreements contain the same events of default as appear in security agreements. Whether or not this is necessary or desirable should be discussed with the attorneys who prepare the documents. The loan agreement, however, may contain additional events of default not appearing in the standard preprinted security agreement.

The usual default clause states that all obligations immediately become due and payable if any of the following should occur:

1. The borrower fails to make any payment or meet any obligation as it becomes due;
2. Any warranty or representation is found to be false;
3. Any acceleration takes place in the maturity of a debt due to the lender or to others;
4. Any loss, theft, or damage to collateral takes place;
5. Any dissolution, insolvency, business failure, or bankruptcy of borrower takes place;
6. The lender feels insecure with respect to the performance by the borrower of all or any part of the borrower's obligations.

Miscellaneous   Miscellaneous clauses which may be included in a loan agreement may
Clauses   cover such points as the following:

1. The agreement is to be covered by the laws of a specific state named by the lender.
2. Another bank (or other banks) may participate in loans to the

borrower in an amount not to exceed a specified dollar amount or a specified percentage of the total loan.

3. If the lead lender is to get a percentage override on the total of the participant's share, to compensate for the costs of handling the participant's share, it should be so stated.

4. The rights of the lead bank should be spelled out in the event that the participant wishes to withdraw from the loans. Among other things, these rights may be that the lead lender can terminate the loan arrangement simultaneously; that the lead bank will have the right but not the obligation to secure a new participant; and that the lead lender can take over the entire loan if he so desires.

5. A termination clause may be included in the loan agreement if substitution or amplification is needed of the termination clause in the security agreement.

UNIFORM COMMERCIAL CODE FINANCING STATEMENTS

UCC financing statements used by the various states are substantially similar and are simple to prepare and file. The forms used as examples are all used in the Commonwealth of Massachusetts. The Code will allow some minor errors in preparation as long as it can be demonstrated that the intent of both borrower and lender is as represented on the forms. However, every effort should be made to prepare the forms with great accuracy.

When preparing the UCC-1 form, shown in Exhibit 4, be sure that the correct legal names of both borrower and lender are shown. A certificate of corporate existence furnished by the state's corporation division will establish the existence of the corporation and its true name.

The security taken for the loan should be amply and accurately described. The two boxes marked "proceeds of collateral" and "products of collateral" should be checked unless, for some reason, agreement has been made that proceeds or products are not taken as collateral.

A final detail is that the signatures of both the signers should be made with a ball-point pen and with a firm hand in order for signatures to carry through to all copies.

The UCC-3 form, Exhibit 27, is used to notify all concerned of the continuation of the lender's security described in the initial filing, UCC-1. In Massachusetts, renewal must be made within five years of

EXHIBIT 27

UCC-3

122

UNIFORM COMMERCIAL CODE

STATEMENTS OF CONTINUATION, PARTIAL RELEASE, ASSIGNMENT, ETC. — FORM UCC-3

INSTRUCTIONS

1. PLEASE TYPE this form. Fold only along perforation for mailing.
2. Re...ove Secured Party and Debtor copies and send other 3 copies with interleaved carbon paper to the filing officer.
3. Enclose filing fee.
4. If the space provided for any item(s) on the form is inadequate the item(s) should be continued on additional sheets, preferably 5" x 8" or 8" x 10". Only one copy of such additional sheets need be presented to the filing officer with a set of three copies of Form UCC-3. Long schedules of collateral, etc. may be on any size paper that is convenient for the secured party.
5. At the time of filing, filing officer will return third copy as an acknowledgement.

This **STATEMENT is presented to a filing officer for filing pursuant to the Uniform Commercial Code.**

1 Debtor(s) (Last Name First) and address(es)	2 Secured Party(ies) and address(es)	3 Maturity date (if any):
		For Filing Officer (Date, Time, Number, and Filing Office)

This statement refers to original Financing Statement No.

A. Continuation............ ☐	B. Partial Release ...... ☐	C. Assignment .... ☐	D. Other: .... ☐
The original financing statement between the foregoing Debtor and Secured Party, bearing the file number shown above, is still effective.	From the collateral described in the financing statement bearing the file number shown above, the Secured Party releases the following:	The Secured Party certifies that the Secured Party has assigned to the Assignee whose name and address is shown below, Secured Party's rights under the financing statement bearing the file number shown above in the following property:	

Dated:................................., 19........

Dated:..................................., 19........

By: ....

(Signature of Secured Party)

Filing Officer Copy — Alphabetical

STANDARD FORM — UNIFORM COMMERCIAL CODE — FORM UCC-3

Forms may be purchased from Hobbs & Warren, Inc. Boston, Mass.

the original filing or of the last renewal; otherwise, the lender's security interest will automatically terminate.

An instance of such a termination occurred when a Boston area bank missed the renewal date by one day and an alert creditor filed a lien on that day. The bank was unaware of the filing of the lien, and filed its continuation statement the day after the five-year period expired; the bank then continued to finance the company for another three years. The continuation statement itself was of no effect whatsoever since the original financing statement had terminated by the provisions of the five-year statute and could not be continued. The only thing the bank could have done at that point was to refile a new financing statement; they failed to do that, not realizing it was necessary. As a result, they had exposure not for just one day, but continually after the first five-year period expired. When the company filed under Chapter XI, counsel for the creditors took the position that the bank did not hold a perfected lien and that the bank's lien was invalid in the bankruptcy proceeding. The bank did not litigate the point.

The UCC-3 form is also used by the lender in order to give partial release of collateral described in the body of the form or to assign its rights to another lender.

THE STRUCTURING AND DOCUMENTATION OF TWO UNUSUAL LOANS

For the most part, loans to receivable borrowers may be structured along traditional lines whereby the amount loaned against collateral is based on a prudent percentage of the face value of receivables or of receivables and inventory. In most cases, the documentation of such loans may be handled by preprinted documents such as the Accounts Financing Security Agreement shown in Exhibit 17 and the Inventory Loan Security Agreement in Exhibit 26. Additional forms might include the Certificate of the Secretary/Clerk Relating to Minutes of a Meeting of the Shareholders, a Certification of a Vote of the Board of Directors, guaranties, and UCC statements. No matter how simple the loan may be, however, the documentation should be approved or prepared by the lender's attorney.

The two loan arrangements discussed below were the result of situations that may be unique. They are described here, however, to show how substantial loans may be made safely to businesses that are in substandard financial condition. It may be done as long as the problems are fully understood, the loan is structured to give the lender maximum safety and the borrower maximum accommodation, the value of the collateral is solid, and the documentation is carefully and completely drawn.

Seaport Oil Company is the fictitious name of a wholesaler/retailer of number two fuel oil and kerosene. It is located on the Maine coast about 400 miles from its major source of supply. We are a commercial finance company, and the account was referred to us by a moderately large bank that had extended as much credit to Seaport as was thought prudent. They knew, however, that Seaport needed considerably more accommodation, especially during the winter season. When we first reviewed this situation there appeared to be so many negative factors that we almost turned it down, but because we had considerable experience and expertise in the fuel oil business, we continued to try to find a way to meet the company's financial requirements.

The several serious negative factors that we had to overcome were as follows:

1. The management (which consisted of one principal owner) was suffering from a bad case of "conglomeritis." In addition to his fuel oil business he owned a wholesale lobster business, an insurance business, and the local theatre. He also owned fuel oil tanks with a storage capacity of approximately one million gallons.

2. Seaport Oil Company was located far from its major suppliers, so to avoid the prohibitive cost of trucking oil to fill its storage tanks, Seaport erected the tanks at the water's edge. This permitted shipment by ocean-going barges. The large investment in these tanks, together with the problems of financing the owner's other businesses, prompted the bank to withdraw its support and the suppliers of petroleum products to restrict their lines of credit.

The factor of distance was also a problem to us because of the expense of sending examiners on a regular basis and the time and expense of sending our executives to administer the loan. This would diminish our net income to the point where the account would be unprofitable.

3. When we first were introduced to Seaport the company's debt to its major bank was $208,000 and debts to its principal oil supplier and others amounted to an additional $250,000.

4. For the most part, Seaport's retail customers were fishermen, farmers, and other local people of low to moderate incomes. Their incomes fluctuated widely on a seasonal basis and sometimes were erratic because of adverse weather conditions.

Seaport also sold to several small independent fuel oil and kerosene dealers within a fifty mile radius of Seaport's storage tanks. In our initial investigation, we found that many of the dealers were friends or relatives of Seaport's management, and the relationships between the parties was casual and unfathomable, at least in regard to who owed what to whom.

For these reasons Seaport's receivables were not acceptable collateral.

5. Seaport's books were in deplorable condition and we were uncertain of the solvency of the company.

These negatives loomed large, but there were compensating positive factors as well:

1. Fuel oil as collateral has a continuous stable value; it is fungible; it has no fashion or style element; it is easily measured; and it is one of life's necessities.

2. Seaport's storage tanks were located on the only deep-water terminal between Portland, Maine, and the Canadian border. This permitted shipment by barge from Providence, Boston, or Portland, depending on the availability of the product, in shipments of over 400,000 gallons each.

3. The known savings in transportation costs not only were sufficient to pay all interest costs but also enabled the company to slowly and consistently reduce its overall debt.

These positive factors encouraged us to come up with a lending arrangement for Seaport. The success of this program hinged on the following documentation, and the intelligent and patient cooperation of the company's bank, suppliers, and other creditors:

1. Because of the nature and condition of the company, we drew up a special loan agreement which incorporated all of the conditions shown in Exhibit 17, as well as the requirement that a CPA acceptable to us be retained to straighten out the company's bookkeeping and to issue financial statements. Specific minimum working capital and net worth amounts were established. The wording of our standard agreement was altered to apply to this particular business and the industry in general.

2. We secured from Seaport's only supplier of petroleum products a repurchase agreement that included two major requirements:

   a. The supplier agreed to repurchase any oil in Seaport's tanks (as determined by warehouse receipts) *at its landed cost any time upon our demand.*

   b. They also agreed to subordinate the amount due them from Seaport to our loan, and to accept payment against it on the basis of one-quarter of one cent per gallon only as long as we permitted it.

The supplier was willing to do this because they wanted the volume business and they felt that our financing and financial guidance would give Seaport a chance to stay in business and to prosper.

3. We required that Seaport enter into a contract with a field warehouse company, which would take possession of the storage tanks, issue warehouse receipts for all oil going into the tanks, and issue release forms for all oil removed from the tanks.

We permitted Seaport to withdraw oil without payment for up to three consecutive days, but after that interval the warehouse company had instructions to stop withdrawals until we had received a bank or certified check.

4. To be absolutely sure that the quality and quantity of the oil that was our collateral was exactly as reported to us, we required Seaport to engage E.W. Saybolt and Co., Inc., an international company that performs independent petroleum inspections. Upon the arrival of the oil in Maine, Saybolt would monitor the transfer of the oil from the barges to the storage tanks and would test it for quality. Part of our agreement with Seaport permitted adding Saybolt's charges to the cost of the oil.

5. Upon receipt of Saybolt's certification of quality and quantity, supported by warehouse receipts from the warehouse company, we would send our check directly to Seaport's supplier for *100 percent of the cost of the oil, including Saybolt's charges.* During the winter a barge of oil cost about $50,000. (Today's price would be considerably higher.) Our agreement with Seaport included permission for us to pay the supplier directly, with none of the funds passing through Seaport's hands. This was done to prevent Seaport from being tempted to use the cash for his other businesses.

6. To further strengthen our position, we required cash deposits from Seaport totalling $20,000. Of this, $5000 was to protect us against any evaporation or leakage of product from the tanks, and $15,000 was to be applied against any amounts owed to use for product withdrawal or interest charges that were not remitted by Seaport in a timely manner.

7. The bank that referred Seaport to us subordinated their balance of $208,000 but took a second position to us on all collateral. Within two years of the start of the arrangement, Seaport was in a position to make payments to the bank on the basis of one-half cent per gallon.

8. Because the oil business is seasonal, during four to five months of the year our funds were not sufficiently employed to produce an income

that would cover our handling costs. Therefore, we instituted a minimum annual fee of moderate size. This made the entire transaction worthwhile.

Our demands on Seaport were stringent and our control over collateral was firm, but we accomplished some very worthwhile things.

Because of the necessity for paying us on short terms for oil withdrawn from their tanks, Seaport became more firm in its credit and collection policies with its own accounts. As a result of their insisting on being paid more promptly by their customers, and by cutting out chronically slow-paying accounts, they created a better cash flow. This enabled them to pay off old debts and keep current creditors happy. It has been a number of years now since Seaport paid its loans in full as well as its old debts to its bank and to its petroleum suppliers. Without the kind of financing we provided, it was a virtual certainty that Seaport would have failed, with a consequent loss to its bank, its suppliers, and of course to its owner.

If some or all of the above tactics had been used in the De Angelis oil affair, perhaps the tremendous losses suffered in that instance could have been greatly reduced or even avoided.

In the accounts receivable and inventory lending business, it is usual and proper to place primary reliance on the collateral of receivables and only secondary reliance on the security of inventory. In Seaport's case, we judged the receivables to be poor collateral because of the large delinquency rate, the uncertainty of how much each customer owed, and the very sloppy bookkeeping methods then in use. We considered Seaport's inventory to be excellent collateral, however, not only because of its intrinsic value but also because of the repurchase agreement we had from a major oil company. With a professional warehouse company to keep track of the quantity, and Saybolt to keep track of the quality, we had no apprehension about making a loan of 100 percent of the landed cost of the product under these conditions.

In another situation, a loan to the Archer Wholesale Book Company, the conditions were reversed: we made an 80 percent loan on the company's accounts receivables, but only a 5 percent loan on its inventory valued at approximately $1.3 million.

Archer Wholesale Book Company was one of three affiliated companies, all with the same ownership. The other two companies consisted of a small bindery, which did business with Archer and others and which occupied part of the same premises; and the Archer Realty Company, which owned the fine building in which Archer and the bindery were housed. This building was located on a large lot of level land at the junction of three of New England's major highways.

Archer was an old company and had been successful for years, but after the founder died, the company went downhill and eventually went into bankruptcy. The new owners, Fred and Carlton Carlson, bought the assets of Archer from the trustee in bankruptcy, but mistake number one was that the cash investment made by the brothers was minimal; too much reliance was placed on a bank loan and a long term payout of the purchase price.

The bank struggled with the loan for several years, but the company suffered continuous losses and the loan was finally classified by the bank examiners. We were then asked if we would like to examine it as a prospective account.

As with almost every other loan prospect, there were well-defined negative and positive aspects of the company. The most obviously negative were:

1. Archer's carrying charges for the building it occupied were too high. The combined outflow of cash for taxes, mortgage payments, interest, and maintenance placed a heavy burden on the company's meager working capital.

2. The bindery was inadequately equipped and too small to be profitable. Archer could not keep the bindery busy with its own work, and the plant was not modern enough to get sufficient volume from outside sources.

3. The biggest problem of all was Archer's management. Fred Carlson was a kindly, compassionate, and paternalistic man who never made a decision without his brother's approval. He never had the heart to terminate employees, especially those who were old and infirm. As a result, the ratio of payroll to other operating expenses was excessively high and productivity was very low.

Fred was the on-site manager of Archer's business; brother Carlton owned and controlled over 70 percent of Archer's stock and managed his own business, which had its headquarters in California. Carlton's business consisted of the management of more than 300 leased book departments, primarily located in department stores and spread across the country. The frustrations and delays encountered in trying to reach Carlton for a decision were aggravating and costly, and when he was finally contacted his decisions were often at odds with his lender's beliefs.

When the bank invited us to take a look at Archer, we recognized all these problems, but felt that if we could set up a good collateral loan we might, over a period of years, help the management to institute the efficient practices necessary to turn it around.

On the positive side, Archer's receivables were excellent. They mostly consisted of sales of supplementary reading material and reference books to public and school libraries and to college book stores. Because most of the accounts were with municipalities, receivables turned more slowly than is generally desirable, but the loss through bad debts was negligible. We therefore decided to carry the receivables as good collateral for 120 days from the invoice date, rather than for the usual 90 days.

Appraisals of the building were excellent. We considered our second mortgage, after a moderate-sized first, to be excellent protection if by chance, proceeds from receivables could not cover our loan.

In addition to the receivables, we also placed a lien on the company's machinery and equipment and on the equipment in the bindery. We were fortified further by the guaranties of the principals, their wives, the bindery, and Archer Realty. The corporate guaranties, of course, were approved by the board of directors and the shareholders of each company. The securing of the votes of the shareholders was a long and tedious task—there were more than 60 stockholders who were friends or relatives of the brothers. Attempts to get acquiescence to the pledge of the company's assets were particularly frustrating because most of the task had to be done by Carlton, who had sold the stock in the first place. Not only could he not be located much of the time, but also he had no stomach for trying to sell the idea to family and friends.

While all of the work of securing the necessary votes, placing mortgages, and preparing documentation was going on, Archer's bank was becoming increasingly nervous. Its loan to Archer had reached $545,000, and that was stretching the bank's legal limit. If the loan was called, a loss was very likely. In addition, the bank lacked experience in receivable and inventory lending and was most anxious to have the problem handled by specialists in the business.

After studying Archer's situation for some time, we determined that, in addition to the $545,000 owed to the bank, the company needed an additional $600,000 to reinstate or maintain its relationships with its suppliers. Some publishers had shortened credit lines and some had put Archer on C.O.D. terms. To arrive at the necessary amount, we split the loan into three parts:

1. An 80 percent loan on accounts receivable within 120 days from invoice date produced approximately $800,000. This was enough

to repay the company's bank and to make significant progress on accounts payable.

2. We made a long-term (ten year) loan of $250,000 on the machinery and equipment of the bindery, and a second mortgage on Archer's building. These loans were made to the bindery and the realty company and reloaned to Archer Wholesale Book Company.

3. We made a $50,000 loan on inventory. We would have preferred not to make any such loan, but it was necessary to perfect our lien on the collateral, and it rounded out the arrangement so as to meet Archer's needs. Although Archer's financial statements showed an inventory cost value of $1.2 million, we discovered that the liquidation value of book inventories is small. The usual disposition method is to sell to a "remainder" house, which will pay only between 5 and 15 percent of cost, depending on the types of books and their conditions. We were certain that if we needed to take this route, the return to us would be minimal; for this reason, the loan to Archer was only slightly more than 4 percent of the cost value of the inventory.

The number and kinds of documents used in structuring and securing the loan were almost overwhelming, but they were necessary because of the nature of Archer's business, its financial history and condition, the characteristics of its principals.

A summary of the documents follows:

1. An Accounts Financing Security Agreement (Exhibit 17);
2. An Inventory Loan Security Agreement (Exhibit 26);
3. A chattel mortgage on machinery and equipment;
4. A collateral installment note;
5. A second mortgage placed on the building owned by Archer Realty Company and occupied by Archer Wholesale Book Company and the bindery;
6. An assignment to us of rents paid by Archer Wholesale, the bindery, or any others. This assignment allowed Archer Realty to use these rents for taxes, maintenance costs, heating, and other such costs, so long as we permitted it;
7. A participation agreement with the bank that referred Archer to us. The bank participated with us up to 50 percent of the loan, or an amount not to exceed $545,000;
8. Custodian agreements with a first and substitute custodian who would verify the accuracy of all collateral assigned to us;
9. Guaranties, including a 100 percent guaranty by Fred and

Carlton Carlson, and a *validity* guaranty by Fred's son, Robert. Although Robert was a principal in the company, he had no investment in it and he held the attitude that Archer's condition was not of his doing; therefore he felt no responsibility for guarantying payment of debts for which he was not responsible. We agreed with this attitude and therefore accepted his validity guaranty, which assured the accuracy of all data given to us, but which did not guaranty the collectability of any collateral on which we had a loan;

10. In addition to the foregoing, our documentation included a special loan agreement which, among other things, requested that Archer's counsel give us a letter affirming that the company was duly organized under the laws of the state in which we were doing business, that the company and its principal had the power to execute all agreements, and that the company was involved in no litigation and had none pending.

Affirmative covenants included the following:

1. Archer was to provide us with monthly financial statements written within 45 days of the end of each month.
2. They were to provide us with certified annual statements within 90 days of the end of each fiscal year.
3. Archer promised to advise us of any litigation started against the company in which the claim was for $30,000 or more.
4. They also were to advise us of the placement of any lien against the company for unpaid state or federal taxes.
5. We made a provision requiring Archer to carry all insurance we considered necessary, with all policies naming us as loss payee as our interest appeared.

Negative covenants included the following:

1. The company would pay no stock or cash dividends without our consent.
2. No return of capital would be made to any shareholders.
3. No mortgages would be placed without our consent.
4. No consolidations, mergers, or acquisitions would be consummated without our consent.
5. No loan or advance would be made to any person, firm, or corporation without our consent.
6. Because of the length of time needed to put this transaction together and because of the unusually high legal expense (we paid

all legal costs), we required that this loan arrangement continue in effect for at least two years. If Archer wanted to terminate the arrangement for any reason other than the opportunity to make an advantageous merger or consolidation, Archer would pay us a termination fee based on our estimated average earnings for the number of months from the notice of termination to the anniversary date of the contract.

Even though neither Seaport nor Archer qualified for unsecured loans, they both were candidates for loans secured by receivables, inventories, and other assets. Both loans had to be structured around the assets, the situations, and the principals themselves. The descriptions of these loans demonstrates that, by giving loan applications sufficient study, it sometimes is possible to provide the banker with good security, and at the same time provide the opportunity for a borrower to turn a poor situation into a good one with consequent benefits to all concerned. Another reason for reciting the details of these two loans is to show the factors involved in determining the amount that may be loaned on a company's assets.

Loans on receivables traditionally are held to 80 percent of receivables outstanding from 90 days of their invoice date, and loans of 50 percent are often made against the cost price of goods. In the case of Seaport we were unwilling to loan anything on the company's receivables because of their age and the inaccuracy of the company's records. The inventory, however, was considered to be good collateral in itself, because oil is a necessity of life and is fungible. The inventory was also considered good collateral because of the guaranties we had from responsible guarantors.

When structuring our loan to Archer, we determined that the company's inventory had a very little liquidation value but the receivables, as well as the liens on machinery, equipment, and the building, were sufficient to provide a substantial line of credit. We therefore were able to extend our loans to include accounts 120 days old rather than 90 days old and to fill out the loan package with meaningful loans on the other assets.

The Seaport Oil Company loan turned out well. Within seven years of the inception of our loan, the company repaid its bank the total of its old indebtedness of $208,000, and paid its major supplier $250,000. In both cases, Seaport has returned as a valued customer on an unsecured basis. Needless to say, our loan was also paid in full. The company continues to prosper, and we feel gratified because we kept this company alive during its period of financial distress, and the business and financial assistance we provided helped Seaport to tighten up its entire operation to the point where it became a successful business.

Archer Wholesale Book Company did not fare as well. The under-capitalization of the principals at the time they purchased the business and a string of poor business decisions, made mostly by brother Carlton, finally led to Archer's demise. From our standpoint, the loan worked out well because both we and our bank participant were paid in full without the necessity of notifying account debtors to pay us directly. The sale of the bindery, the building, and the inventory yielded enough to pay all creditors with a small amount left over for the principals. The ultimate test of the security taken for loans is whether or not it yields enough on a liquidation basis to pay a loan in full. The loan to Archer passed this test with flying colors.

We invested a great deal of time and money in our investigations and documentations of both of these accounts because we felt that our financing would provide the borrowers with a reasonable chance of success and would give us collateral sufficient to cover our loan even under distressing circumstances.

It sometimes is easy, however, to become so engrossed in a prospective borrower's affairs that one loses sight of the fact that one or more of the four fundamentals of secured lending (see p. 15) may be missing, and that the deal may be economically unsound. It is imperative, therefore, that an early determination be made that your prospective loan will be profitable to handle. Otherwise, time, money, and brainpower may be wasted in a losing cause.

CHAPTER 6

Administration of the Account

INTRODUCTION

In all of the following discussion of the daily administration of the account, it should be understood that the assignment of invoices, the submission of collections reports, and the report of credits and returns are to be handled on a *bulk* basis.

The posting of a lender's records on a bulk basis means that the total of each day's sales, rather than separate totals of each of the borrower's customer's accounts, are to be recorded. This should also be the manner of posting each day's collections and credits. The individual posting of each debtor's accounts would be excessively time consuming and costly, even when computerized, and would give no better control over collateral than using the procedures recommended here. The record-keeping involved in posting sales, collections, and credits is outlined in the section dealing with bookkeeping in this chapter.

It is also assumed that a *non-notification* system of financing will be used—meaning that the lender does not notify the borrower's customers that accounts due from them are being used as collateral by the borrower as security for loans. The lender, of course, retains the right of notification any time he thinks, in his sole judgment, that it is necessary in order to protect the lender's rights. Non-notification financing also presumes that the lender has recourse to the borrower for any individual accounts which cannot be collected from account debtors.

Before establishing any loan pattern with a new borrower, consideration must be given to the minimum loan that can be made without becoming involved in any small loans statute in the lender's state. For example, loans made in Massachusetts on any given day must be at least $3001.00 in order to avoid possible limitations, licensing, or consumer regulations having to do with the small loan. It must be understood that this applies to *every* loan made and not just to the initial loan or to the total of the borrower's loan balance.

Some states do not specify any minimum loan, and in others the minimum will vary. It is necessary, therefore, to seek guidance in this matter from the bank's legal counsel.

An overriding consideration in determining the validity of collateral is the financial health of your customer. The receivables of a continually sound borrower are always good collateral, and the total of these assets is a measure of the amount that may be borrowed against them. However, if your borrower fails, the receivables may be adversely affected and their collectability reduced substantially—even to zero. An example taken from the recent past is the experience of a commercial finance company which made loans to a wholesale door and window company on the security of its accounts receivable. For a number of reasons the company became unprofitable and eventually ended up in Chapter XI proceedings. When the finance company attempted to collect the receivables, customers claimed many deductions because of dents in doors, broken glass, missing hinges, or missing locks. It was impossible to determine whether or not all of these claims were justified. The finance company had neither the time nor the facilities to cure the alleged problems and had to make generous allowances in order to get the remainder of the invoice paid. The allowances that had to be made reduced the value of the receivables to such an extent that the finance company sustained a loss. Because of situations of this kind, security agreements must give the lender the right to make any adjustments necessary, based solely on his own judgment.

Another, and even more dramatic, example of the almost complete deterioration of a list of receivables involved loans made to a shoe manufacturer on receivables due from a long list of leading department stores throughout the country. After financing this company for a couple of years, the lender was suddenly notified that the borrower had made an assignment for the benefit of creditors. At the time of this notification, the lender was not unduly alarmed because the borrower's current list of receivables was made up almost entirely of stores with top Dun & Bradstreet ratings. As it turned out, however, a serious loss was realized when attempts were made to collect, because practically all account debtors claimed that they bought the goods on a consignment or guaranteed sales basis. The borrower insisted that all sales were final, but the stores fortified their opinions by cleaning their shelves of unsold merchandise and returning it to the now defunct manufacturer.

Imagine the plight of the lender in such a situation! The lender now had to be concerned with such matters as providing a place for storage; arranging for unloading freight cars or trucks and stacking the goods in an orderly way in a warehouse; paying rent for the warehouse space; insuring the goods until disposition; finding a buyer for an inventory that contained a wide variety of styles, sizes, and colors, which were then out of season; and paying a warehouseman for taking care of the goods and for arranging shipment when they were sold. All of this resulted in reducing the recovery value of the receivables by about 65 percent. That plus the cost of liquidation, added up to a very serious loss.

In retrospect, it seems that the lender failed to protect himself in at least three primary respects; 1) he did not insist upon getting at least quarterly financial statements from the borrower, and when he did get them, they did not get sufficient study; 2) accounts receivable were not verified properly; and 3) copies of invoices were not reviewed. A review of these copies might have shown that some, or all, sales were made only on a guaranteed or consignment sales basis, in which case the lender might have been able to reduce his exposure or even withdraw gradually from the account.

The financing of the receivables due from volume buyers are interesting because of the ways such customers operate. Generally, their financial strength is more than satisfactory, although notable exceptions to this have shown up in the past few years. What must be realized is that the buyer for any department in a department store is usually allotted a certain amount of money with which to purchase goods. If the goods show a satisfactory turn, then a good return on the employed funds results, and the buyer's position and his or her future become more secure. If, on the other hand, the buyer is left with broken sizes, colors, and styles, or if the goods are seasonal, the items no longer can be promoted, nor can replacements for faulty merchandise be gotten easily. A situation such as this ties up the allocated funds, and there is a great temptation (to which many buyers yield) to return all unsold goods to the supplier.

In such cases, the lender on receivables is put into a very untenable situation—particularly if there are several returns made. If the lender refuses the goods, the lender usually has to pay the cost of freight for the return trip or guarantee the trucking company that it will be paid. Also, the lender usually gets involved in lengthy discussions with the account debtor relative to the correctness of the billing and, in many cases, has to supply proof of an order and proof of delivery. If the store does not respond and suit has to be brought, the legal costs and the time consumed may reduce any net recovery substantially. Volume buyers know all of these things, and know that in many cases it is less costly for the lender to accept returns and sell off the goods than it is to attempt to collect through lawsuits or other means.

The lesson here is that the liquidation values of any collateral may be very different from the numbers shown on a balance sheet, and one should not be lulled into a sense of security because most of the receivables are due from strong companies.

FRAUD

One of the great dangers of accounts receivable and inventory lending is that fraud will be perpetrated on the lender by the pledging of fictitious invoices, false inventory reports, or by the diversion of collections.

When frauds appear, they often come in giant sizes, such as the salad oil swindle of the 1960s and the fertilizer storage tank fraud of the same era. These were dramatic examples but, while there are no statistics to prove it, it is believed that such frauds account for a small part of the losses taken on accounts receivable lending. Fraud often comes about when a previously honest businessman is put under pressure because of a series of losses, or when, because of personal problems, one or more of the principals feels forced to borrow for a little while from the bank or finance company. In spite of the fact that deliberate frauds are infrequent, the lender should always be alert to the fact that they *can* happen. When they do, they may lead to serious losses before being detected.

Frauds may be perpetrated in so many ways that it is pointless to try to list them all. One of the more common types involves the issuance of fictitious invoices to a nonexistent company that has been given a name very similar to a large and creditworthy company. For example, false invoices could be made out W. *A.* Heller Corporation, *107* Adams Street, Chicago, Illinois, and could easily be assumed to be due from Walter *E.* Heller & Company, 105 W. Adams Street, Chicago—a billion dollar company with a top credit rating. If such invoices were issued in collusion with an outsider who would give affirmative answers to verification requests, the fraud could continue for a long time.

When checking aging schedules, daily assignments, invoices, or bills of lading, therefore, one has to be inquisitive as well as somewhat suspicious in order to be sure of the validity of all collateral accepted for loans. In addition to checking the accuracy of names of customers and in following prudent verification procedures, the activity of accounts should be observed. For example, frauds are sometimes concealed in accounts that are kept consistently within thirty days from invoice date, either by cash payments or credits. When the borrower has been sufficiently lulled into a sense of security, a flood of sizeable bills are issued that are never paid. Conversely, fraudulent accounts may be hidden in consistently overdue balances where the slowness is related to a new bookkeeper, a new computer, or the general practice of paying bills. This also may be allowed to go on for a long time until the perpetrator is ready to make his killing.

There is no formula for combating such situations. It can only be said that the validity of receivables has to be viewed with some cynicism and some suspicion; it has to be tested continuously notwithstanding the fact that the lender must have confidence in the general trustworthiness of the borrower. No honest person should object to a lender taking every reasonable precaution to ensure that the collateral against which funds are advanced is bona fide in every respect.

By the same token, no lender should relax his or her vigilance because the borrower objects to the checkings that have to be made or simply because the lender has a "gut feeling" that the borrower is completely honest. What a person or a company did yesterday is history, but what will be done tomorrow is unpredictable. One of the most astute lenders in the commercial field, whenever told that the integrity of a prospective borrower was above reproach and that the possibility of fraud was nonexistent, very often would comment, "Many men will die tomorrow who never died before." The point is well taken. The weakest defense that a lending officer can give after a fraud has been discovered is that he or she did not think it necessary to maintain at least routine checks on the borrower.

The daily supervision and policing of collateral is of prime importance. The following sections of this chapter are intended to help in this respect, although the list of checkpoints is in no way complete. One of the aspects of receivable and inventory lending that makes it both fascinating and challenging is that each account is different, so each account requires its own special checklist which can change with changing circumstances. Imagination, practical business experience, realism, and the knowledge of a borrower's business will dictate the type and number of tests and reviews that are needed to inspire and maintain the lender's confidence in the borrower and the pledged collateral. Care must be taken, however, that overzealousness in this respect does not unnecessarily harass the borrower.

The checks and verifications that follow keep the lender informed on what is currently happening to collateral, rather than waiting for quarterly audits, verification reports, or financial statements that reveal only what happened weeks or months ago. Many circumstances may lead to a rapid deterioration in pledged receivables and inventory. There is, therefore, a great urgency for keeping up to date on collateral and for making prompt corrections or adjustments whenever there appears to be any irregularity or diminution in value.

REVIEW OF ACCOUNTS RECEIVABLE SCHEDULES

Before funds are advanced on a new borrower's schedule of accounts receivable, the schedule should be checked against the receivable and general ledgers. A verification should be made (by telephone, if necessary) of a significant portion of the balances outstanding. It is particularly important that the larger accounts be verified. In addition, the initial schedule and subsequent schedules should be reviewed for the age of accounts and for credit risks.

Age of Accounts   There is no absolute rule in judging the validity of a list of accounts receivable only from its aging. Generally speaking, though, if the total of over-ninety-day accounts (from the invoice date) goes beyond about 15 percent of the total of all receivables, the reason for the slowness should be discovered and attention should be focused on the particular accounts making up the old balances. Some lenders will establish a policy which is referred to as the *10 percent rule*—meaning that if that portion of an account which is over ninety days old is equal to 10 percent or more of the account's total balance, the entire account is deducted as unacceptable collateral. The account is then not restored to the borrowing base until it has been brought into a satisfactory condition.

The rationale of the 10 percent rule is that if an account debtor has to let a large portion of his balance run over ninety days, something is wrong either with his ability to pay or with the invoices involved. In either case, a cloud is cast over the collectability of the account. The lender, of course, retains his lien on such accounts but puts them in "special reserve."

Terms of sale vary greatly between industries; while a large number of accounts over ninety days old in one industry would be sufficient cause to reject a loan application, in another industry they might be considered acceptable. For example, a great many old accounts due from banks should raise many questions, but old accounts in the plumbing and heating industry are not unusual.

A large number of overdue accounts might indicate, among other things, an extension of credit to poor credit risks, undetected contra accounts, poor collection policies, undisclosed and unissued credit memos, or quality problems with merchandise causing customers to withhold payment until a satisfactory adjustment is made. Balances could represent charges for goods that have since been returned and for which customers are awaiting credits. An example of this is the examination which was once made of a prospective borrower; it revealed over $125,000 of credits which should have been issued for returned goods but which, for the prospect's own reasons, had been held up. The lender considered this to be an attempt at deception and declined the loan.

A large number of overdue accounts also may exist when a borrower offers cooperative advertising to his customers; fairly sizeable balances may remain outstanding awaiting credits to be issued. Credits for advertising are usually held up until *tear sheets*—copies of the printed ad —are accumulated; these credits are often settled quarterly or seasonally, rather than on a monthly basis.

Credit Risks   When a schedule of receivables is submitted that consists of one hundred or more names, the majority of the balances are usually in moderate amounts and the lender is somewhat protected by the diversity and size of the accounts. The initial acceptance of such receivables as good collateral may be based on a review of the paying habits of a portion of the accounts as shown on the borrower's records, and positive verification of some of the larger and older accounts.

The lines of credit extended to larger accounts should be substantiated by reviewing whatever credit information is in the borrower's files, by checking credit agency ratings, and, if necessary, by obtaining new agency reports and bank references.

Ledgering of Individual Accounts. If one or more receivables are particularly large and constitute a large percentage of the total receivables, it is often advisable to keep a detailed ledger for such accounts in the lender's office. Posting of debits and credits to such a ledger would duplicate the borrower's records, but when one or just a few accounts constitute a large percentage of a borrower's total receivable balance, they may be dangerous to both lender and borrower. For instance, if a borrower normally makes substantial shipments to a large customer, and if the borrower should ever harbour evil intent, a fictitious invoice in a sizeable amount may be made out which will not be detected for quite a long time—particularly if such accounts were not ledgered in the lender's office. If a borrower falls out of favor with a large customer and sales stop, it could have a serious, and sometimes fatal, impact on the borrower's business; or, if a large customer phases out with a borrower, numerous adjustments may be made in the payment of final invoices which could bring recoveries below the amount of the lender's original advance.

The lender can gain some protection from the dangers of concentration not only by ledgering large accounts but also, with the consent of the borrower, by notifying such accounts that the lender is advancing funds on his receivables. It should be the option of the lender to ask the customer to make payment directly to the lender or to state in his letter of notification that the customer may continue to make payments to the borrower until otherwise directed by the lender. The latter route is usually followed and is more acceptable both to the borrower and the lender. In either case, it should be made clear to the borrower that notification does not alter in any way the lender's recourse rights against the borrower in the event of the account debtor's failure to pay.

There are many advantages to the lender in maintaining individual receivable ledgers on some accounts. The lender is constantly aware of the frequency and size of the sales made to the account; it can be verified that the borrower does not allow the account to run above any credit line which has been established. Then, slowness in payment can be detected quickly, making it possible for the lender to lower an established credit line if it seems advisable. By keying payments to specific invoices, any skipped invoices can be spotted easily, enabling the lender to determine promptly the reason for this. Further, credit memos can be watched for size and frequency; and finally, the issuance of invoices and their cancellation by credit memo within the same month can be caught quickly. This latter example is a fairly familiar fraudulent practice, whereby a borrower issues an invoice at the beginning of the month, obtains funds against it, and then cancels the invoice with a credit memo later in the same month.

On the occasion of each examination, the examiner should take with him a copy of every detailed ledger to be sure that it compares in every respect with the borrower's records.

Contra Accounts

Contra accounts should not be accepted as collateral unless the borrower's purchases from the customer are consistently very small in comparison to the customer's purchases from the borrower.

When a borrower is asked about the existence of contra accounts, a frequent answer is that there really is not a contra situation because the borrower and the customer exchange checks rather than offset the balances due to each other. This answer is unacceptable; it would be nonsensical under liquidation conditions for a supplier to pay an account, knowing that the amount due would be heavily discounted or not paid at all.

Checking for contra accounts should be a routine procedure on the occasion of every examination of the borrower's records. A list should be made of all contra accounts and given to the department head for continuous checking against new sales. All contras should be removed from the borrower's total of good collateral and added to special reserve.

Datings

Extended terms are given in many industries to conform with seasons of the year or to cover special holiday sales. Datings are standard accommodations offered by many companies and give buyers the opportunity to arrange for the sale of the goods before the dating terms mature. Because the seller can ship early, he is relieved for several months of the substantial costs of storing, handling, and insuring the goods.

Dating terms generally run from 60 to 120 days, with some extending as much as eight months, although lenders are not too enthusiastic about loaning against receivables with such slow maturity. Experience has proved, however, that credit losses on long-term invoices are about the same as on goods sold on regular terms.

The form for aging accounts receivable should contain a column where datings may be listed, and all such balances should show in this column. These balances should be considered current until thirty days after the maturity date of the invoice. After thirty days beyond the net terms, the unpaid dating balance should be deducted from the borrowing base and added to the special reserve.

If, during the dating period, news reaches the borrower or lender that casts doubt on the collectability of any account, that account should, of course, be removed from the borrowing base at once.

Comparison of
Aged Schedules

As aged schedules are received each month, it is a good practice to set up a separate columnar sheet for each borrower, and to record the total balance of each column showing:

Total   Dating   0-30 days   30-60 days   60-90 days   over 90 days

As time goes on, the most recent month-end balances may be compared with the receivables of three months, six months, a year, and more; trends may be observed regarding growth, seasonal fluctuations, and customer payment practices. Information gathered from this source may alert the borrower to firm up his collection efforts or to tighten up on the extension of credit; it may also inform the lender of progress through growth or, conversely, a deterioration of this important asset.

REVIEW OF DAILY LIST OF ACCOUNTS ASSIGNED

Every list of accounts assigned should be checked to ensure that it is legible, properly dated, consecutively numbered, and correctly totalled; that it shows adequate identification of the customer; and that it is signed by an authorized party. If the form is lacking any of this information, it should be returned to the borrower for correction. Keep in mind that this form and its attachments are the fundamental collateral for loans; any incorrect or missing information may weaken the lender's claim upon the proceeds in the event that the lender has to collect directly from the account debtor.

As is indicated in Exhibit 10, some borrowers issue invoices in strict numerical sequence and file copies accordingly. When this is done, a complete explanation for any missing numbers should accompany the assignment sheet, and copies of the voided invoices should be attached if possible.

Review of
Invoices

The review of invoices is a very important control function of the accounts receivable lending department and should be done as frequently as possible. Ideally, invoices should be at least fanned on a daily basis, but if a daily review is not possible, a day's invoices should be studied no less frequently than every ten days. A great deal may be learned about a borrower's business from a study of his invoices: the names and addresses of steady customers, the terms of sale, whether regular or dating; the normal size of invoices; the type of goods sold; the discounts offered; and whether goods are sold on a consignment or guarantied basis.

Some discounts offered by borrowers to their customers are very high, such as the 8 percent usually offered to the retail clothing trade. The rates of advance on invoices with more than the usual 2 percent discount should be adjusted to allow for the discount and still keep the lender's advance within a prudent percentage of the amount expected to be paid by the account debtor.

There usually are clues on invoices representing consignment or guaranteed sales, among which could be the word "special" or "per agreement" in the space provided for terms. Any indication of this type of sale should be questioned immediately and, if confirmed with the borrower, should be removed from the borrowing base and added to the special reserve. Such invoices are not good collateral because a receivable is not created until title passes or, if a service is involved, until the service is satisfactorily performed.

When a new product has been manufactured or a new customer has been obtained, goods sometimes are sold on a trial basis, which in effect is the same as selling on consignment or guarantied terms. The invoices resulting from thése are not acceptable as collateral; unless the borrower specifically spells out the period of time or the total dollars that may be involved, there may be a continuing uncertainty as to when the goods stop being sold on a trial basis and when sales become final. Invoices arising from trial orders should be added to special reserve and should not be included in the borrowing base.

Invoices for progress payments are also usually identified by such words as "Per Contract Dated _____," "Payment Number _____," or "Contract Dated _____." Any indications of progress payments should be investigated to determine the extent to which progress billing is employed. If it is done on a regular basis, it would be sufficient justification to ask your borrower to pledge another type of collateral to support the loan or even to seek financing elsewhere.

Bill-and-Hold Invoices. Bill-and-hold situations may arise when a manufacturer finds it more economical to make an entire order at one time rather than on a piecemeal basis, but the customer can only use the goods in smaller quantities and at intervals of his or her choosing. If the borrower is a wholesaler, he may buy a customer's entire order at one time, at truckload or carload prices, with considerable savings over the cost of buying only for current needs.

From a lender's standpoint, bill-and-hold invoices are questionable collateral because title for the goods may not pass until they are delivered to the buyer's premises. Such invoices should be added to special reserve, or the borrower should be asked to secure a letter from the customer (see Exhibit 11) that acknowledges that the goods are the borrower's and that he will accept and pay for any invoice rendered on regular terms.

Bill-and-hold invoices usually may be identified by such words as "Partial Billing," "per your contract" (or "order"), or "Billing Number _____ against your order," and will appear in the body of the invoice or in the section reserved for terms. When goods are held for an account debtor's shipping instructions, it should be determined who has the responsibility for keeping the inventory insured until shipment is made.

Other invoices which should be questioned are invoices for services to be performed, invoices issued in round numbers, and invoices without proper description of the product or services rendered. One of the worst accounts receivable accounts ever reviewed involved all of these three categories. The borrower in this case was a manufacturer of displays used at conventions or exhibitions; an additional service rendered was the storage of the displays in between the times they were to go on exhibit. Many of the invoices were for storage charges for periods of up to twelve months *subsequent* to the date of billing. The borrower was not financially strong. In this situation, should the business fail, the account debtor would have every right to refuse to pay because a great percentage of the invoice was for service yet to be rendered. Furthermore, a great number of the invoices issued by this borrower were in round numbers. Except for invoices issued by professional people, billing in round numbers are unusual; when they occur, they should be questioned. If a borrower is intent on fraud, it does not matter if invoices are issued in round or odd numbers, but if a bank will accept invoices in round numbers, it is much easier for a potential thief to defraud the lender. To compound the bank's problems in this particular case, the bank also accepted, without question, the cancellation by credit memo of many of these invoices within the same month they were issued.

As if this were not enough, the bank also accepted invoices that contained little or no information about the product or the service that was rendered. Numerous invoices showed legends such as:

Display for Bicentennial Exhibit $5,000.00
For exhibit per quote 4,000.00
Display for Managers Meeting 1,000.00

These invoices not only contained insufficient descriptions of the items produced, but also did not advise whether the goods had actually been built or whether the function for which they had been built *had been* held or was *to be* held.

The bank involved in this situation had allowed its loan to more than quadruple in about six months time, and at the time of review the loan had reached a total of almost $600,000. It is not known whether this loan arrangement still exists; however, even if the bank has been paid, it still may be severely criticized for accepting collateral of such dubious value, and for not supervising and policing the activities of its borrower more closely.

*Review of
Warranties*

Many items manufactured and sold carry warranties that they are free from quality defects. The goods involved may cover a wide spectrum of merchandise from simple kitchen devices to large specialty equipment, and the period of the warranty may vary from three months to a year or more.

The terms of warranties seldom show on invoices; therefore, it is necessary for the lender to check the company's sales literature, including inserts that go in packing boxes, to be sure of the exact nature and extent of any product guaranties.

At times of liquidation, the collection of accounts receivable covering products with extended warranties may be very difficult and troublesome. For example, if loans are made on the security of accounts receivable arising out of the sale of television sets sold to volume buyers throughout the country, it presupposes that the seller must have a service organization consisting of parts and repair depots at strategic locations to quickly, efficiently, and economically service the sets as needed. This kind of a service organization may work well under normal and profitable operations, but under liquidation conditions, the organization may rapidly fall apart with increasing frustration to sellers, consumers, and lenders. Volume buyers know these things and often will delay payment until they are assured that warranties will be fulfilled, or will withhold payment until the warranty period has expired. When such circumstances exist, the lender has to make an early decision about the need to hold a service department together; if it is deemed necessary, the lender must estimate what the costs would be of doing so. If the loan to be liquidated is large, it is sometimes advisable to retain the service manager on the payroll to supervise the service organization and to phase it out when conditions warrant it.

If a borrower is in financial trouble and it appears that accounts receivable will have to be collected by the lender, it is always best to review the warranty situation carefully and to keep public awareness of the borrower's problems as quiet as possible. This does not imply in any way that the lender should commit any dishonest act or deal in subterfuge, but it is obvious that the more receivables collected before warranties become an issue, the greater the lender's chances will be of coming out without a loss.

Review of Bills of Lading

Every invoice covering goods shipped by common carriers or by a borrower's own trucks should be supported by a bill of lading or a trucking receipt. This requirement sometimes presents a problem, however, as the invoice often may be prepared before the goods are picked up and signed for by the carrier. As a result, invoices may have to be withheld from assignment until they can be matched with bills of lading. If the lender agrees, the invoices may be sent at once with the bills of lading to be sent later. This leaves the matching process up to the lender. The former procedure is preferable, but, in either case, the bill of lading should be reviewed carefully for dates and signatures, and to determine that the amount of goods shown on the bill of lading makes sense when compared with its matching invoice. Even though everything may appear to be satisfactory, the lender is still at the mercy of the borrower, since the boxes, barrels, or crates shown on the bill of lading actually may contain rocks or partial shipments instead of what is shown on the invoice. This points up the necessity of constant verification of accounts and the need to act promptly whenever any discrepancies appear.

When, because of the daily volume of sales, it is impractical for the borrower to submit a copy of each invoice, the lender's examiner should review—on the occasion of each visit—a representative selection of invoices and bills of lading with all of the foregoing considerations in mind. Any invoice that is incomplete or questionable in any way should immediately be brought to the attention of the bank's accounts receivable department head instead of being put aside until the examination report is completed.

Guarantors of Receivable Accounts

Many lenders require borrowers to use the services of companies that guaranty the validity of the accounts receivable which are pledged. Such companies as NYTCO Services, Inc., and Lawrence Systems, Inc., provide such guaranties and will certify the quantity of the collateral through the use of their custodial set up. Furthermore, through the use of custodians, some companies will guaranty a lender against the diversion of collected funds.

These are good and valuable services, but it must be pointed out that the guaranties are restricted to fraudulent acts; they do not guaranty that the accounts are collectable or that they are free of the offsets mentioned in this chapter. It is of prime importance, therefore, that the lender constantly police accounts receivable for collectibility. No one else is in a position to do it as promptly or as accurately, nor can anyone else stay on top of the rapid changes that may take place in this important asset.

It is good psychology to call a borrower from time to time and ask an innocent question about an invoice, bill of lading, remittance report, or credit memo, or even to congratulate him on an unusually large sale or on the first sale to a new account. This makes the borrower aware that the invoices are being looked at closely, and it might inhibit any possible intention of wrongdoing.

In spite of taking every possible precaution and of handling every account with all due diligence, fraud is an ever-constant possibility. Fraud may be perpetrated by a borrower alone or in collusion with an outside party, and sometimes with the help of a company employee. There is a sameness about fraudulent acts, but they always come as a surprise because of the attitude, "I never thought this could happen to me," or because of the sudden revelation that a friendly borrower or a loyal employee is a thief. Those lenders who are heavily involved with large accounts receivable loans should discuss fraud coverage with their insurance departments or insurance brokers to determine what protection may be afforded in the event that a large fraud is encountered.

Review of Credit Memoranda

When a prospective borrower's financial statements are being analyzed at the time of an initial examination, it is important to review the company's returns and allowance account, and, if possible, to compare the activity in the account on a year-to-year basis. This should give the lender an idea of the number of credits issued during a month or a season, and, if a norm can be established, it may serve as a basis of comparison for future transactions.

The issuance of credit memos is a normal activity for almost any business, but credits should be studied just as frequently as invoices are reviewed. A plethora of credits or credits of unusual size could indicate the beginnings of quality problems with goods manufactured or sold, the incidence of poor business practices, or the issuance of credits covering fraudulent invoices . For example, a certain shoe manufacturer borrowed on his receivables. He ran into a bad batch of adhesives used in the gluing of soles and heels. Before the problem surfaced, a very large quantity of shoes was manufactured and sold to volume buyers throughout the eastern part of the United States. About four months after the shoes were built, they started to come back in large quantities, with nearly disastrous results to both the manufacturer and the lender. In this case, many receivables were completely wiped out and others were drastically reduced in value.

The lender first learned of this problem by a study of credit memos. (The borrower was reluctant to advise the lender when the situation first arose because he feared that the lender would not cooperate with him.) As it turned out, the manufacturer of the adhesives, the principals of the shoe company, and the lender all worked together and provided enough funds and extended enough credit to enable the shoe company to work itself out of its troubles.

A fraudulent practice that comes to light with some frequency involves the issuance of fictitious invoices that later are cancelled in full with credit memos. When credits are issued in the same month as the invoice, the fraud cannot be caught by verifying month-end balances. When a credit is issued to cancel an entire invoice, it does not necessarily mean fraud. When billing errors are made, many companies will credit out the wrong invoice in full and issue a corrected invoice at once. Such credits should be investigated, however, to be sure that the transactions involved are legitimate.

Credits also may be issued for unordered merchandise that is actually shipped, or overshipments may take place to enable the borrower to get extra funds to take care of a temporary shortage of funds.

Sizeable credits also may arise when a manufacturer or wholesaler shares in the expense of advertising a product (cooperative advertising). In addition, some companies will extend special volume discounts if a certain amount of their products are sold within a specified time. In either case, credits have to be withheld until tear sheets are accumulated or until the volume agreed upon is reached. As a result, credits may build up, and, when issued, they may eliminate the "available to borrow" funds and even create an "over advance" position in the lender's records.

There are many other reasons for issuing credit memos—for instance, adjusting for contra accounts, or charging accounts to bad debts. In almost every instance credit memos will dilute the value of receivables; this, of course, results in a smaller return covering any loan made against them. The lender, therefore, should review credits consistently and should insist that each one show a clear explanation for its issuance.

As has been noted earlier in this book, the Memo of Returns and Credits form should be sent to the lender at the end of each week, whether or not any credit memos have been issued. If a succession of reports are received with only a few credits, or with none, it might mean that credits are accumulating and the only reason for not issuing them is to keep the borrower's borrowing base at a higher level than it should be. An indication of this might be that some receivables which appear to have slowed down in reality are waiting for the credits to be issued.

Review of
Collection
Reports

Basic to the concept of accounts receivable lending is that the borrower must remit all collections to the lender as soon as they are received. There are three important reasons for this: first, upon assignment, the proceeds of receivables (customer collections) become subject to a lien in favor of the lender and must be sent to the lender promptly upon receipt by the borrower; second, the lender's insistence on the immediate forwarding of collections will reduce the possibility of a misuse of the funds; and third, because collections are credited to a borrower's account as received, the borrower's loan balance is thereby reduced, resulting in lower interest costs.

All customer remittances should be sent to the lender exactly in the same form as received by the borrower. The bank should provide the borrower with an endorsement stamp that reads:

Deposit to the Account of
XYZ Manufacturing Company
Special Account Number 0000

The special account number is the bank's own account number, and as the bank's name does not appear on the endorsement, the non-notification feature of receivables financing is preserved. The bank's right to endorse checks made out to the borrower in this way or by showing its own name should be part of the Accounts Financing Security agreement.

Vouchers should be left attached to checks so that they may be inspected by the lender for deductions, corrections, or any other changes. It is especially important that this information be available to the lender when a borrower's larger accounts are being ledgered in the lender's office. Checks and vouchers will also show partial payments and deductions which may or may not reconcile with information supplied by the borrower.

Checks should be compared with the names or remittance sheets to be sure that the check actually received applies to the account listed on the sheet. It has been known to happen that a borrower has collected funds on one invoice, has kept it for his or her own use, and, at a later date, has used another check to substitute for the one appropriated; if there was a difference, it would be wiped out with a credit memo or another invoice.

Most companies that borrow on the security of their accounts receivables receive checks almost daily from their customers. Borrowers should make it a routine to send checks to the lender as they are received—whether there is only one check or many, whether the total remittance is small or large. If remittances are not received from a borrower for three consecutive days, an inquiry should be made as to why this is so. If answers appear to be unclear or evasive, an examiner should be asked to call on the account promptly in order to trace the disposition of collections.

THE REVIEW OF ACCOUNTS PAYABLE SCHEDULES

At the time of the initial examination of a prospective borrower's business, an aged list of accounts payable should be reviewed to determine a number of conditions. First, it should be determined that the amount of the proposed loan will be enough to put the prospect in a comfortable position with creditors and leave some excess working capital to take care of contingencies. This does not mean that all payables have to be put onto a discount basis, but suppliers should be made sufficiently happy to induce them to sell adequate amounts, on a continuous basis, thus providing the borrower with a smooth flow of raw material or goods for resale.

Any review of accounts payable has to take taxes (federal, state, and city) into consideration. This is particularly true of federal and state taxes which, if not paid, might result in liens that could have priority over the lender's claim to the proceeds of receivables.

If the amount available from receivables provides only partial relief for the prospect and would result in a number of accounts remaining unpaid or only slightly reduced, the account should be declined. This is particularly true if the prospect's recent operations showed losses rather than profits. Many receivable loan losses have been suffered because of the belief that the extra funds provided by a revolving line of credit will almost automatically enable a failing company to become profitable. Although this sometimes happens, the chances of success are much greater when receivable financing is used to make a profitable company more profitable; taking a risk on a failing company often means that continuing losses will absorb the extra funds and only add to the borrower's woes.

The accounts payable should be checked for contra accounts that may reduce or eliminate some accounts receivable. It is also important to determine the extent of concentrations in accounts payable. Big suppliers may exert big pressures by withholding goods which could shut down the plant of a manufacturer or might eliminate the top line of a distributor or wholesaler. For example, if a distributor or wholesaler bases his or her business primarily on one or more national brands, the cancellations of purchase and sale agreements could prove fatal. When large concentrations appear in payable agings, it is advisable to review purchase and sale agreements to determine whether any sales quotas established by the seller can be met, and if payment terms can be adhered to.

When a manufacturer or a national distributor of a product is selling through subdistributors or wholesalers, it must be realized that the manufacturer or distributor is interested primarily in two things: one, where to get the biggest volume; and two, who will pay on the shortest terms. The credit aspect of selling is only a necessary evil to companies geared principally to sales, and patience quickly wears thin when volume does not meet expectations or when collection problems arise.

When a new loan arrangement is made and funds are advanced, the next accounts payable aging list should show the expected improvement. If not, inquiries should be made about the disposition of the funds advanced.

It is good practice to obtain accounts payable on a monthly basis if possible. If this is too difficult for the borrower, accounts payable should be submitted at least quarterly and, of course, verified with the borrower's general ledger at the time of the lender's regular examination.

The age and general condition of accounts payable should be reviewed carefully. Old accounts may be a worry to the borrower, and not only may result in pressure from suppliers, but also may cause the suppliers to raise prices or to impose late payment charges to compensate for the costs of carrying the old account. Such action would naturally reduce profits, and, if the borrower were already marginal, it could accelerate a downhill slide.

It is suggested that the totals of payables be posted to a ledger each time they are received; as time goes on, they may be compared to determine whether they are changing for the better or for the worse. If receivable availabilities are being fully utilized but payables are deteriorating, it could mean that losses are being suffered or a diversion of funds is taking place.

ANALYSIS OF BORROWER'S FINANCIAL STATEMENTS

*General
Considerations*

Careful analysis of financial statements is crucial to prudent lending not only before the initial loan is made but also as a basis for the continuance of a lending arrangement.

Sometimes a loan officer may study the financial reports of large national companies whose reports are supported by detailed schedules of assets and liabilities, comparative statements for years past, and voluminous auditors notes. These companies often have such a margin of safety in strong net worth positions that the analyst can feel comfortable with his position even if fairly substantial losses take place before the next statement is issued. When companies are borrowing on accounts receivable and inventory, however, it generally means that such borrowers are leveraged to a significant degree. It is therefore imperative that the loan officer has detailed knowledge of the assets being pledged as collateral, of the amount and term of liabilities, and of the various items appearing in the income statement. The *acid test* —the ratio of current assets to current liabilities—has little meaning when applied only to the numbers appearing on the balance sheet of marginal borrowers, unless the lender has specific and current knowledge of the hard value of the assets being studied and of the amount and term of all liabilities.

Annual financial statements should be prepared by a competent certified public accountant, and, unless there is some compelling reason to the contrary, they should bear an unqualified certification by him. It is also desirable that interim statements, such as monthly, quarterly, or semiannual statements, be prepared by a CPA, but such statements do not have to be certified. The great majority of accountants are careful, capable people, but as in any profession, some are better than others. It is always important for the lender to review and test all figures shown to be sure of the statement's completeness and accuracy.

Any financial statements submitted by the borrower should include the accountant's foreword, which spells out the scope of the audit, and should also include comments which give pertinent details about the statement itself. The auditor's comments should cover some of the following areas:

1. The basis of evaluation of inventory—is it based on FIFO, LIFO, or Lower of Cost or Market? If, at the end of a fiscal year, the inventory evaluation has changed from one basis to another, not only should it be noted, but also at least the last fiscal statement should be restated in order to give the analyst a true comparison between the current and prior statement;

2. The rate of depreciation applied to various fixed assets such as real estate, machinery and equipment, and automobiles;

3. An analysis of term debt with supporting payment schedules showing payments made during the year under review, to whom they were made, and the payments that must be made over the agreed term of the loan. If the auditor's notes do not include any comments regarding penalties that could be invoked if payments are not made on time, the analyst should inquire about the possibility. If the information received from the borrower or the accountant is unclear, the bank's examiner should be requested to review the borrower's purchase contracts to be sure that all terms and conditions are understood;

4. A breakdown of all taxes due, such as real estate, excise, income taxes, withholding taxes, and whether they are due to the federal, state, or city government. The auditor's notes naturally should state whether any of such taxes are delinquent, and, if so, how long they have been overdue;

5. An analysis of any notes payable arising from loans made on the security of any of the company's assets. The analysis should give the amount due on short-term and long-term bases and should state whether payments are being made on time;

6. Remarks as to whether the borrower has any contingent liabilities, and, if so, what impact they might have on the company's cash flow;
7. A recitation of any lawsuits outstanding and an expression from the borrower's attorney as to the probable outcome of such suits;
8. Remarks pertaining to union negotiations that are currently under way or which may be started within the next fiscal year.

The nature and volume of an auditor's comments will vary with the size and type of business for which a statement is prepared. From an analyst's standpoint, an auditor's notes to a financial statement are fully as important as the numbers themselves, and in order to gain a complete understanding of a financial report, the notes should be clear and in detail.

Particular attention also should be paid to any exceptions to generally accepted accounting procedures, such as not verifying accounts receivable or not being present during an inventory count. The reasons for such exceptions should be discussed with the borrower.

When a financial statement covers the activities of two or more affiliated or subsidiary companies, it is important to get *consolidating* as well as *consolidated* statements in order to determine the relationship of each company to the other and to check on the profitability of each company.

If there is a possibility that an affiliated or subsidiary company may drain the resources of the company being financed, the lender should consider the following alternatives: encourage the weaker company or companies to arrange for their own financing; consider financing the weaker company as a separate operation; or obtain corporate guaranties from the affiliated companies for all debts due from the borrower to the lender.

Of course, it is preferable that each company stand on its own merit so that the lender is relieved of the work and the anxiety of closely following the progress of each company.

Frequency of Financial Statements

The frequency with which a borrower should submit financial statements to a lender depends on the strength of the borrower's financial condition. For example, if a company has a good net worth and is making satisfactory profits, statements on a quarterly or semiannual basis could be satisfactory. On the other hand, if the borrower has a small net worth and is losing money or making only small profits, the lender should insist on at least quarterly statements, and if the situation is really tight, monthly figures should be submitted.

The preparation of statements on a quarterly basis will cost a borrower more than if only annual reports were required. The extra cost, however, should be moderate; an accountant may keep running records throughout the year and, accordingly, may cut down on preparation time at the end of the year—a time, incidentally, when the accountant may be busy with many year-end statements. Frequent statements are fully as important to the borrower as to the lender; they give the borrower an opportunity to correct any problems on a current basis, rather than having them multiply during the whole of the fiscal year.

Early in the negotiation stage, a prospective borrower should provide copies of at least the last three annual statements as well as the most current interim figures. These, and subsequent statements, will show the lender the trend of the business and will give timely warning of any deterioration. Spread sheets should be set up for all statements, in order to give an easy comparison of trends in the borrower's business.

When the financial statements of a borrower are being reviewed by the accounts receivable lending department, it must be realized that any financial statement purports to show the financial condition of a company at a specific time and that a good statement is no guaranty that the assets or liabilities will remain as favorable to the borrower for even a short time into the future. For this reason, the lender must constantly review pledged collateral, as recommended earlier, to be sure of its value regardless of what is shown on financial reports.

Review of Assets

The review and verification of pledged assets are covered earlier in this book, but additional considerations follow.

Analysis of Accounts Receivable. When reviewing statements and comparing the figures to the company's records and history, a few questions concerning the accounts receivable are important. For example, does the amount shown on the statement reconcile with the amount on the lender's records? Is the reserve for bad debts adequate in relation to the borrower's historical record of write-offs? What is known about the accounts from verifications, credit agency reports, or amounts known to be in litigation?

It is advisable to calculate the turnover rate of accounts receivable by dividing the net credit sales by the receivables. This will show the number of times the receivables turn over on an annual basis and may indicate the effectiveness of the borrower's collection policies and the overall collectibility of the accounts. This ratio also may be compared with industry standards to see whether the condition of the borrower's accounts is better or worse than a competitor's accounts.

Analysis of Inventory. As has been noted earlier, the constant evaluation of inventory is a difficult and sophisticated task; inventory often is the place where losses are taken when a combined accounts receivable and inventory loan has to be liquidated. Accountant's statements should always break down the inventory of a manufacturer into raw materials, work-in-progress, and finished goods; each category may have very different liquidating values and each should stay in proper proportion to production and sales.

Inventory turnover should be calculated by dividing cost of sales by the inventory; this ratio will show the number of days inventory is tied up in this asset. This, then, may be compared with industry averages to determine if the borrower is meeting or exceeding the norm. A slow turnover of inventory does not necessarily mean bad news. From time to time many businesses accumulate a temporary excess of inventory. If this happens to be the case, the sale of such inventory could help cash flow or, if an acquisition is involved, could provide some of the funds for the purchase.

When computing inventory turnover, consideration has to be given to the type of inventory involved and to the industry in which the borrower does business. For example, an inventory of goods made only for the Christmas season may give a negative turnover answer if calculated just before the start of the company's shipping season. A turnover figure will also be entirely distorted if taken when inventory is at its lowest point, just after the holiday has passed.

Analysis of Other Assets. Generally speaking, "other assets" will include such items as prepaid rent, prepaid insurance, and airline deposits; they are not usually a significant part of a company's working capital or net worth. Occasionally, however, an item such as amounts due from employees or officers may be large, and if no specific repayment schedule has been established, the item should be deducted from current assets before computing both working capital and net worth. The same applies to such assets as good will, cost of acquisition over net book value, or any other item which, from a practical consideration, is not likely to produce cash in the event of liquidation.

This does not imply that intangible assets of this kind have no value and should not be shown on a financial statement. For an on-going concern they may have real worth. On a liquidation basis, however, they may be heavily discounted and often entirely ignored.

When working capital turnover is calculated (net sales divided by working capital) and it shows a high rate of turn, it may indicate that the borrower will have very little staying power in the event of trouble. It is a good and sometimes revealing exercise to try to calculate what might happen to a borrower if sales suddenly fell 10 percent or 25 percent. Under such circumstances, the depth of working capital becomes extremely important.

Analysis of Fixed Assets. The bulk of fixed assets is usually centered in machinery, equipment, and real estate. When negotiating with a prospective borrower, if the company's net worth is in any way questionable, or if it depends heavily on the value of only a few assets, it is advisable to have these assets appraised by professional appraisers on at least two bases—a *going business* value and a *knockdown* or *forced sale* value. Equipment, because of age or hard use, may not be worth as much as shown on the statement; real estate, because of a deterioration of the property or the neighborhood in which it is located, may depreciate faster than the depreciation schedule that is in use. If a proposed loan package includes loans on fixed assets, it is particularly important that professional appraisals be made in order to establish realistic liquidation values.

Conversely, it is often found, because of inflation or a rising market, that one or both of these fixed assets may be properly reappraised upwards and the increased value may be brought on to the statement. If at the time of initial review an upward appraisal has already been made and added to the balance sheet, consideration should be given to employing another appraiser to confirm the first appraiser's estimate. In order to keep appraisal costs down, often it is satisfactory to have the second appraisal made on a *walk-through* basis rather than to have a full, formal appraisal which may be costly and time consuming. A walk-through appraisal is one in which an experienced appraiser inspects a plant and its machinery and equipment and, on the basis of this cursory examination, states whether or not the first appraiser has been conservative in assigning values. If a wide difference results from the two appraisals, it should be discussed with the prospect and a decision should be made as to what steps should be taken to arrive at realistic figures.

Review of Liabilities

Analysis of Accounts Payable. The affect of accounts payable on borrower and lender and the need to verify have been discussed earlier in this book. There is no need for amplification here except to say that when considering the amount of money needed to put the borrower in good shape with the trade, it is rarely necessary to bring all accounts to a prompt and discount basis. Payments to the trade should be scheduled to keep the required lines of credit open and to keep creditors satisfied. If the cost of borrowing cannot be covered by discounts earned, a moderate leaning on the trade may help cash flow a great deal.

Many suppliers offer either no discounts or such low discounts that it is more economical to schedule payments either on a net basis or even on sixty-day terms rather than to pay interest on the borrowed funds needed to discount bills.

Analysis of Notes Payable. Notes payable may be divided into several categories such as notes payable—bank, notes payable—machinery and equipment, and notes payable—trade. Each of these may be broken down further into *current* and *long-term*. Current is that portion which must be paid within the next twelve months, and long-term is the balance due over various periods beyond twelve months.

The notes payable—bank may actually be due to a bank or could be due to another lender such as a commercial finance company. Whether or not the amount shown is secured by the assets being considered, the previous lender undoubtedly will have to be paid in full before the new lender may take the assets for security on a new loan. This being the case, the amount involved may take such a big bite out of funds to be raised on pledged collateral that the money remaining available may be insufficient to satisfy the trade and to provide a safety valve for contingencies. There is an old adage to the effect that if you can provide a way for a man to get only halfway across the river, it is better not to attempt the trip at all. Insufficient financing may lead to aggravation, acrimony, and frustration; if financing cannot be done correctly, it is better to leave it alone altogether.

The notes payable on machinery and equipment and mortgages payable are usually divided into current and long-term. It is important to know whether the current principle payments have been comfortably met out of income or out of the cash flow created by the combination of income and depreciation. If this has been a tight squeeze in the past, or if there has been a deficit in this respect, it could mean trouble ahead unless a known source of funds can be tapped to make up the shortage. Notes and mortgages payable should be examined to make sure that all terms and penalties for default are understood. For example, notes and mortgages often will contain default clauses whereby the entire balance will become due and payable immediately in the event that current payments are not met within a certain number of days of the due date. If this should happen, and if there is no foreseeable way for the borrower to bring payments up to date, the auditor for the firm has no alternative but to add the entire amount of the note or mortgage to current liabilities with the possible result of wiping out working capital entirely. If the lender has a working capital default clause in his own agreements, it could put the borrower into default and immediately raise discussions about the continuance of the lending arrangement and the initiation of liquidation procedures.

Notes payable to the trade may be issued, making it easier for a customer to pay for a large purchase over a period of time; this is better than having the borrower use up a large portion of working capital by paying for an invoice all at once. Notes payable also are frequently issued by cash-short borrowers in order to convert overdue accounts onto a more manageable payment schedule. Some borrowers get carried away with this device to the point where the larger part of the debt to suppliers is in notes payable rather than accounts payable. When such a situation exists, the effect is to force suppliers to provide some of the borrower's financing needs through the medium of extension of their regular terms. When used carefully and thoughtfully, with proper recognition of how payments may be met with current and projected cash flow, it may be very helpful to borrowers with small working capital. On the other hand, the payment of trade notes must be considered along with the payment of other term debt to be sure that all obligations are paid according to the agreed-upon terms and that default problems are not created.

When trade debt remains as accounts payable it retains a degree of flexibility, because partial or full payments may be made on a somewhat selective basis. When converted to notes payable, however, a rigid payment schedule is established which, if it is not properly maintained, may incur severe penalties resulting from default.

Debts Due to Officer. An account that appears with some frequency on the statements of closely held companies is "Due to Officer $____." Such amounts should be subordinated in full to the lender using a form similar to Exhibit 22. The original note covering the amount due should remain in the possession of the lender. In most cases, the payment of interest on the amount involved may be allowed, but no payment of principle should be made without the lender's written permission.

Occasionally, statements will be studied that show a prospective borrower to be insolvent, and the only thing that keeps the company afloat is the amount of debt that can be subordinated to the lender. A subordination of debt may have the practical effect of curing an insolvency in a business sense, but it does not cure the insolvency in a legal sense. Care should be taken, therefore, to determine that the company is currently meeting its obligations in a satisfactory manner, that it is profitable, and that at the least its short-term prospects are good. If this is not the case and debt due to officers is subordinated only to one or a few creditors, other general creditors—in the event of liquidation or failure of a business—may claim that preferential payments have been made to the lender detrimental to the interests of general creditors. If the complaint of general creditors prevails, the lender may have to yield up any payments received within four months of bankruptcy, whereupon the amount involved will be shared on a *pari passu* basis with all creditors.

Payment on a pari passu basis is payment to each creditor in the same proportion as his debt is to the company's total unsecured liabilities.

Analysis of Accruals. Accruals may be made for many items of expense such as taxes, rent, wages, utility bills, or fuel bills. Except for taxes, such accruals generally do not become a significant portion of the borrower's liabilities. If accruals increase over a period of time and are not detailed on the balance sheet, the borrower should be requested to supply information about them.

Accruals for taxes should be broken down into categories such as federal withholding taxes, state withholding taxes (if any), income tax, and real estate tax. It is desirable to secure copies of state and federal income tax reports to compare them with the amounts shown on balance sheets and on income statements. It is imperative that taxes be sufficiently current to avoid the placing of government liens that could take priority over the lender's rights to the proceeds of collateral.

Analysis of Total Liabilities. When reviewing balance sheets, total liabilities should be compared with the borrower's net worth to determine the amount of money that is owed to creditors in comparison with the owner's own investment. If the ratio of the amount due creditors is high in relation to the owner's equity, the lender should investigate—by periodically verifying accounts payable—the borrower's rapport with suppliers to be sure that they cannot exert any undue pressures upon him.

Undisclosed Liabilities. Undisclosed liabilities often do not pose a problem for lenders unless acquisitions are being financed. However, it is advisable to bring up the subject and to ask a prospective or present borrower what may take place in the near future regarding long-term leases, new contracts that may require investment in time (such as contracts for new plant machinery), or negotiations with unions for new labor contracts. Any such projects may need financing. It is important for all concerned to know how they are to be handled and whether they will have any adverse effect on the present or proposed financing.

If acquisition financing is involved, it is the usual practice to secure a statement from the borrower's attorney that no contingent liabilities exist at the time of negotiations, as far as is known, but that if they should be discovered, the purchaser will not be held liable for them.

Net Worth. Net worth is literally the bottom line on a balance sheet and purports to represent that which should be left over after all assets are liquidated or sold and all liabilities are paid in full. The assessment of net worth by a prudent lender must be made with all of the foregoing considerations in mind. Some now unknown sage (perhaps a sad and experienced lender) made the observation years ago that "the liabilities of a company in liquidation will always amount to at least the amount shown in the company's books, but the assets will frequently melt away at an unknown and alarming rate."

Analysis of Income Statement

The Income or Profit and Loss Statement shows a company's results—either good or bad—for the period under review. A statement issued by a competent CPA firm should present fairly a company's earnings and, through notes that are made part of the report, should spell out the assumptions made and all considerations used in arriving at the conclusions shown.

Generally speaking, a certified financial statement is reliable, but it is always good practice for an analyst to review statements in order to test them for practical values and to inquire of the borrower or the accountant whenever particular items are not clear.

Analysis of Sales. Sales sometimes are expressed as Net Sales. It is always advisable to find out the total of gross sales in order to determine the company's experience with returns and allowances. This information helps in establishing the proper advance rate to make on the face amount of invoices; on a continuing basis, the information may reflect quality problems, a too liberal return policy, or fraudulent invoices cancelled by fraudulent credit memos.

Analysis of Gross Profit. The percentage of gross profit to sales of a prospect or borrower often may be reliably compared with the industry average as a measure of efficiency. Care must be taken to determine what makes up the cost of goods sold, to be sure that a valid comparison may be made with industry gross profit figures. Answers are needed to such questions as: What method is used in costing inventory—LIFO, FIFO or the Lower of Cost or Market? Are the beginning inventory and ending inventory valuations consistent? Are production and purchasing figures accurate and do they indicate efficiency?

If gross percentages appear to be low, it could be an indication of poor or lagging pricing policies. In the past few years it has been difficult for many companies to increase prices strictly in concert with increasing costs of manufacturing and operations. However, management that is timid in this respect may incur loss of revenue that is difficult to recoup.

Analysis of Expenses. The listing of a business's expenses may vary a great deal depending on whether the borrower is a manufacturer, wholesaler, or retailer. When the net income of the borrower is low, as a percentage of sales, it is advisable to review such items as selling and travel expenses, office and officer salaries, and the many other items that contribute to overhead. A study of a series of statements of a prospective borrower will indicate whether expenses as a *percentage of sales* are going up or down, and may help in making a decision as to whether the company in question is headed in the right direction.

If management is paying itself and its supervisory personnel well, it is of no consequence to the lender provided that the percentage of these salaries relative to sales is kept within reasonable bounds. However, it is strongly recommended that spread sheets of income statements be kept on a continual basis and that all major items of income and expense be computed as a percentage of sales. The rise and fall of such percentages are very meaningful in keeping track of the financial health of the borrower.

EXAMINATIONS

When a bank contemplates opening an accounts receivable and inventory lending department from scratch, it naturally wants to retain a conservative control over start-up costs. The largest start-up expense involved is the salaries of the required personnel; this may be controlled to a degree by using present employees on a part-time basis until sufficient volume has been built up to warrant full-time persons. Some banks prefer to hire an experienced person from the outside to organize and run a department, in which case the department's breakeven point may run somewhat higher at the beginning. Assuming that the right person is employed, the breakeven point may be reached more quickly this way than by trying to build the department entirely from within.

A problem that sometimes has to be dealt with in starting a department is what to do about an examiner until volume is sufficient to support a qualified person on a full-time basis. Although it is true that a full-time, experienced examiner is desirable, he or she can represent a fairly large item of expense. The department, however, has to start somewhere, and many banks temporarily have used the services of a junior accountant employed by a professional accounting firm, a retired bank or tax examiner, a retired or unemployed credit manager, or any person familiar with financial and accounting matters. Such persons may use an examination form similar to Exhibit 3. They may need more guidance than a full-time, experienced examiner to be sure that all required information is obtained, but they may do a creditable job until a permanent employee can be hired. Part-time examiners may be paid on an hourly or per diem basis.

Examination Reports on Accounts Receivable

The examination report form referred to above is particularly well suited to reporting on the existence and the quality of accounts receivable and the general financial condition of the borrower. This form may be supplemented as required by the addition of other schedules. For example, spread sheets of annual balance sheets and income statements may be used; these should be kept up to date for as long as the borrower's loan account remains unpaid. Schedules may be kept showing changes that may have occurred in the borrower's working capital. There is also a form for the analysis of accounts receivable control. This schedule records in a columnar form the date (the name of each month), the net sales for each month, and the total of each month's collections.

Such information pinpoints changes as they occur in a borrower's business; it is of great assistance to the loan officer in determining the trends in monthly and seasonal sales, collections, and month-end balances. Distortions in such figures may tell a great deal about changes that take place in a borrower's affairs.

Examination Report on Inventory

As has been mentioned before, inventory is an uncertain type of collateral, whose value, under changing conditions, may shrink dramatically if goods have to be sold on a crash basis, particularly in an off season. Certain inventories with stable value, ready markets, and little or no seasonal fluctuations may be good collateral, particularly if quantities are controlled by professional warehouse companies. Such items may include certain metals whose prices are quoted daily on commodity exchanges, alcoholic beverages, grocery items of well known brands in case lots, and petroleum products in cases or bulk storage. However, inventories that have any aspect of seasonality, styles, colors, or sizes may lead to disappointment if they have to be sold quickly, either privately or through an auctioneer.

Whenever a loan on inventory is needed to fill out a financing package, great care should be taken in evaluating the inventory on its probable liquidation value and in determining the percentage of cost of inventory that must be advanced to meet the borrower's requirements. If it appears that a moderate advance will be sufficient, the bank must then consider who will be responsible for monitoring inventory collateral; the bank must realistically determine whether there is anyone in the bank that has the experience in inventory financing to protect the bank's loans at all times.

Ideally, one person should be given the responsibility of determining the collateral value of inventory, not only at the beginning of the loan arrangement, but also for as long as any inventory loan is outstanding. Over time, such a person's expertise not only may help in the supervision of the loan, but also may be of great assistance in arranging the sale of the goods if liquidation becomes necessary.

In spite of the known hazards in inventory financing, if the bank either wants to gain expertise in this area or if it feels compelled to make an inventory loan because of special customer relationships, the examination report should contain a major addendum to report on the following:

1. A description of the inventory being offered as collateral. This should specify whether it is raw material, work-in-process, or finished goods, and a collateral value should be assigned to each category;
2. A comparison of inventory turnover of various items taken as collateral in order to determine which inventory may be slow-moving or even obsolete;
3. A specification of where inventory is located. If multiple locations are used, the problems of control over quantities and quality become magnified;
4. Comments on how inventory is stored. Is the area suitable for the storage of the type of inventory involved—is it too wet, too hot, too cold?

5. An explanation of how inventory is valued. Is it based on cost of production? Do you have confidence in the accuracy of the records and the efficiency of the company's production? If inventory is purchased for resale, are purchase orders or suppliers' invoices available to confirm costs? Can the value of major items of inventory be substantiated on a current basis by reliable sources such as commodity listings in periodicals such as the *Wall Street Journal?*

6. Whether or not quantities have been computed either by a full physical count or by test checks made from perpetual inventory records to the goods on the borrower's shelves;

7. Whether occasional cases or barrels have been opened to be sure that they contain the goods and the quantities indicated on the labels;

8. Whether inventory records are adequate to show dates, quantities, and costs of goods received or shipped, and whether they are prepared on a current basis;

9. Whether the borrower's security measures are adequate to prevent any serious pilferage problems. For example, are goods of high value kept under lock and key and available to only a limited number of employees? Are alarm systems used that inhibit breaking and entering? Are perpetual inventory records maintained by the warehouseman or within the front office? It is recommended that the responsibility for perpetual inventory record keeping be in the hands of someone other than the company's own warehouseman. When control over inventory and record-keeping rests with one person or even one department, the possibilities of illicit sales are magnified, and frequently the integrity of the people involved is tested unfairly.

Frequency of Examinations

The frequency of examinations must be left to the sole judgment of the lender. Quarterly exams usually are satisfactory to both lender and borrower, but it should be the prerogative of the lender to shorten the interval between examinations if the nature or financial condition of the borrower warrants it.

As often as possible, examinations should be made on a surprise basis—there should be no forewarning to the borrower of the examiner's visit. On the other hand, it is only courteous to try to cooperate with the borrower by not planning examinations during his busiest time of the month or season. The security of the bank must be paramount in this consideration, but scheduling usually may be made to coordinate with the borrower's quieter periods of business.

When a borrower does not submit copies of invoices, the bank's examiner should take along a few days' assignment sheets in every visit. They should be checked not only against the invoices in the custodian's files, but also against postings on accounts receivable ledger cards. Checks should be made not only for the accuracy of information that has been submitted to the lender, but also to determine the goodness of the receivables.

A thorough examination also should include a review of slow payables to determine the extent of creditor pressure, if any, and to investigate the possibility that some of the payables are contra'd against any of the accounts receivable. In this respect, it sometimes is necessary to check correspondence files to determine the basic reason for the slowness of either accounts payable or accounts receivable.

In many ways an examiner must play a dual role when on a borrower's premises. First, he or she always must be courteous and as unobtrusive as possible in order to perform the work with the least interruption to the borrower's business affairs. Becoming too friendly with the principals or employees must be avoided in order not to have comments or recommendations prejudiced by friendly feelings. In this respect, an examiner must walk a fine line: on the one hand, refusing gifts or large discounts when buying the borrower's products, and on the other hand, joining management or employees at lunch or coffee breaks. Helpful hints or comments are often made to the examiner on such occasions, and may lead to the checking of items not necessarily on the examiner's agenda.

It is imperative that the examiner check the accuracy of the borrower's records to be sure that they agree with the lender's books. However, an examiner's real worth is in the ability to relate reported sales and collections to the activity observed in the plant or warehouse. Inventory must also be observed in order to evaluate housekeeping and record-keeping, to see whether any significant amount of inventory has gathered dust because of slow movement, and to see whether the inventory is stained, rusted, broken, or in any way deteriorated so that its collateral value will be reduced.

The examiner also should observe the general behavior of the principals. Are they attentive to business? Do they have penchants for expensive clothes, boats, big cars, or expensive vacation trips?

While all of this seems like cloak-and-dagger activity, it is nevertheless important information to gather. Trouble in one or more of these areas may mean either that the financial health of the company is not as good as represented on the company's financial statements, or that excessively good living is draining funds from the business and might eventually bring it to a financial crisis. It often happens that once an expensive lifestyle is adopted, it is extremely difficult to cut back, and, in order to maintain it, borrowers sometimes have turned to fraud.

The conjectures and opinions of the examiner should be a separate part of the report (particularly references to the character of the principals), and submitted only to the loan officer to whom the examiner reports. However, it is recommended that an unedited copy of the balance of the report be given to the borrower. Such reports are greatly appreciated by borrowers and frequently inform them of things going on in their offices or plants of which they were unaware. These reports also tend to bring the managements of borrower and lender closer together and help each to better understand the problems of the other.

VERIFICATIONS

A constant verification program is a key security device in the policing of accounts receivable collateral. The very fact that your borrower knows that the accounts are being verified will help to curb any latent dishonesty. However, one always must be aware of the possibility of fraud being covered up by the collusion of the borrower with an outsider who will verify fictitious invoices.

The verification of accounts is an arduous, monotonous, and expensive procedure, and often is considered a nuisance by the borrower's customers—particularly if account debtors are consumers. However, it is an indispensible part of receivables financing and ultimately receives the cooperation of practically all borrowers and account debtors. Most borrowers find that verifications tend to speed up collections; this results in a reduction of borrowing requirements which in turn lowers interest costs. From the lender's point of view, a verification program has several salutary effects: it helps to keep an honest debtor honest; it may ferret out fraud; and it helps to keep accounts receivable free of disputes, contras, and unapplied credits.

*Use of an
Assumed Name*

In order to protect the non-notification aspect of accounts receivable financing, verifications should be made using a name that sounds like an accounting firm such as "Metropolitan Audit Associates" or "Boston Auditors." Whatever name is selected should be checked with the Department of Corporations in the lender's state to ensure that there is no conflict with an already-established firm of the same name. It also is advisable to check the adoption of any name with the bank's attorney to determine whether it obligates the bank to payment of any taxes or filing fees, and whether such adoption violates any state or federal law relating to the use of assumed names.

Frequency of Verifications

As a regular procedure, about one-tenth of a borrower's accounts should be verified each month unless the receivables list is very short. In such cases, about twenty-five percent of the accounts may be verified quarterly. Positive verification forms should be used, similar to Exhibits 28 and 29, with a postage-paid return envelope enclosed. Exhibit 28 may be used for verifying month-end balances, and Exhibit 29 applies only to the verification of specific invoices.

For purposes of verifying about ten percent of month-end balances, the alphabet may be broken down as follows:

1. A-B	4. G-H	8. S-T
2. C-D	5. I-J-K	9. U-V-W
3. E-F	6. L-M-N	10. X-Y-Z
	7. O-P-Q-R	

When starting a borrowing arrangement with a new account, a representative selection of accounts taken from the first schedule of aged receivables should be verified by mail or, if time is pressing, by telephone. A sufficient number of accounts, by volume of accounts and by dollars, should be verified to assure the bank that all of the accounts are legitimate.

Discrepancies

The verification clerk is an important member of the accounts receivable lending department. He or she must be able to endure the frequent monotony of the job, must have sufficient imagination to identify possible problems, and also must be able to discuss discrepancies with borrowers in a diplomatic, businesslike, and dispassionate manner. The head of the receivables department should work closely with the verification clerk until a clear understanding is reached as to the difference between a *serious* discrepancy and a *small* discrepancy. Small discrepancies may be handled by the verification clerk directly with the borrower, but serious discrepancies should be reported at once to the department head, who should give priority to their handling by a telephone call to the principal of the borrower or by a personal visit.

METROPOLITAN AUDIT ASSOCIATES
Financial Place
Receivables City, USA
Tel. [617] 123-4567

_____

THIS IS NOT A REQUEST FOR PAYMENT

_____

_____

_____

Gentlemen:

      Re: _____

We are examining the books of the client named above.

Their records show a balance owed by you of

$ _____ as of _____ .

For verification purposes, kindly compare their balance with your records.

If correct, please sign below.

Please give us details on the reverse side if -

    I. Above balance is not correct.

    2. Our client owes you money; or if you now expect them to
       owe you money in the future.

    3. Any part of the amount owed to our client is based on a
       guaranteed sale or a consignment arrangement.

    4. Credit (s) are due to you.

Kindly return this letter in the enclosed postage paid envelope.

Your cooperation will be very much appreciated.

The balance shown above IS CORRECT _____

                                     (Signed)

EXHIBIT 29   171
Verification Form—Specific Invoices

METROPOLITAN AUDIT ASSOCIATES
Financial Place
Receivables City, USA
Tel [617] 123-4567

_____

┌───┐
│ **T H I S   I S   N O T   A   R E Q U E S T   F O R   P A Y M E N T** │
└───┘

_____

_____

_____

Gentlemen:

We are examining the books of: _____

For verification purposes, there are listed below certain unpaid invoices due from you as shown by their records as of _____

These may not constitute your entire outstanding account.

Kindly compare this statement with your records. If correct, please sign below. If not correct, explain under "Remarks".

Please explain on reverse side if your account is offset by contras or is subject to guaranteed sale or consignment arrangements.

Kindly return this statement in the enclosed envelope.

INVOICE DATE	INVOICE NO.	ORDER NO.	AMOUNT	REMARKS (any additional remarks use other side)

This statement of unpaid invoices is correct, subject to remarks.

Signed _____

Title _____

The definition of a small or serious discrepancy is relative to the nature of the borrower's business, his products or service, and the seasonality of his business.

One good example of a serious difference is the verification form that reports a payment has been made when none of the collection reports submitted by the borrower shows that the payment has been received by the bank. This, of course, may be a clerical error in which the payment has been credited to the wrong account or in which the check was mismailed; but it also could mean that the borrower has purloined the check. This would constitute a conversion of funds that could result in criminal liability, and is a very serious charge. Not always is it easy to pinpoint conversion and to establish that an actual fraud has taken place. It helps to establish a case, however, if the account debtor is willing to send a photostat of the check to the bank. In such instances, the non-notification feature of receivables must be given up, but the right to notify at any time must be included in loan documents in order to give the lender the right to take immediate action if any wrongdoing is suspected.

When a borrower's customer claims that the merchandise is faulty or the service is unsatisfactory, the lender may be hurt. If one customer complains about quality, it is only reasonable to assume that other customers may have the same problem. It is always possible that a customer is trying to get a price concession by complaining; but if it proves that the goods or services are of poor quality, collections of invoices may slow down or dry up. Extensive losses because of poor quality cannot be readily absorbed by marginal borrowers, and this may result in the loss being pushed off on to the lender.

The lender should be wary when the customer reports that the balance or invoice in question will be offset against a payable due from the borrower. In such cases, the bank's examiner should recheck all possible contra items to determine the number and amount of receivables that can be offset against payables. On the occasion of each visit, examiners should check for contra accounts and give a list to the bookkeeping department to be sure that invoices that can be contra'd will not be accepted as good collateral.

Sometimes a borrower will argue that a receivable due from a customer is always much larger than the payable due to the customer, and the point may be proved by going back over many months' records. It must be recognized, however, that contra items may fluctuate constantly between aging reports, and there always may be an uncertainty as to which party has the greatest amount due.

Another serious situation which should be investigated occurs when a customer claims that merchandise was really sold on a consignment or guarantied sales basis. This happens with some frequency when a seller is trying to break into a volume account or when a new product is being introduced. If such selling terms are used extensively, the financing of receivables should be discontinued as they would be worthless under liquidation conditions.

A situation arose a few years ago in which a borrower, who unfortunately went bankrupt, emphatically denied that goods were sold on a consignment or guarantied basis, and there was nothing evident on invoices that such terms existed. When the lender attempted to collect the receivables, he found that there was general agreement among account debtors that verbal agreements had been made by the principal of the borrower and by the borrower's salesmen to the effect that goods were sold on consignment. The result was that the lender had to permit the return of unsold goods because proof of final sale and litigation in attempts to collect would have been prohibitively costly.

Finally, a situation should be checked when instinct seems to indicate that replies are not normal. For instance, are the replies too consistently good and free from exceptions? Do they arrive in batches, which might indicate that they were all signed on the same day? Is there a similarity of signatures indicating the possibility of collusion? Do names on verification replies look like the names of nationally known companies that might be unlikely to do business with your borrower?

If there is any suspicion about verification replies, prompt direct contact by telephone or in person should be made with the account debtor. Continuing discrepancies with unsatisfactory explanations should be sufficient reason to ask your borrower to seek financing elsewhere.

Length of Time to Keep Verification Replies

Keep all verification replies until a receivables account has been paid in full. If there is collusion which includes the verification of a consignment sale as a bona fide invoice or the verification of a fictitious invoice as a good one, the verifier may be held liable for the amount involved. An example of this is taken from a panel discussion held by the National Commercial Finance Conference. It relates the experience of a large commercial finance company with a consignment sale, and the collusion of an account debtor with a borrower.

We had a client in New York State, possibly eighty miles up the Hudson. He was in the business of manufacturing clay brick for the building trade. His method of transporting it was to put it on barges. Since this clay bank was on the Hudson, it was very easy to float the barges down the Hudson to the customers in the metropolitan area.

He had a rather large customer in the metropolitan area who had docking facilities. This customer had some very large contracts with the municipal buildings at the time. It was approaching November. All the reports in the almanac said it was going to be a very cold winter and the river would probably be frozen. This client had loads of inventories of brick and he wanted to convert it into cash. What better way than to float it down the river to somebody who might possibly be able to use it later on?

So he called his friend Joe, who had these docking facilities, and said, "Joe, I wish you would do me a favor. I have $150,000 worth of brick on the barges, ready to go, and I wonder if you would take it into your docking facilities, and then if I sell it locally I can move it out." Joe said, "Anything for you, Sam."

So Sam proceeded to ship these bricks down by barge to Joe's docking facilities. Joe signed the receipt for them and the client took the shipping receipt and gave us an invoice, or several invoices, since this was done over a period of two weeks and said, "Here's $150,000 to Joe, and he's rated triple A-1!" And we gave him $120,000.

We sent out a verification on this. An independent accountant was used. And lo and behold! two days later the independent accountant got a reply, "We don't know what you are talking about."

We immediately called the client down and said, "Sam, take a look at this." Sam, looked at it and said, "Is something wrong? Well, I'll let you know today." Two days later we got a letter, not to the independent accountant, but to the accountant of our company, saying, "There is a big mistake. We got the merchandise and everything is fine." Well, we relied on that verification. That was a positive verification of $150,000. We continued to make advances on other invoices that this client gave to us.

Several months later our client was forced into involuntary bankruptcy. We used this notification form to notify the customer and said "How about it?" And he sent back an answer, "I don't know what you are talking about." Well, we took him to court, and we were able to prove that we relied on his verification dating two months ago that this was OK. And we collected every nickel that he verified to be OK. Therefore, I cannot stress too much the value of retaining verification replies.

Verification Procedures   If verification is handled by the bank under an assumed name, which implies that it is an auditing firm, a new telephone should be installed in the accounts receivable department under the chosen name. When answering, the verification clerk should always answer under the assumed name and not the name of the bank.

Whether verification requests are mailed on a new or old account, this activity should be coordinated with your borrower's accountant so that no verifications will be mailed within about sixty days of the end of the company's fiscal year. This assumes that the accountant will do his or her own verifications at the company's fiscal year-end. An understanding should be had with the borrower that the lender has the right to review any or all verification replies. Cooperation with a borrower and his accountant is common courtesy, but should there be any conflict in the matter of verifications, it must be made clear that the bank has first legal claim on accounts receivable collateral. Accordingly, the borrower's interests in the handling of verifications must be subrogated to the bank.

As often as possible, prepare verification requests from balances appearing on month-end accounts receivable aging schedules. Because many firms will not reply to the first request, it is advisable to follow up with at least two requests at two-week intervals. Further follow-ups become too expensive, and if a consistently small response is received, it should be discussed with the borrower to find out why.

It is sometimes helpful to get an alphabetical segment of statements from your borrower and to mail them out from the bank with verification requests enclosed. However, do not ask for a selection of statements until the last moment. Ideally, a borrower should never know which accounts will be verified in any month. The verification clerk should take A to B one month, L to M another, and X, Y and Z another. Never form a verification pattern that may be followed by your borrower.

Verifications generally are made at the end of a month's billing cycle, but it is not necessary to adhere to a rigid verification schedule. Verifications may be sent out at any time during the month to confirm especially large sales made to one or a few customers. They also may be used whenever there is the slightest suspicion of irregularity in either receivables or collections.

Department stores, chain stores, and some others will almost never reply to verification requests based on month-end balances. The most successful verification may be obtained by verifying individual invoices by telephone directly with the account debtors' accounts payable department. Some department and chain stores will respond to a request to verify individual invoices. When such is the case, the forms where invoices may be listed should be used.

Verifications will always turn up some differences between buyer and seller, such as errors in the amount of goods shipped, wrong goods, goods broken in transit, or items that do not meet quality standards. Such matters are to be expected and may be handled in a routine fashion by the borrower issuing a corrected invoice or a credit memorandum. If, in fact, verification replies come back consistently with no differences, it might indicate that collusion is taking place and false invoices are being verified. If this is suspected, a double checking of some of the larger accounts should be done by telephone. If this still does not produce satisfactory answers, the bank's examiner should be requested to visit a few account debtors to be sure that they actually exist, and that the amount shown on aged schedules is due according to the aging that has been provided.

Good and prudent policing of accounts receivable collateral makes a constant verification program imperative, but it must be realized that it may take up to ninety days or more after a sale is made before it is verified. It may take up to thirty days from the date of a sale until it appears on an aging schedule, another thirty days to receive the schedule from the borrower and to prepare the verification request, and an additional thirty days before the answer is received. Because of this delay, it is extremely important that aged receivable schedules are received as early in the month as possible and that verification requests are mailed promptly. Because of the time involved in verifying, it is important to handle all discrepancies expeditiously. The receivables of most companies are their fastest turning asset; if differences are not settled quickly, they become difficult to straighten out and, especially if fraud is involved, they may compound any possible problems.

Verification Report

At the end of each month the verification clerk should prepare a report similar to Exhibit 30 for the department manager. A brief explanation of the columns follows.

Account. The name of the borrower whose accounts are being verified.

Collateral. The total amount of the accounts receivable schedule for the month indicated.

Verified. The number of accounts to which verification requests were mailed.

Verified—Amount. The total dollar value of all the accounts to which requests were mailed. Under the amount shown is the percentage of the dollar amount verified with respect to the total of the month's receivable balance.

EXHIBIT 30

Verification Report

177

METROPOLITAN NATIONAL BANK

Verification Report for Period Ending _____

Prepared by _____
Approved by _____

Account	Collateral	VERIFIED		O.K.		EXCEPTIONS					NO RESPONSE		UNABLE	
		No.	Amount	No.	Amount	No.	Amount Verified	Amount O.K.	Cleared	Uncleared	No.	Amount	No.	Amount
U.S. Supply	657,467	26	89,786 / 14%	16	45,496 / 51%	2	2,849 / 3%	2,363	486		7	38,306 / 43%	1	3,135 / 3%
Star Gear Co.	234,679*	6	33,412 / 14%	2	3,269 / 10%	6					4	30,143 / 90%	0	
Atlantic Print	118,092	6	5,420 / 5%	6	5,420 / 100%									
Strong Paper	FISCAL													
Liquid Chemical	39,464	4	7,444 / 2%								4	7,444 / 100%		
Bodwell Supply	260,830	42	26,090 / 100%		20,324 / 78%		788 / 3%		788		7	4,304 / 16%	2	674 / 3%
Bloomfield Metal	238,256	9	14,075 / 6%	5	5,549 / 39%	1	1,815 / 13%		1,815		3	6,711 / 48%		
Business Forms Co.	542,529	13	71,075 / 13%	8	50,285 / 71%	0					5	20,790 / 29%		

Remarks: * Star Gear—One large account (Kollsman) $23,573 paid $16,167.00.
　　　　　† Liquid Chemical—3 accounts paid in full this month. One not yet paid.

OK. The number of the accounts which verified their balances to be correct.

OK—Amount. The total dollars represented by the accounts which verified balances to be correct. Under the number is the percentage of dollars of correct verification to the total dollars verified.

Exceptions. The number of accounts not agreeing with the receivables as reported by the borrower.

Exceptions—Amount Verified. The total value of accounts where discrepancies are claimed.

Exceptions—Amount OK, Cleared, and Uncleared. When a verification reply indicates a disagreement with the total shown, it often will state that the account debtor agrees with a part of the total but not all of it. For example, if a form requests verification of a balance of $1,000, the debtor might reply that his records show only $800. In such an instance, the $800 that was verified would be shown in the exceptions amount OK column and the balance of $200 would be posted to the cleared column if agreement is reached at a later date. Differences often represent a missing invoice, or returned goods for which the debtor has not received credit, However, if the difference remains unreconciled, it would be posted to the uncleared column. If the difference is insignificant compared to the borrower's total receivables, extensive effort to reach agreement might be more expensive and troublesome thán it is worth. The settlement of small exceptions must be a matter of judgment of the accounts receivable department head.

No Response. This is the number of accounts to which verification requests have been sent but from which no replies have been received.

No Response—Amount. The total dollars represented by the accounts that did not reply to verification requests. Under this is the percentage of dollars of no response accounts with respect to the total dollars of the accounts to which requests were sent.

Unable. The number of accounts that expressed a willingness to verify but claimed an inability to do so. Many such replies state that the companies are on a voucher system and, therefore, have no facilities to verify month-end balances. When the amount or number of such accounts is significant, verification should be requested using forms as in Exhibit 29 to verify specific invoices. Alternatively, the account debtors may be called on the telephone.

Unable—Amount. The total dollar amount of accounts which claim an inability to verify. Under this is the percentage of dollars relative to the total of the accounts to which verification requests were sent.

At the bottom of the report, the verification clerk should make comments about any information which is not self-explanatory.

INVENTORY AS COLLATERAL

Introduction

"Caveat emptor" is never a more apt or cogent expression than when applied to the consideration of the financing of inventory. Inventory *may* be good collateral, but one always must be aware that in order to recover a loan in liquidation, the inventory must be sold at favorable prices and to creditworthy customers. This presupposes that the merchandise involved is of good quality, is in sufficient depth to be interesting to likely buyers, and is of current collateral value at least sufficient to cover the amount of money loaned on it after applying liquidation costs such as assembling, shipping, tagging, and auctioneer's fees.

Because of the kaleidoscopic nature of inventory—its often sudden changes in quantity, quality, and value—no lender looks with enthusiasm on the possibility of having to recover inventory loans through the sale of the collateral. As a consequence, lenders want to follow the financial affairs of a borrower very closely to determine whether or not he maintains a capacity to repay inventory loans. Two of the basic reasons for making inventory loans are to obtain purchase discounts and to carry broader lines in greater depth in order to create more sales, which, in turn, should create greater profits. If this fundamental plan is successful, then the reduction or elimination of an inventory loan over a reasonable period of time should be possible without undue strain on the borrower. If this happy turn of events does not take place and the borrower's financial condition deteriorates, the lender may find himself frozen into a loan that can be paid off only by liquidation of the collateral.

It is in this area of financing that some of the most difficult and careful judgments must be made. For instance, if the borrower's financial condition is deteriorating, the lender should make every attempt to reduce the exposure on inventory. When establishing a rate of reduction, great care must be taken that any increase in payments requested from the borrower will not precipitate insolvency.

When attempting to establish a proper rate of advance, a determination should be made during negotiations with the prospective borrower as to the *real* collateral value of the inventory offered. A percentage of advance should be proposed that will take into consideration the possible costs of liquidation plus any shrinkage that might take place because of broken lots, slower moving goods, or a deterioration in the quality of the inventory.

If a borrower experiences troubles and possibly faces liquidation, it is axiomatic that good inventory will be sold off as fast as possible, and at the time of liquidation the lender will be left with poor or slow moving goods.

It therefore seems prudent either to negotiate repayment schedules that are geared to a seasonable payment or to request repayment at a slightly higher rate than the advance that was made. For example, if an advance was made of 50 percent of the cost of merchandise, the repayment of any goods sold might be set at 55 percent of the cost of goods sold as defined by the borrower's accountant in conjunction with the lender's department head and examiner. This type of reduction could be raised or lowered depending on the borrower's circumstances, the nature of the collateral, and the initial advance rate. The reduction may be continued until the loan is paid in full or until it is reduced to a point where losses through liquidation seem highly improbable.

Usually, lenders consider loans on inventory to be supplemental to accounts receivable financing; as a result, loans on inventory without a loan on receivables are made only in very rare instances. There are exceptions when goods of high or stable value are involved.

Before you consider any loan on inventory, it should be agreed with your prospective borrower that no other lender shall have a lien on accounts receivable. The interest of a lender in inventory flows naturally into the accounts receivable created by the sale of the goods; the existence of a separate lender on receivables would create confusion and probably law suits. For this reason, factors generally will not permit any factored client to pledge inventory to another lender. Should inventory be pledged inadvertently or intentionally, factors would probably cancel their factoring arrangements. Occasionally, however, it will be advantageous to all parties for loans to be made on inventory even though a factoring arrangement exists. In such cases a *parity letter* should be written which constitutes an agreement between the receivable and inventory lenders that the lien of the inventory lender does not extend to the proceeds of the receivables. If loans are made only on inventory because the borrower objects to a lien on the accounts receivable, security agreements should contain a negative clause prohibiting the borrower from pledging the receivables to anyone else.

When goods such as precious metals or whiskies are a part or all of inventory, it must be determined whether or not a lender would have the right to sell such merchandise. It is quite likely that they may be sold only by a firm having a license to do so. Whenever there is a doubt in this regard, it should be checked with your attorney.

In every case possible, all inventory should be pledged to the lender even though loans will be made on only part of it. For example, loans are not often made on work-in-progress inventory as it rarely has any collateral value; yet, because of the difficulty of separating it from other inventory, it is included in the overall package and considered to be other collateral for whatever it may be worth. Furthermore, particular items of inventory should not be excluded from collateral unless they are physically separated from the pledged collateral and are of a completely different nature than the items that are pledged.

The controlling of inventory in regard to quantity, quality, and value is difficult, but if the merchandise is housed in several locations over a wide geographical area, the problems increase. When a borrower has many locations, and the lender is secured by the inventory in only some of them, the lender must watch the movement of goods between the various storage facilities. Such movement may take place to reduce the carrying of duplicate inventories in several places and therefore is a sound economic activity of the borrower. From the lender's viewpoint however, pledged collateral may be moved out of his control, and, unless it is paid for according to strict and short credit terms, the lender's secured position may be weakened.

"Sales" of goods may also take place between the borrower and parent, subsidiary, or affiliated companies. These sales do not create good receivables; therefore, the cost of the inventory involved should be paid to the lender on cash or on very short terms.

Another area of leakage is in cash sales made by some companies, such as wholesale lumber yards, that include a cash-and-carry retail operation, or by shoe manufacturers that have retail stores on their premises. Inventory sold in this way, of course, is subject to the lender's security interest and should be paid for as it is sold.

Maintaining
Inventory
Records
of Quantity

Of the three tests that must be made, for quantity, quality, and value, keeping accurate records of the quantity of inventory pledged is the easiest, although there are numerous ways to defraud a lender if a borrower is intent on so doing. The most common methods of checking quantities are either by the lender's own staff or through the use of a public or a field warehouse.

Using Own Staff. When a lender's own staff is charged with the responsibility of keeping track of inventory quantities, a report and designation of inventory form is used, similar to Exhibit 14, which reports additions and deletions to inventory. It is desirable to get such reports weekly, but occasionally, because of the volume of goods, designations can be prepared only semi-monthly or even monthly. When reports cannot be made frequently, the risk to the lender can increase substantially; therefore, the risk should be compensated for by lowering the rate of advance on inventory. Borrowers who are relatively strong financially involve less risk and may not be required to provide information as frequently.

When designations are received with such supporting documents as production reports, copies of purchase orders, and cost of sales data, they should be studied and compared with previous designations. It is important to determine if all inventory is moving satisfactorily or if any category is slowing down and becoming either slow-moving or obsolete. Designations should also be compared with reports from like periods in the year before to determine whether the quantities reported bear a good relationship to sales and to company projections. When a borrower is losing money and wants to conceal the fact from the lender, a frequent hiding place for losses is in inventory. Any suspected distortion of this asset should be investigated promptly.

During the initial and periodic review of inventory, the borrower's security measures should be observed in an attempt to determine the possibilities for pilferage, and in order to estimate how serious the problem might become.

In addition to reviewing inventory designations, the department head or the bank's examiner, perhaps both, should spot-check inventory quantities to designation reports at least on a quarterly basis, and more frequently if the borrower's record-keeping systems are less than adequate. It is also recommended that the examiner and department head be present when the borrower's accountants take an annual physical inventory. In this way they may observe the operation for completeness and accuracy, as well as learn any inventory-taking techniques that will help expedite future spot-checks.

When inventory is kept in boxes of uniform size and stacked in rows, the taking of inventory may be a fairly simple operation, but when it is kept in bins or barrels—as are plumbing parts—it may be a difficult and time-consuming job. Whether taking an annual physical inventory or spot-checking inventory, a few containers should be opened at random to be sure that the boxes or barrels contain the quantities and kinds of goods that they are supposed to contain.

The maintenance of accurate inventory records by the bank's staff is a difficult and uncertain task, particularly when a great many items are involved. The borrower quite naturally likes this arrangement because the bank bears the cost of policing the collateral. Greater accuracy may be achieved, however, through the use of either a public or field warehouse company.

Using a Public Warehouse. A public warehouse is a firm that is lawfully engaged in renting space for storage purposes to the general public. When inventory is stored in a public warehouse, the warehouse will issue warehouse receipts, in the name of the lender, for all goods received, and will provide the lender with a record of all goods shipped. The usual arrangement made in regard to shipments is to allow the warehouse company to ship up to a specified dollar amount or number of units (which amount has been negotiated previously with the borrower) before payment is required from the borrower.

Although a public warehouse can provide a good means of assuring the lender of the number of cartons or cases on hand, it has limitations that restrict its use. The public warehouse is mainly geared to the handling of standardized cases or cartons of goods of a wholesale operation in which goods may be shipped directly from suppliers to the warehouse, and directly from the warehouse to customers. In many situations, the use of a public warehouse would be impractical, especially in a manufacturing operation where there is an immediate need for access to inventory in order to maintain a smooth and even flow of production. The cost of transporting inventory to and from the public warehouse, and the time lost in doing so, would make a public warehouse prohibitively expensive.

Using a Field Warehouse. Field warehousing is an operation conducted on a borrower's premises by professional warehouse companies. Among these are such highly regarded and competent companies as NYTCO Services, Inc., Lawrence Systems, Douglas-Guardian Warehouse Corp., and St. Louis Terminal Warehouse Co., all of which operate throughout the United States.

The space used for the field warehouse may be either inside or outside the plant, is restricted to the use of only authorized personnel, and is leased at a nominal fee by the warehouse company from the borrower. Signs will be posted outside of the warehouse area giving public notice to all concerned that the goods enclosed are under the control of the warehouse company.

After agreements have been signed between the borrower and the warehouse company, employees of the warehouse will screen off the portion of the premises to be used and will count the inventory pledged or to be pledged to the lender. For this, a one-time set-up charge will be made, after which monthly charges are billed to the borrower based on a percentage of the dollar value of the goods stored, the volume of inventory, and the number of transactions involved.

In order to handle the day-to-day operation of a field warehouse, one or more of the borrower's employees is removed from the payroll and moved to the warehouse company's payroll. These employees then become custodians for their new employers. The warehouse company, however, bills the borrower for all such out-of-pocket expenses. Obviously, such an arrangement does nothing to change the employee's loyalty to the borrower, with whom he may have had a long employment record and from whom he is accustomed to taking orders. There is little that may be done about this conflict of interest despite the existence of a fidelity bond. The warehouseman must, without antagonizing the custodian or the borrower, remind the custodian frequently of his responsibilities to the warehouse company. The warehouseman must also review and check the custodian's reports to be sure that they accurately set forth the turnover of the collateral.

One of the fundamental reasons for using a field warehouse instead of a public warehouse is that withdrawal of goods for sale may be made almost as easily when a warehouse is employed as when it is not. The only extra steps are segregation of the goods involved and the preparation of receipts and releases. To keep the operation as flexible as possible, lenders usually will allow a few days' shipments to be made before requiring payment from the borrower. The number of days generally does not exceed one working week. The number of days and the volume of goods allowed is a matter of the lender's credit judgment.

Purpose and Use of Public or Field Warehouses

The principal purpose of using either a public or field warehouse rather than the bank's own staff is for the bank to benefit from the professional expertise of a warehouse company in gaining control and maintaining possession of inventory collateral. This includes making an accurate count of the inventory pledged at the beginning of the lending arrangement and maintaining it until the loan is paid in full or until the lender releases the warehouse company.

There are many warehouse companies—both public and field—in existence; naturally, there are differences of financial responsibility among them. The lender should check the credit standing of a prospective warehouse company before entering into any arrangement with it. The financial demise of a warehouse may lead to complications and aggravations in regard to regaining physical possession of the inventory collateral. Before selecting a warehouse company, it is prudent to ask each candidate company for its most current annual financial statement, to ask for a copy of its warehouseman's Legal Liability Policy, and to check with its bank for a credit reference.

In both public and field warehouses, the possession by the *bailee*—the warehouse—is considered to be possession by the lender with two conditions: one, the warehouse has received notice of the lender's secured interest in the goods; and two, the warehouse has issued nonnegotiable receipts for the goods in storage. When these things are done, the lender is considered to have physical possession of inventory in a warehouse.

Practically all warehouse receipts will be issued for a quantity of cartons, cases, or barrels "said to contain" goods as described in the security agreements between the borrower and the lender. This wording limits the responsibility of the warehouse company to certifying only the number of boxes or containers received; the lender is charged with the responsibility of assuring himself as to their contents.

Most warehouse companies, for a fee, will periodically open a specified number of cartons at random and certify to the lender that the cartons opened contain the number of items specified on the borrower's tally sheet. In some cases, however, it is impossible to verify that the contents within a container actually represent the goods described by the borrower. For example, imported maraschino cherries in brine are white, and, when viewed by the uninitiated, could just as well be floating mothballs as cherries.

When containers are opened for inspection by a warehouse company, no real assurance can be given about the quality of the contents. A warehouseman, for example, cannot assure a lender that food stuffs are select quality as purported on a case. All the warehouseman can do is to report on the obvious breakages of merchandise, such as broken furniture, or glass.

After the initial inventory count is made, the first warehouse receipt, as in Exhibit 31, will be issued showing the count of the containers "said to contain" the goods being pledged. The subsequent receipts should be issued in strict numerical sequence, and a prompt explana-

EXHIBIT 31   186

Warehouse Receipt

NOT-NEGOTIABLE WAREHOUSE RECEIPT

NYTCO SERVICES, INC.

MAIN OFFICE: 444 LAFAYETTE RD., ST. PAUL, MN. 55101

ISSUED AT	Receivables City, U.S.A.	
RECEIVED FROM	Food Wholesalers Inc.	**DEPOSITOR**	**WHSE. No.** 702
FOR ACCOUNT OF	Metropolitan National Bank	**RECEIPT HOLDER**	**RECEIPT No.** 18-2
IN WAREHOUSE AT	101 1st Avenue, Receivables City, U.S.A.		**DATE** January 2, 1970

in apparent good order, except as noted, the following property. The Warehouseman, at his discretion, will treat property of a like kind or character as fungible. Property will be delivered to the Receipt Holder or in accordance with the Receipt Holder's instructions.

Lot No.	Quantity	Unit	Said to be or to Contain
18	59	CTN	PEACHES, SLICED, DEL MONTE 24/1 1/2
			"SPECIMEN"
			R.R. #2

NOT NEGOTIABLE WAREHOUSE RECEIPT

Storage and other charges as per contract with the Depositor, the provisions of which will be disclosed to the holder hereof upon request to the Warehouseman.

PROPERTY NOT INSURED BY THE WAREHOUSEMAN

Location of property is not given for insurance purposes and the Warehouseman disclaims all liability for error or insufficiency of the location shown.

Values shown hereon are declared by the Depositor and the Warehouseman disclaims all responsibility therefor.

The Warehouseman's liability shall not exceed the following value as declared by the Depositor:

UNIT: 4.39   **TOTAL VALUE:** 259.01

NYTCO Services, Inc. certifies it has no financial interest in the property covered by this receipt, except it claims a general lien on all property stored by Depositor for all lawful charges for the storage, handling and preservation of the property.

NYTCO SERVICES, INC.

By _____

Authorized Signature

RECORD OF DELIVERIES AND BALANCES ON HAND

Date	Confirmation of Delivery No.	Quantity Delivered	Balance	

tion should be given for any break in the numbers. While the receipts themselves may be used as a ledger of all pledged inventory, most warehouse companies will issue monthly summaries showing the totals of all goods on hand as well as the daily activity in dollars and quantities. This gives better visual control than merely leafing through many receipts.

Warehouse Receipts. Warehouse receipts may be issued by a public or field warehouse on either a negotiable or non-negotiable basis. There appears to be a limited number of advantages to the use of negotiable receipts. For example, a negotiable receipt limits a warehouseman's lien for charges to the actual charges rising out of the goods underlying one particular receipt. In addition, goods cannot be released without the surrender of the receipts; in the case of a partial release, goods cannot be released without the endorsement on the original warehouse receipt. Negotiable warehouse receipts are not widely used in the United States except in the case of readily marketable commodities such as whiskey, cotton, or wool.

If a negotiable receipt is lost, a bond must be posted, and a court order has to be obtained to issue a duplicate receipt. A lost non-negotiable receipt, however, may be reissued simply by a written agreement between the parties.

It also must be kept in mind that a negotiable receipt is a document of title, and the holder—whoever it may be—has priority over a secured lender with regard to the collateral involved. This makes it imperative for the lender to retain possession of negotiable receipts until satisfaction is received for the goods that they cover.

Non-negotiable receipts give the lender much greater flexibility in administration as these receipts do not have to be surrendered each time goods are released. Partial releases of goods shown on any receipt may be made by written instruction from the receipt holder.

Priority of Warehouse Fees. Storage and handling fees of a warehouse company are based on a percentage of the dollar value of the goods stored. The actual charge may vary, however, depending on the quantity and the quality involved, the bulk of the items being stored, their rate of turnover, and the distance of the inventory from the regional office of the warehouse company.

As warehouse charges take precedence over a lender's lien, the lender should see that such charges are kept current. In deteriorating situations, fees may accumulate rapidly and may take a sizeable bite out of any monies realized through the liquidation of collateral. In this connection, agreements with the warehouse company should contain a clause whereby the warehouse company will advise the bank monthly of any overdue warehouseman's charges.

Whenever inventory is used as collateral, an inventory loan security agreement, such as the one in Exhibit 26, should be negotiated with the borrower. If the borrower is a corporation, the clerk or secretary should certify that such an agreement has been adopted by a vote of the corporation's board of directors.

The use of an experienced, responsible warehouse company is the best known way of keeping an accurate count of goods coming into and going out of a company. The warehouseman usually accepts the dollar value placed on the goods by the borrower and, consequently, is liable to the lender for whatever amount may be represented by any missing containers. It is also important to note that the warehouse is required to exercise reasonable care in the handling and storing of inventory so as not to cause loss to either the borrower or lender.

From time to time, it is prudent for a lender to visit a field or public warehouse to view the conditions of storage and to explore any questions that might arise in regard to quantity. A note of caution, however: any count made by a representative of the lender should be in the presence of the warehouseman and agreed to by him in writing. This obviates any disagreement as to quantity that might arise sometime in the future.

Testing Inventory for Quality

When a new inventory lending arrangement is being negotiated, it usually may be determined that the inventory is acceptable collateral by reviewing its turnover through sales records and by studying the company's recent returns and allowances experiences. A further check on quality may be made with a few select customers. It is quite another story, however, to be sure that the quality of inventory is maintained during the entire span of the lending relationship.

The maintenance of quality for an established and profitable company usually is not a formidable problem, although there may be sudden and catastrophic events that make a large part, or even all, of a company's inventory worthless. A good example of this is the large shoe company which nearly failed when half of its spring production of shoes was returned because of a bad batch of adhesives. In another instance, a food canning company was put out of business because botulin was discovered in one of its products. This cast so much doubt on all of the company's other items that sales were reduced to a hopeless level.

These events are unexpected and, thankfully, rare. When they occur, all concerned must get together, examine the problem, do the best they can, and hope for an offsetting miracle.

There is no checklist that can cover all of the conditions that alter the quality of inventory. It should be assumed that changes may take place, and probably will. Careful thought should be given to various possibilities, not only as a guide to establishing a conservative rate of advance, but also as an alert to what might reduce the value of collateral.

The following are just a few examples of what may happen to some products to greatly reduce their saleability: metal products may rust by being stored in a damp area; candles or candy may melt in areas that are too warm; foodstuffs may spoil because of storage conditions or diseases; doors may be dented in shipment or by rough handling in the warehouse; glass may be cracked or broken; and boards may warp or become cracked or chipped. In addition to considerations such as these, a manufacturing borrower who is suffering financial reverses sometimes will cut corners in production in an attempt to reduce costs. This often leads to a deterioration in quality and a consequent reduction in sales which may hasten insolvency.

Where perishable goods such as grains in silos or foodstuffs under refrigeration are involved, warehouse companies will exclude themselves from any loss caused by diseases or by the breakdown of refrigeration equipment. Accordingly, a lender should insist that the borrower carry insurance against such hazards and name the lender as his interest may appear.

When the department head is considering as collateral a type of inventory that is unfamiliar, he or she should check with people in the prospective borrower's business to determine what potential problems there might be in establishing and maintaining values. Such sources of information can be competitors of the borrower, other lenders, or auctioneers.

Testing Inventory for Value

The value of inventory not only is affected by the quality of the pledged goods, but also may change drastically and suddenly for a number of other reasons. Styles in women's clothing, hats, and shoes change quickly, and last season's inventory must be heavily discounted in value, if it can be sold at all. The style factor also applies to many mechanical devices such as kitchen equipment and automatic equipment, which are subject to model changes. Inventory of such technical equipment as electronic devices, calculators, computers, and cameras may quickly become obsolete because of the swiftness of technological advances.

If inventory has to be sold at auction, or even at a private sale, values may be greatly reduced from normal if seasonal goods have to be sold in the off season; if any significant part of the inventory consists of slow-moving or obsolete goods; if there are numerous types of inventories in small lots (auctioneers usually are not interested in small quantities, and often will accept sacrifice prices in order to dispose of them quickly); or if sizes are involved and many popular sizes are missing.

Repayment of Inventory Loans

Usually, repayment for inventory removed because of sale is handled by charging receivable availability for the account involved. For example, assume that a 50 percent loan of $500 is made to a manufacturer on finished goods that have a cost value of $1,000 and which may be sold for $1,250. Further, suppose that the accounts receivable agreement calls for an advance of 80 percent of the face amount of the invoice.

When the invoice is created for this sale, the lender makes available to the borrower 80 percent of $1,250, or $1,000. The inventory loan then is credited for $500 to repay the original advance, and the remaining $500 is paid to the borrower either at once or when requested.

Accounts receivable and inventory agreements always should be cross-collateralized so that all collateral is collateral for all debts. When this is done, there is no necessity to match particular inventory with particular invoices; therefore, any availability may be used to cover any of the borrower's debt.

Liquidation of Inventory

The liquidation of an inventory loan through the sale of collateral may be costly and messy, time-consuming, and a very aggravating situation; yet it is an experience that all inventory lenders have to face from time to time. Each situation is unique and must be decided on its own merits, but there are a few simple guidelines to follow.

Keep the news that you, as a lender, now own this inventory as quiet as possible for as long as you can. When it is learned that a lender owns inventory, prices usually slide off rapidly. Those who attend auctions or otherwise buy close-out inventories know that lenders have no facilities for storing goods nor do they want to stay involved with the handling or insuring of the collateral. As a result, bargain prices are usually offered.

If it is possible to keep the borrower's sales force together to dispose of most or all of the inventory, it sometimes is advantageous to do so. Of course, this entails the cost of salaries and travel expenses which have to be considered in light of the hoped-for sales results. It may be desirable to hold only the sales manager or the principals of the business to aid in the disposal of inventory, or to work through brokers if trade custom allows it.

You may work with both domestic and foreign competitors of the borrower (depending on the size of the inventory involved) and try to arrange for a private sale. This frequently may bring the best results at the lowest cost.

Inventory loans require continual policing to determine current values and quantities of the borrower's merchandise in its various categories. It has been shown time and again that if losses are taken on a combined receivable and inventory loan liquidation, the losses almost invariably are higher when disposing of inventory than when collecting receivables.

A dramatic example of this is the recent experience of an eastern lender who financed both the receivables and inventory of a company that imported women's shoes and slippers made in Italy and Spain. The financing program was in two parts. First, the lender guarantied the letters of credit covering the cost of the goods; second, the lender financed the receivables arising from the sale of shoes after they were imported.

This "round robin" of financing worked well for a couple of years, but the fault in the situation—the weak financial responsibility of the borrower—showed up when shoes made for a fall season arrived two months late. The borrower did not have the capacity to absorb the losses inherent in a case like this, and he promptly took refuge in Chapter 11.

After a normal amount of difficulty, the accounts receivable were collected with only a small loss on this portion of the loan, but the inventory became a large and aggravating problem. The shoes, which covered a large range of styles, colors, and sizes, normally sold at retail for about $15 to $35 for dress and casual shoes, with high boots for as much as $60 per pair. Landed cost was about half that of retail.

The number of pairs involved was about 14,000, and of these, 2,000 were sold at an average price of $4.50. The cost of selling shoes piecemeal, however, was very high, and the lender concluded that the balance of the inventory should be sold at almost any price so that the personnel involved could turn their attention to more profitable projects. Bids were asked for from six "liquidators," and the *best* offer was accepted at $1.25 per pair!

In spite of all due diligence in the policing of inventory, there may be an additional hazard if the borrower is declared bankrupt and, in order to recoup, the inventory must be sold by private or public sale. In some cases, the bankruptcy court will stay the sale on the assumption that a sale of all inventory will ruin a business and make it impossible ever to reorganize. There have been cases where a foreclosure sale on inventory was delayed by as much as two years. This may mean disaster to an inventory lender, as there are few inventories that will maintain their value over extended periods.

Regardless of the negatives and precautions in the foregoing, inventory may be good collateral if evaluated carefully and supervised diligently. The best inventory is that which is fairly stable, where style factors are small or nonexistent, and where additional fabrication is not needed to make it saleable—petroleum products, alcoholic beverages, packaged or canned food products are examples. However, there is no question of the necessity of supervision of collateral.

If a bank does not have the staff or desire to get into this type of loan, there are alternatives to rejecting the loan application entirely. One alternative is to participate with a bank that does have the staff and experience; another is to participate with one of the larger reputable finance companies which not only has the know-how but also is happy to consider this type of business.

BOOKKEEPING

While the bank's accounts receivable and inventory program is being established, a very simple daily record of transactions involving collateral and loans should be kept (see the Daily Record of Account Sheet in Exhibit 32). Each entry should be coded as it is posted so that it may be identified and located whenever the need arises. Codes affecting collateral may be posted in the sheet number column on the left edge of the form, and codes affecting loan balances may be posted in the sheet number column beside the reserve column.

Codes for Posting to Receivables

1. For each new assignment of receivables, the number of the daily assignment should be posted in the sheet number column beside the applicable date of the assignment sheet listed in this column.

2. AJ—Adjustment. This may be an increase or decrease in accounts

EXHIBIT 32   193

Daily Record of Account With

Metropolitan National Bank

MONTH OF _____

DAILY RECORD OF ACCOUNT WITH _____

ACCOUNTS RECEIVABLE ☐   INVENTORY ☐   ADVANCE RATE _____ %   INTEREST _____ %

CODE	ASSIGNED RECEIVABLES				CODE	LOAN BALANCE			
SHEET NO.	INCREASE	DECREASE	BALANCE	RESERVE	SHEET NO.	INCREASE	DECREASE	BALANCE	
	Brought	Forward				Brought	Forward		
1									1
2									2
3									3
4									4
5									5
6									6
7									7
8									8
9									9
10									10
11									11
12									12
13									13
14									14
15									15
16									16
17									17
18									18
19									19
20									20
21									21
22									22
23									23
24									24
25									25
26									26
27									27
28									28
29									29
30									30
31									31
TOTALS									
							AGGREGATE		
	FORWARD				CHARGES		FORWARD		

receivable collateral; it is usually an adjustment caused by a difference between the bank's and the borrower's records of gross receivables.

3. RC—Return Check. This is an increase to both the gross receivables balance and the loan balance column.

4. CM—Credit Memo. This is a reduction of the receivable balance caused by returns and allowances, or incorrect billing.

5. JE—Journal Entry. This is any adjustment to collateral caused by posting to the wrong account, by writing off uncollectable accounts, or by transferring monthly interest charges on the inventory loan account to the accounts receivable loan balance account.

6. RA—Reserve Adjustment. The reserve may be increased by adding to it the amount of an account judged to be a poor credit risk, by including invoices representing goods sold on a consignment, guarantied, or bill-and-hold basis, and, at the end of the month, by increasing the overage accounts. The reserve may be decreased by judging a previously unacceptable account as acceptable and, at the end of the month, by decreasing the overage accounts.

Codes for Posting to Loan Balance

1. A—Advance. This is an increase to the loan account caused by a new advance.

2. TR—Transfer. When inventory designations are submitted by the borrower, and the current designation shows a lower inventory than the previous one, a transfer of the difference may be made. This results in increasing the accounts receivable loan balance. The net effect is to repay the lender for the inventory that has been sold.

3. CH—Charges. Charges to the loan balance for UCC filing fees, legal fees, appraisal fees, and others may be identified with this code.

4. CC—Compensation Charges. This identifies an interest charge made at any time during the month.

Posting to Daily Record of Account

One Daily Record of Account sheet should be used for receivables each month, and one for inventory. As soon as the Schedule of Accounts Receivable Assigned form (Exhibit 7) is received from a borrower, the total should be checked against the amount on the Daily Record of Account sheet. If the balance shown by the borrower agrees with the bank's records, the aging sheet should be passed to the department head for review.

If there is a discrepancy between the records of the bank and the borrower, the posting clerk should discuss it with the borrower. If agreement is reached, a calculation of the reconciliation should be shown on the Adjustment of Schedule form, Exhibit 33, which then may be used as a posting medium. A copy should be attached to the aged schedule.

If, in the judgment of the department manager, the differences are insignificant, the bank's balances should be changed to reconcile with the borrower's records. If the differences seem important, they should be discussed with the borrower, and, upon agreement, a Collateral Adjustment Notification form (Exhibit 34) should be sent to the borrower with a request to change his records to reconcile with the bank's. Changes of over fifty dollars should be initialed by the department head. Promptness in making adjustments is important. The older unreconciled differences become, the more difficult it is to make the adjustment. The following is an explanation of how information is posted on the Daily Record sheet in both the assigned receivables and loan balance sections.

Assigned Receivables Section

Increase Column. The total of each day's assigned accounts receivables should be posted in the increase column on the same line as the date indicated in the column on the left edge of the form. This date should agree with the date that the assignment sheet is received by the bank.

Decrease Column. The gross amount of the collateral reduced by customer remittances, cash discounts, or other adjustments should show in this column. For example, if a customer was billed for $1,000 but returned part of the shipment for $200 and took a 2 percent discount on the remainder, the customer's check should be for $784. The collateral in such an instance would be reduced by $800 (the amount of the cash plus discount) and the borrower would be expected to issue promptly a credit memo for $200 to cover the return. If the borrower shows the $200 deduction in the deduction column on the report of collections form, the gross collateral should be reduced accordingly. A credit memo supporting the deduction should accompany the collection report.

As has been mentioned elsewhere in this book, the borrower should be requested to submit a weekly report of returns and credits as shown in Exhibit 13, and, if he does so, the deduction made by the account debtor promptly would be covered. If frequent and significant deductions are made from customer's checks and a weekly report of credits and returns is not made, it is imperative that the bank's examiner or

EXHIBIT 33   196
Adjustment of Schedule Form

Metropolitan National Bank

ADJUSTMENT OF SCHEDULE FORM
AGING SUMMARY

FOR MONTH ENDING: _____

CUSTOMER: _____

PER METROPOLITAN NATIONAL BANK AT END OF MONTH: $_____

ASSIGNMENTS IN TRANSIT:
ASSIGNMENT NO.   #_____ $_____

                        _____   _____
                        _____   _____
                        _____   _____
                        _____   _____

                                       ADD-TOTAL $_____

CREDITS IN TRANSIT:
CREDIT SHEET NO.   #_____ $_____

                        _____   _____
                        _____   _____
                        _____   _____
                        _____   _____

                                       LESS-TOTAL $_____

REMITTANCES IN TRANSIT:
REMITTANCE NO.   #_____ $_____

                        _____   _____
                        _____   _____
                        _____   _____
                        _____   _____

                                       LESS-TOTAL $_____

TOTAL PER METROPOLITAN NATIONAL BANK $_____

TOTAL PER CUSTOMER $_____

VARIANCE $_____

COMPUTATION OF RESERVE:

PRIOR $_____

10%   _____

CONTRAS   _____

UNACCEPTABLE   _____

TOTAL RESERVE $_____

EXHIBIT 34

Collateral Adjustment Notification

197

Metropolitan National Bank

COLLATERAL ADJUSTMENT NOTIFICATION

TYPE _____

CUSTOMER _____   DATE _____

INCREASE $_____

DECREASE $_____

REASON _____

_____

_____

PREPARED BY _____

the department head find the reason. Receivables may be quickly diluted in value by credits due the customer that have not been reported to the lender.

The decrease column also should show any other adjustments which would reduce collateral, such as a write-off of accounts receivable to bad debts; the adjustment should be identified with its appropriate code letters.

Balance Column. This represents the gross amount of the borrower's accounts receivable and should tie in at all times with the borrower's general ledger receivables control account. If it does not tie in, at month-end or any other time, and if it cannot be reconciled either by telephone or correspondence, the bank's examiner should visit the borrower to determine the reason for the disagreement. Month-end balances, as shown on the borrower's aged list of receivables, always should reconcile with the borrower's general ledger and with the total shown on the lender's Daily Record of Account.

Reserve Column. In this column are posted all accounts receivable that are over-age—usually over ninety days from invoice date. Also posted here are other unacceptable accounts, such as poor credits, contras, sales to affiliates, amounts billed on a progress payment basis, foreign accounts, or any account not expected to be paid by check or currency. Deductions from the reserve would result from an unacceptable account changing to an acceptable account, or from a reduction in the over-ninety-day accounts as shown on the last aging schedule. A copy of Special Reserve Change form, Exhibit 35, should be sent, advising the borrower of any changes made in the reserve during the month.

The lender retains a lien on all accounts in the reserve column, but they are not considered to be good collateral.

Loan Balance Section

Sheet Number. This column should show collection report numbers and any appropriate code letters for items that will affect the borrower's loan balance.

Increase Column. All new cash advances should be posted in this column beside the applicable date shown on the right hand side of the sheet. Any other items that will increase the loan balance also should be posted here, such as charges for filing UCC statements, legal fees, or returned checks.

Decreases Column. All net payments received from the borrower's accounts receivable should be posted in the decrease column.

There are times when a borrower may acquire cash other than

EXHIBIT 35

Special Reserve Change Notification

199

METROPOLITAN NATIONAL BANK

SPECIAL RESERVE CHANGE NOTIFICATION

CLIENT: _____ DATE _____

INCREASE FROM $ _____ TO $ _____

DECREASE FROM $ _____ TO $ _____

REASON: _____

_____

_____

PREPARED BY _____

through payment of receivables, such as through the sale of extra machinery and equipment or through the sale of real estate. Such payments should be permitted, because a reduction in the loan balance will mean lower interest charges to the bank's customer. Bulk payments such as this should be identified as "Against Loan Only," and should be recorded on a Daily Remittance Sheet below the total of the day's receipts from receivable payments. Naturally, no equivalent deduction should be made in the decrease or balance columns in the assigned receivable section.

Balance Column. The balance column always should reflect the total amount owed by the borrower to the bank on loans against accounts receivable, and should agree with the borrower's general ledger. The most frequent time of discrepancy is between the tenth and fifteenth of the month, when adjustments to the aged list of receivables for the month before are necessary. Another point of difference may occur when the bank adds its interest charge at the end of each month and the borrower fails to pick it up on his or her records.

Miscellaneous Debit or Credit Forms

Check Order. This form (Exhibit 36) should be made out by the person who received the borrower's request for a loan, and should be signed by the person or persons having authority to make that loan. The form should indicate clearly whether or not the funds requested are within the amount available to borrow.

If the amount requested is large in relation to the borrower's usual borrowing pattern, or if the amount is close to the borrower's full availability, a computation showing collateral and loan position is desirable.

The check order form should also show the name of the person who called in the loan request. After approval, the amount advanced should be posted to the increase column in the loan balance section.

Collection Report. From the collection report (Exhibit 12), post the net amount collected to the loan balance decrease column.

Charge Form. On occasion it will be necessary to charge a borrower for such special services as legal or appraiser's fees or UCC filing charges. For these purposes, the Charge form, Exhibit 37, may be made out in duplicate with one copy for the borrower and one to be used by the bank to post to the loan increase and loan balance columns.

Journal Entry. A standard journal entry such as Exhibit 38 should be used to correct posting errors, to write off bad accounts, or to write off uncollectable interest or principal.

Change Form. During the time an accounts receivable loan is out-

(*Text continues on page 204*)

EXHIBIT 36

Check Order

201

CHECK ORDER

DATE

PAY TO $

ADDRESS

IN PAYMENT OF	ACC'T NO.	DEBIT	CREDIT
	TOTAL		

Order drawn by   Approved   Check signed by

EXHIBIT 37

Charge Form

202

METROPOLITAN NATIONAL BANK
CHARGE FORM

DATE_____

TO:_____

_____

_____   Loan Acct. No. _____

We have today CHARGED your account as follows;

REASON	AMOUNT
By: Total	

EXHIBIT 38

Journal Entry

203

METROPOLITAN NATIONAL BANK
JOURNAL ENTRY

J. E. No. —————

Date ——————

ACCOUNT	ACCT. NO.	DEBIT	CREDIT

EXPLANATION

MADE BY

APPROVED

ENTERED

9WHX006

standing, changes may be made, such as temporary overadvances with varying repayment schedules, changes in rates of advance, or changes in interest rates. Unless such changes are systematically recorded, confusion may result which will create misunderstanding with the bookkeeping department and the borrower.

Change forms such as the one in Exhibit 39 should be prepared by the department head or the loan officer. The forms should be kept in a ring binder, filed alphabetically, and retained by the posting clerk so that he or she may become familiar with the particular requirements of each account.

Computation of Interest Charges

The usual method for computing interest charges is as follows:

1. Compute the sum of the daily loan balances for the month.
2. Compute the sum of collections from receivables, less non-float items such as payments made with currency or by wire transfers, and multiply this figure by the number of days float. Then add this figure to the number resulting from step one.
3. Divide the final number from step two by 360 to get the average daily balance outstanding.
4. Multiply this number by the bank's full rate to get the monthly interest charge.

Interest charges may be added to the loan balance at the end of the month, and the new loan total then becomes the starting balance of the next month. When this system is used, bank charges are automatically paid at the time of the bank's first advance in the ensuing month by reducing the availability for borrowing.

Once in a great while a borrower will question this method because it creates a situation during the first few days of a month in which interest will be paid on the interest charges for the previous month. The amount involved usually is small and adjustments may be made to correct any excess charges.

The system of adding interest charges to loan balances is a good one and is preferable to billing a borrower separately. When billings are made separately, there may be delays in receiving interest payments; if a customer is marginal, there is the risk that the billings might not be paid at all. Interest charges may be charged to the borrower's checking account, but this presupposes that there will always be funds in the account sufficient to fully pay the earned interest.

EXHIBIT 39

Change Form

205

METROPOLITAN NATIONAL BANK

CHANGE FORM

Date: _____

Name of account _____

Nature of Change	From	To
Interest	%	%
Rate of advance	%	%

Special advance $ _____

Repayment Schedule

Other _____

By _____

By _____

*Computation of
Amount Available
to Borrow*

The computation of the amount of funds to which the borrower is entitled is simple; it is a formula which is quickly learned by the borrower. To determine the amount available on any day, it is necessary to:

Example

1. Deduct the amount shown in the reserve column from the amount of the gross receivables of the same day;

Gross Rec.	$120,000.00
Reserve	20,000.00
Acceptable Collateral	$100,000.00

2. Multiply the amount of the acceptable collateral by the agreed upon advance rate of the receivables—for example, 80 percent;

Available Amount	$ 80,000.00

3. Deduct from this figure the total loan outstanding on the day in question.

	$ 70,000.00
Amount Available to Borrow	$ 10,000.00

One of the outstanding features of accounts receivable financing is its flexibility. In this example, any part or all of the $10,000 available could be transferred to the borrower's account immediately upon request and without the bother of signing notes.

*Inventory Loans
Bookkeeping*

The Daily Record of Account form also may be used to keep track of inventory collateral and loans. This is possible when a manufacturing company has an adequate cost system, which frequently and reliably will report the cost of finished goods or where purchase orders may be supplied for raw materials or for goods bought for resale. The fluctuations in the value of pledged inventory and the resulting variations in the loan may be posted, using much the same procedures as with receivables. Additions to inventory may be posted to the increase column from a designation of inventory form that reports the amount of goods purchased. This figure should be supported by copies of purchase orders or by records, supplied by the borrower, reporting the cost of goods manufactured. Deductions from inventory may be posted in the decrease column and may represent the cost of goods sold for manufactured goods, or wholesale prices for goods bought and sold. This presupposes that the lender and the borrower are in complete agreement on the figure used for the cost of goods sold.

New loans on inventory should be posted in the increase column on the loan balance side of the Daily Record of Account, and any repayments will show in the decrease column. Repayments usually are handled by charging the receivable loan balance for the amount of the cost of goods sold, and by crediting the inventory loan in the same amount. Forms for reporting frequent changes in inventory must be custom-made after studying the borrower's inventory and his record keeping. There are enormous variations in the mix of inventory relative to kinds and amounts of goods sold daily, and the amounts remaining on hand. More often than not, daily or even weekly changes in inventory cannot be made without incurring a tremendous amount of record keeping for both borrower and lender. Frequently, inventory balances may be changed only monthly or even quarterly, in which case all of the considerations covered earlier, pertaining to using inventory as collateral, must be observed.

Interest charges for inventory loans may be transferred by journal entry from the inventory ledger and added to the accounts receivable total. This might be a convenient method of payment for the borrower and might avoid collection problems for the bank.

Machine Bookkeeping

When the number of accounts receivable loans increases, machine bookkeeping may be justified. If so, a program that will provide the following will be helpful in keeping better track of the daily transactions and their accumulative effect during the month:

1. A daily accumulative record of sales;
2. A daily accumulative record of collections;
3. A daily record of net eligible accounts;
4. A daily record of amounts available to the borrower;
5. A daily accumulation of aggregate balances.

At the end of each month, a copy of the Daily Record of Account should be sent to the borrower. This may become his bill from the bank because it shows interest charges as well as all transactions that have taken place during the month.

FILING

All information pertaining to accounts receivable and inventory loans should be kept in the main office of the bank in an area that is easily accessible to the department head and staff. Files should be locked when not in use and should be of fireproof construction. The following basic files are required.

Legal File

This file should consist of a folder for each account; the folder should be of sturdy construction, in which legal documents may be held by wire brads. The folder should house original documents, including:

1. Accounts Financing Security Agreements;
2. Inventory Loan Security Agreements;
3. Guaranty Forms—personal and corporate;
4. Subordination Forms. Debts due to principals or affiliated companies should be evidenced by notes, the originals of which should be kept in the bank's vault;
5. Certificates of Secretary/Clerk relating to any actions taken by shareholders or directors pertaining to corporate borrowings;
6. Special Loan Agreements.

Evidence of the pledging of additional collateral, such as chattel mortgages, real estate mortgages, or blanket assignment of corporate stocks or bonds, also should be kept in this file. The actual mortgages or stock pledges with the stock attached should be kept in the bank's vault. From a security standpoint, no negotiable collateral should be retrieved from the bank's vault without the physical presence of at least two bank officers who will sign for its release.

The bank's legal folder should include the originals of Custodian Agreements and Participation Agreements signed with other lenders. Further, any information that alters original agreements in any way should be contained in this folder. Such changes may include changes in the rates of advance on some or all types of collateral; changes in the rates of interest; changes in the terms of a contract; and changes in guarantors.

Credit Files

A credit file for each account should also be maintained in a sturdy folder, and should contain:

1. Annual financial statements in one section and interim financial statements in another;
2. Spread sheets of annual statements;
3. Spread sheets of interim financial statements;
4. Credit agency reports on the borrower and on its principals;
5. Trade references on the borrower's paying habits;

6. Correspondence relating to the borrower's financial health;

7. Information, taken from newspapers or elsewhere, which bears on the credit responsibility of the borrower or its principals;

8. Analysis of accounts receivable control (a monthly comparative record of month-end accounts receivable balances). This is a very informative record which shows the comparative conditions of accounts receivable on a month-to-month and year-to-year basis;

9. Analysis of accounts payable control;

10. Loan officer's comments pertaining to significant events or projections in regard to the borrower's business. It is particularly important that the department head or a nominee add comments whenever any important change takes place, or if a change is contemplated. A continuous flow of the account's history will enable anyone who picks up the file to get an understanding of the account.

Other Files

Examinations. Examination reports should be filed alphabetically by customer, and chronologically by the date of examination.

Verification Files. Replies to requests for verification should be filed alphabetically by customer, and chronologically by date of the verification requests. Subsidiary follow-up files also will have to be maintained for those requests which have not been answered promptly or which are still to be investigated. The subsidiary file may be a standard file cabinet, kept near the verification clerk's desk. Verification files should be retained until a borrower has paid the account in full.

Insurance Files. Insurance folders should contain (as often as possible) original policies with riders attached, showing the interest of the lender as it may appear. It is of utmost importance that the type and amount of coverage be adequate to insure the lender against loss for at least the amount of the loan on the collateral involved.

Insurance cards should be maintained by the department head or the staff; each card should list the name of the borrower, the name of the insurance company, the insurance policy numbers, the type of coverage, the amount of coverage, the expiration dates of policies, and any other data that will assure the bank of adequate coverage. The cards themselves, or a "tickler" file created from them, should be maintained, to warn both lender and borrower, about thirty days before expiration dates, that policies should be renewed and possibly increased in face value.

Daily, Weekly, Proper policing of accounts receivable and inventory loans requires
and Monthly that borrowers submit the following information to the bank:
Reports Files

1. A monthly aging of accounts receivable with assignment sheet attached;
2. A daily assignment of sales;
3. A daily remittance sheet;
4. A weekly report of credits and returns;
5. A weekly or monthly inventory designation.

Each of these data sheets should be filed in folders marked "Monthly Agings," "Daily Assignments," and so on, and should be filed alphabetically by account. The material in the folders should be filed numerically by the consecutive number assigned to it by the borrower.

Whenever it is possible and practical to secure copies of invoices and credit memos, they should be filed with adding machine tapes attached to each group submitted. The tapes should be numbered with the same consecutive numbers that appear on the related assignment, remittance, or credit forms. Each borrower's invoices or credit memos should be filed alphabetically by borrower's name, and then by consecutive number. Borrowers should be urged to file their daily work as described above in order to facilitate recall when discussions about individual copies of any item are required.

The maintainance of files is a meticulous, time consuming, and arduous job, but it is essential to insure the safekeeping of important records and to provide a place for the building of a complete and understandable history of the borrower's business. It is helpful to keep all files as free as possible of outdated correspondence and duplicate financial information. In this respect, it is advisable to check with legal counsel regarding how long it is legally necessary to keep various categories of credit and financial records.

When a borrower's account has been paid in full, he should be asked whether he wants copies of invoices and credit memos returned to him. If he does, the usual practice is to ship them back to him at his expense. If he does not want them, the bank's files may be cleared by destroying them.

USE OF CUSTODIAN

Whenever it is possible for a borrower to provide copies of invoices, credit memos, or inventory records on a daily basis, it is desirable that this be done, because much may be learned about a borrower's business by a review of these records. In certain businesses, however, such as in the department store trade or businesses with thousands of customers, daily sales are so numerous that the borrower would be overburdened with the work and expense of preparing and sending daily copies to the bank, and the bank would be buried in paper.

As an alternative to providing the bank with an avalanche of copies, an agreement may be signed with an employee of the borrower to act as a custodial agent for the bank. The principal duties of a custodian are to review invoices, delivery receipts, credit memos, and inventory records, and to certify to the lender that they are correct in every respect. The custodian also retains custody of such records and should file them as outlined earlier in the section on filing.

Typical Agreement

A typical custodian agreement is shown in Exhibit 23 and attention is called to a few of the highlights. First, the lender does not contribute in any way to the custodian's compensation. Next, note that paragraph 4 includes a satisfactory certification to be signed by the custodian. This may be made up into a rubber stamp or even may be printed on the forms themselves. Paragraph 6 secures the custodian's agreement to fill out and execute an application for a fidelity bond. The last paragraphs call for the consent of the employer to the agreement that specific persons shall be under the bank's control regarding their duties as custodian, and that all necessary space and equipment will be available to the custodian without charge to the lender.

Selection of a Custodian

While documents for closing are being prepared, the principals should be asked to select at least two custodians—a regular and an alternate. The alternate is to act for the regular custodian in the event of his or her absence from work. Almost anyone in the company may serve as a custodian, but in regard to invoices, it should be someone, such as the bookkeeper, who is familiar with the company's accounts receivables. In regard to the movement of inventory, the custodian should be someone in the shipping department. In both cases alternate custodians should be selected to maintain a flow of information to the lender.

It must be recognized that when a custodian is used, a slight breach is created in the lender's security procedures; no matter what kind of an agreement is signed, the custodian's loyalty in all likelihood will be first to his employer. If a custodian happens to be a long-time employee and any irregularities appear in the quality of pledged assets, it would only be reasonable to expect that the custodian would try to work out such irregularities rather than inform the lender of the first instance of an apparent breach of the rules. Because of this inevitable situation of dual loyalty, it is imperative that the lender impress upon the custodian the seriousness of his or her duties and the necessity of quickly informing the lender of any instance that might lessen the value of collateral. It also is important that no principal of the company should sign assignment sheets, remittance sheets, reports of credits and returns, or inventory records. The signature appearing on these records should be only that of the custodian. If the regular custodian is not available, the alternate should assume the duties. If both custodians are absent, the borrower should call the lender for instructions regarding the signing of any documents having to do with collateral.

When a lender has to forgo the privilege of frequently reviewing invoices, an important control function is relinquished; as a substitute, the lender has to place great reliance on the honesty, integrity, and intelligence of the custodians. Custodians should be chosen carefully and investigated through credit and character reports before agreements are signed.

Use of a
Fidelity Bond

As a matter of course, a prospective custodian should be requested to fill out a fidelity bond application. As indicated by the sample form in Exhibit 40, the questions asked by the bonding company are very personal; they presume that if the custodian is dishonest in any way, the bonding company may place attachments against his or her personal assets. Prospective custodians often will object to providing all of the information called for. It then becomes a matter of the lender's judgment as to the minimum information and commitment that will be required to have a specific person act as a custodian.

It also becomes a matter of judgment as to whether the bond is actually applied for, or is simply filed with the custodian agreement. Before a determination of this kind is made, it is advisable to make a few checks. First, check with a reputable bonding company to find out exactly what their attitude is about the bonding of custodial agents. Also find out under what circumstances they would protect the bank against dishonesty or defalcation. Next, check with the bank's insurance department or insurance company to determine whether the bank may already have, or could secure, a blanket policy that would cover custodian dishonesty even though no fidelity bond was secured. Finally,

EXHIBIT 40

213

Application for Fidelity Bond

APPLICATION FOR FIDELITY BOND

INSURANCE COMPANY
OF NORTH AMERICA
HOME OFFICE:
PHILADELPHIA, PA.
(Print or Type)

USE SERVICE OFFICE STAMP IN PROPER BLOCK	
B.B.B.	ALL OTHER

SPECIFIC EXCESS INDEMNITY
$_____ INDIVIDUAL AMOUNT ON APPLICANT
(Cross Out One)

I, _____ _____ _____ Soc. Sec. No. _____
First Name / Middle Name / Last Name

hereby make application to the INSURANCE COMPANY OF NORTH AMERICA for or to be included under a
fidelity bond as may be satisfactory to my Employer, for $_____
(Amount of Bond)

to cover my position as _____

at _____

from _____ 19____ in favor of _____
(Month) (Day) (Employer)

whose address is _____ City of _____ State of _____
(Street and Number)

and whose business is _____
and I hereby affirm that the following declarations and answers are true without any reservations whatsoever:

1. Present Residence _____ _____
(Street and Number) (City and State)

   Last Previous Residence _____ _____
(Street and Number) (City and State)

2. Age: ____ years.
3. Married, single or divorced? _____ Wife's (husband's) name and address? _____

4. How many persons are dependent on you for support? _____
5. Have you ever had an application for bond cancelled or declined? _____ By whom? _____
   State reasons _____
6. Were you ever discharged from any position? If so, give particulars with dates _____

7. Give below consecutive record of your employment during the past ten years and show places of residence if not employed continually during that period. If unemployed, in business for yourself, or with a concern that has since retired from business, supply the names and addresses of references who are in a position to confirm dates and other details.

PREVIOUS EMPLOYMENT, ETC. DURING PAST TEN YEARS
Please Print Names and Addresses Plainly

FROM		TO		Name and Address of Employer	Nature of Position and Place where Employed or Located	Name and PRESENT Address of Immediate Superior	Why Did You Leave?
Month	Year	Month	Year				

IN BUSINESS FOR MYSELF

FROM		TO		Name of Business and Address	Names and Addresses of Business Houses or other references who can confirm details
Month	Year	Month	Year		

8. **REFERENCES**   *Give at least five. Print names and addresses plainly.*
Do not name a relative, former employer, or any one in the service of this employer.

NAMES OF REFERENCES	OCCUPATION	P. O. ADDRESS (Number, Street and City)

FB-1b 2-15-69 Ptd. in U.S.A.

EXHIBIT 40—continued

214

Application for Fidelity Bond

9. RELATIVES	Name	Occupation	Address
Father			
Mother			
Brother			
"			
Sister			
Father-in-Law			
Mother-in-Law			

If not living, other nearest relatives

10. Are your parents possessed of any property? Value $

11. How long have you been in the position for which bond is desired?
    How long in the service of this employer?
    State fully the duties of the position you will occupy

12. What salary or compensation will you receive? State amount of income, if any, other than salary or allowance above named $ Source

13. Have you ever been in arrears or default in this or any previous employment?

14. Do you owe your employer any money? Amount $

15. Do you own any real estate in your own name? If so, state particulars below.

LOCATION	DESCRIPTION	VALUE	INCUMBRANCE

16. Give conservative valuation and description of your personal property? $

17. Is your life insured; if so, state amount and nature of policies and to whom payable?

18. Give details of your personal debts or liabilities other than liens on property and what effort you are making to liquidate same

19. Do you ever engage in speculative transactions? Of what nature?

20. Have you ever been bankrupt or insolvent? When? What settlement was made with your creditors?

21. Will you have any business interests other than those incident to the position for which this bond is required? Give particulars

In consideration of the INSURANCE COMPANY OF NORTH AMERICA'S (hereinafter called the "Company") issuing the bond herein applied for, I hereby agree to protect and immediately indemnify the Company against any and all loss, liability, cost, damages, charges and expenses of whatsoever nature it may sustain or become liable for by reason of the issuance of the said bond or any changes in or continuations thereof, in my present or any other position, including counsel and attorney fees which it may incur in connection with any litigation relative to its rights or liabilities under the bond (or if the Company has issued a blanket form of bond to my employer then in consideration of the Company's inclusion of me under the coverage I agree to be bound to all the terms of this agreement as respects any and all loss resulting from my dishonesty or fraud even though the said blanket bond may cover other and different hazards). I further agree that all vouchers and other evidence of payment of any such loss, liability, costs, damages, charges or expenses of whatsoever nature incurred by the Company or its attorneys shall be taken as conclusive evidence against me and my estate of the fact and extent of my liability to the Company, provided that such payment shall have been made by the Company in good faith, believing itself to have been liable therefor.

I hereby further agree that the Company shall have the absolute right to decline to issue any such bond (or to accept or continue to cover me thereunder), or if any such bond be issued to decline to continue same, and to cancel at any time any such bond or any continuation thereof; and that the Company shall be under no obligation to disclose its reason therefor or to give any information in connection therewith, unless required by law to furnish a statement of the ground or grounds for such action to me.

IN TESTIMONY WHEREOF, I hereunto set my hand this day of

, 19

Witness:

(Applicant will sign here)

PHYSICAL DESCRIPTION OF APPLICANT

Applicant will please fill out this blank.

Date of Birth Height Weight lbs.

Color of Eyes Color of Hair Color of Mustache

Color of Beard Birth-marks, prominent scars or other distinguishing features

EMPLOYER'S CERTIFICATE

The applicant has been in the employ of the undersigned during years and to the best of my knowledge has always performed his duties in a faithful and satisfactory manner.

His accounts were last examined on the day of , 19 , and found correct in every respect. He is not to my knowledge, at present, in arrears or in default.

Dated at the day of

(Signature)

On behalf of

NOTE:—Agents will please see that the physical description of Applicant is given.

check with the bank's attorney to be sure that he or she agrees with the department head's ultimate decision.

The custodian should file copies of invoices, delivery receipts, credit memos, and inventory records in the same manner as the bank keeps its records; each batch of invoices or other data should be stapled together, with an adding machine tape attached, on which should be noted the date of its corresponding assignment sheet and its proper consecutive number.

On the occasion of each examination, the bank's examiner should check a random selection of assignment sheets, remittance sheets, and credit memos against the custodian's records to be sure that they match properly. The examiner should also check to be sure that the information in the custodian's records corresponds to the postings on individual receivable or inventory records.

CHAPTER 7

Participations

INTRODUCTION

The outstanding characteristic of participation is flexibility; it permits banks to participate with one another or with commercial finance companies. This fine financing device enables both borrowers and lenders to take advantage of the endless facilities available in the marketplace for handling large or complex loans on a domestic or foreign basis. It also permits banks of various sizes to share a loan either on an equal basis with other participants, or on a specified percentage of the loan. That percentage may be determined either by a participant's size or by the amount of funds it wishes to put to work.

Participations among banks have played a tremendous part in our banking system; they have contributed enormously to the system as a whole and to the financial well-being of countless businesses, both large and small. They usually result in benefits to all parties concerned. The lead bank or the participant is able to make a loan that is larger than its legal lending limit, or that represents more dollars than it wants to have in a particular industry or company at a given time. The participant bank is able to keep funds employed, usually with less cost of handling than if it made the loan itself. Furthermore, through a participation of lenders, the borrower is able to obtain the funds needed that otherwise might not be available from the borrower's own bank, either because of legal restrictions, credit considerations, or a lack of the necessary skills or expertise to handle receivable financing.

There seems to be a proliferation of participations that are made more because the participant has faith in the lead bank's ability to service and protect the loan, than because of any independent credit decision of its own about the borrower's ability to repay the loan within a reasonable period. Participation with any lender—whether it be a "sister" bank, a suburban bank, a big city bank, or a finance company —should be approached with the same credit considerations as though the participant were to handle the loan itself. In fact, rather than better securing a loan, a participation may add another element of risk, involving the ability of the lead bank to evaluate the credit risk properly, and to administer the loan constantly, efficiently and prudently. Before making credit decisions on the loan, therefore, the participant should satisfy itself that the lead bank has a sophisticated accounts receivable and inventory lending department which can handle the loan in question for the entire period of the lending arrangement. This would include a review of the type and frequency of examinations made of the borrower, the type and frequency of information to be supplied by the borrower, and the kind and frequency of verifications made. If a substantial percentage of the loan is to be made on inventory, the participant should be sure that the lead bank can keep track of inventory quantities and values, that the collateral is properly insured, and that policies name the bank as loss payee.

TERMS OF THE PARTICIPATION

When a decision has been made to participate, a Participation Agreement similar to the one in Exhibit 24 should be signed. As may be seen in the sample agreement, this form not only spells out the warranties and responsibilities of the lead lender itself, but also includes such terms as the percentage of the loan to be taken by the participant, the dollar limit, if any, of the participant's share of the loan, the frequency of notification of the account's status, and the frequency of settlement between the lead bank and the participant. It is preferable to keep notification and settlement on a weekly basis; a suggested report form for notification of the account's status is shown in Exhibit 41. The rate of interest to be charged by the participant also will be written into the agreement. Rates should be tied to prime, but an additional charge sometimes is warranted which will keep the interest rate from dropping below an agreed minimum.

There should be a termination clause that will permit the participant to withdraw on a specified number of days' notice. Preferably, the time involved should be sixty days or fewer, although some lead banks will

EXHIBIT 41

218

Participation Report

METROPOLITAN NATIONAL BANK

FINANCIAL PLACE
RECEIVABLES CITY, USA

PARTICIPATION REPORT

_____
DATE

PARTICIPANT :

_____

Att: _____

Re: _____

% _____
RATE OF PART.

The status of the above account in which you participate with us in accordance with agreement, at the close of business_____ was as follows:

ACCOUNTS RECEIVABLE COLLATERAL ACCOUNT

COLLATERAL PREVIOUS BALANCE	NEW COLLATERAL RECEIVED	DEBIT ADJUSTMENTS	GROSS COLLECTIONS	CREDIT ADJUSTMENTS	COLLATERAL CURRENT BALANCE
$	$	$	$	$	$

Special Reserve $

INVENTORY COLLATERAL (if any)

Previous Balance $ _____ Date of Designation: _____ $

ACCOUNTS RECEIVABLE LOAN ACCOUNT

CASH LOAN PREVIOUS BALANCE	SERVICES AND OTHER CHARGES	CASH ADVANCES	NET COLLECTIONS	LOAN CURRENT BALANCE
$	$	$	$	$

INVENTORY LOAN ACCOUNT (if any)

$	$	$	$	$

Present Participation $ _____

Previous Participation $ _____

Check Due _____You _____Us $ _____

TOTAL $ _____

By _____

This participation statement is submitted for your review and approval. All transactions appearing therein shall be deemed confirmed by you unless written objections shall be forwarded to us with—in **7** days from the date hereof.

A-800

require ninety days. It must be recognized that the lead bank is under no obligation to buy out the participant's share upon receipt of notice. Usually, termination clauses will contain choices stating:

1. The lead bank may purchase the participant's share of the loan, but it is not required to do so;
2. The lead bank may make an effort to secure another participant to buy the terminating participant's share;
3. The loan may be liquidated with collections paid to the participant in proportion to its share of the loan. (This choice also should spell out the fees, such as attorney's or accountant's fees, and expenses that must be paid before lenders may share in the proceeds.);
4. The rights and duties of both parties in the event liquidation of collateral takes place.

INFORMATION TO BE SUPPLIED BY LEAD BANK

When a participation is being offered in a new loan or in a share of the lead lender's existing loan, the lead lender should be required to provide the prospective participant bank with credit information and history of the borrower sufficient to enable that bank to make a prompt, but not hasty, decision. Investigation might include a visit to the borrower's plant to talk with management and to make whatever inspection of records or collateral seems justified.

It also is entirely in order for the participant's examiner to accompany the lead lender's examiner on an initial or periodic examination. This not only will help the participant to become better acquainted with the borrower, but also will enable the participant to become more familiar with the lead lender's examination and policing procedures. A participant's examiner should be welcomed; the additional help will save time and money when conducting an examination. Generally, however, a participant's examiner will join in an annual examination rather than on every visit.

The lead bank should provide the participant with:

1. Complete copies of all documents pertaining to the loan, for review by the participant's attorney;
2. Complete copies of all examination reports promptly upon completion;
3. Copies of all financial statements as received;

4. Information pertaining to any sudden deterioration in the borrower's financial condition;

5. Information on requests from the borrower for unusually large loans, for a change in terms, or for any release of collateral or reduction in subordinated loans.

All information received from lead banks should be studied as received, and any items that require clarification or questioning should be discussed with the lead lender.

LEGAL CONSIDERATIONS

Whenever a bank is involved in a participation, whether as a lead bank or as a participant, it should be aware that loan participations may be legally classified as securities and, accordingly, should comply with SEC regulations. An important article on this subject appeared in the *Journal of Commercial Bank Lending,* from which the following excerpt is taken:

> Four securities laws principally affect loan participation arrangements: (1) the registration provisions of the Securities Act of 1933, (2) the antifraud provisions of the Securities Exchange Act of 1934, (3) the broker-dealer registration requirements of the 1934 Act, and (4) the Glass-Steagall Act. Although I will discuss only the Federal securities laws, state securities laws should also be consulted.
>
> **Securities Act of 1933**
>
> The Securities Act of 1933 requires that securities be registered with the SEC before they may be offered for sale. Certain securities, such as securities of a bank, are exempt from such registration. In addition there are certain exempt transactions.
>
> *Definition of security*—Although many people are surprised by this fact, it is pretty well established that loan participations are securities. The 1933 act defines the term security to include any "note ... bond, debenture, evidence of indebtedness ... or certificate of interest or participation in ... any of the foregoing." In the only reported case directly in point, *Lehigh Valley Trust Co. v. Central National Bank of Jacksonville,* 409 F. 2d. 989 (5th Cir. 1969), the 5th Circuit Court of Appeals held that a loan participation agreement between banks was a security within the meaning of the Federal securities laws.
>
> The *Lehigh* case was decided under the antifraud provisions of the 1934 act, rather than the registration provisions of the 1933 act. It is possible to argue under the 1933 act that even if a loan

participation is a security, it is exempt from registration when it is issued by a bank. However, this position is dubious, at best, and prudence dictates that the sale of a participation be structured as an exempt transaction.

Exempt transactions—There are two principal exemptions which may be available in the case of loan participation sales—the *intrastate offering* and the *private offering* exemptions.

To qualify for the *intrastate offering* exemption, all solicitations and offers must take place within a single state. Further, the securities must "come to rest" within the state—that is, they must be purchased by residents of the state and cannot be transferred to a nonresident for nine months after the purchase.

It is very difficult to qualify for the intrastate offering exemption, especially when a bank is continuously offering loan participations to correspondents.

A better exemption to pursue is the *private offering* exemption. This exemption requires that participations be sold only to sophisticated investors who have sufficient knowledge and information to make a rational decision to buy or not to buy. These investors must purchase with the intention of holding the participations for their own account. Subsequent resales are prohibited unless accomplished in an exempt transaction.

The SEC has promulgated Rules 146 and 147 to aid in determining whether the requirements for a private or intrastate offering have been met. However, Rules 146 and 147 do not purport to be exclusive, and it is possible to qualify for a private or intrastate offering without meeting the tests of these rules.

Summary of 1933 act—Before proceeding to the 1934 act, let me briefly summarize the 1933 act. This act requires registration of a security unless the security is exempt or is issued in an exempt transaction. A loan participation is generally regarded as a security and is probably not exempt, even when issued by a bank. Thus, it should be sold in an exempt transaction—that is, in a private or intrastate offering. It is difficult to qualify for an intrastate offering, so the private offering is the better alternative. This requires that the participation be offered only to sophisticated investors who have access to sufficient information to make an intelligent judgment regarding the investment. Presumably, it is safe to sell participations to banks, provided they are furnished adequate information regarding the loan. They may not resell except in another exempt transaction. I normally include, in participation agreements that I prepare, a provision prohibiting transfer unless the participation is first re-offered to the lead bank.

Securities Exchange Act of 1934

The Securities Exchange Act of 1934, and Rule 10b-5 of the SEC promulgated thereunder, make it illegal:

—To employ any device, scheme or artifice to defraud,

—To make any untrue statement of a material fact or to omit to state a material fact necessary in order to make the statements made . . . not misleading, or

—To engage in any act, practice, or course of business which operates or would operate as a fraud or deceit upon any person, in connection with the purchase or sale of any security.

These provisions have been read broadly by the courts, and it is relatively easy to be found guilty of making a false or misleading statement, or of failing to provide material information. This judgment is made after the transaction has already gone sour and with the benefit of 20/20 hindsight.

Lessons of the *Lehigh* case—The *Lehigh* case is a perfect example of what can happen under 10b-5. In that case, the lead bank sold a participation in a corporate loan which was secured by personal guarantees. The guarantors were described to the participants as "high type individuals," "outstanding lawyers" and "outstanding citizens," and the principal guarantor was described as a "good customer of our bank, had been for a long time and . . . was all right."

The lead bank failed to mention that it had had difficulty in collecting on several of its loans to the prime guarantor, and that the bank examiners had criticized some of these loans. Nor did it disclose that other banks had recently foreclosed on some of the collateral securing the participated loan, or that the prime guarantor had recently advised the lead bank that he had "had an extremely bad year and had suffered a large decrease in net worth."

The loan was not repaid and the participant lost $106,000 which it sued the lead bank to recover, alleging a violation of 10b-5. The lead bank raised three defenses: (1) loan participations are not securities, (2) the fraud provisions of the 1934 act do not apply to transactions between banks, and (3) the omitted and misstated facts were not material. The Court of Appeals found the defenses without merit and upheld the lower court's judgment against the lead bank for $106,000. The court's discussion of its reasons for applying 10b-5 deserves quotation:

Furthermore, the facts of this case show the wisdom of not excepting banks from the protections and restrictions of §10b-5. Although Lehigh Trust was experienced in the intricacies of loan participation agreements, it still had to rely upon the representations of Central Bank to determine the soundness of the transaction. Lehigh Trust, being located in a small Pennsylvania town, had no way independently to verify the information supplied by Central Bank which was on intimate terms with the borrower; consequently it had to rely upon the truth of the recommendations of Central Bank. . . .

[490 F.2d, at 993]

It's important to emphasize two points concerning *Lehigh*. The case involved some rather serious misstatements and omissions. It is entirely possible that a 10b-5 violation could be found on even better facts. On the other hand, the case does not mean that the lead bank is, in effect, the guarantor of every participation it sells. It imposes on the lead bank a duty to provide the purchaser with full and accurate disclosure of all material facts in its possession regarding the loan. As I noted earlier, I believe this same disclosure is required in order to qualify for the private offering exemption under the 1933 act.

Broker-dealer registration—Under the 1934 act, brokers or dealers in securities are required to register with the SEC. A broker is defined to mean any person engaged in the business of effecting transactions in securities for the account of others. A dealer is defined to mean any person engaged in the business of buying and selling securities for his own account.

Both definitions *expressly exclude banks*. However, they do *not exclude non-bank subsidiaries* of banks and bank holding companies. Thus, if you have a mortgage banking firm, for example, engaged regularly in selling loans or loan participations, you ought to consider, with your counsel, the advisability of registering the company with the SEC as a broker-dealer. There are criminal penalties for failing to register, and purchasers of securities from an unregistered broker or dealer may bring a civil action for rescission of their purchases.

This area of the law is still developing and it's extremely complicated, so I won't go into more detail. However, the SEC doesn't appear anxious to force mortgage banking firms to register, and it has adopted Rule 3a12-4 to provide an exemption for many mortgage banking firms.

Glass-Steagall Act

This law prohibits banks from engaging "in the business of issuing, underwriting, selling, or distributing . . . stocks, bonds, debentures, notes, or other securities . . . ."

The Glass-Steagall Act was enacted in the 1930's in an attempt to separate the banking and securities industries. It's inconceivable to me that its drafters could have intended it to prohibit banks from selling loans and loan participations.

However, one provision of the act raises a serious question regarding its meaning. Following the act's prohibitions, two exceptions are listed. The second exception states that (emphasis added):

> Nothing in this paragraph shall be construed as affecting in any way such right as any bank . . . may otherwise possess to sell, *without recourse or agreement to repurchase, obligations evidencing loans on real estate . . . .*

Note that the quote above states that Glass-Steagall does *not prohibit* the sale of real estate loans without recourse. If this provision were not in the act, no one would have interpreted the act as applying to sales of loans or loan participations. However, the provision is in this act and it expressly permits sales of real estate loans without recourse. Does it by negative implication prohibit the sale of loans with recourse or the sale of all loans other than real estate loans?

Unfortunately, there is no clear answer to this question. No court has considered the issue and the banking agencies don't care to do so. Unless and until we receive some definitive ruling to the contrary, it seems appropriate to ignore Glass-Steagall as it relates to sales of loans and loan participations.

Summary. In purchasing a loan participation, know your seller well, but just as important, do a complete credit review of the borrower. Whether you are a buyer or seller, make sure that the participation agreement is well drafted and covers the seller's warranties, rights and responsibilities.

In the securities area, sell participations only to sophisticated purchasers. Provide complete and accurate disclosure of all material information you have in your files concerning the loan. If you have a non-bank subsidiary selling loans or participations, consult your counsel regarding the broker-dealer registration provisions of the 1934 act. Finally, in the Glass-Steagall area, be aware that there is a potential problem, but there's little or nothing you can do about it.*

In the past few years, a few banks and other financial institutions have experienced serious financial problems, even to the point of failure. While these problems occur very infrequently, they raise the question of what the participant's legal position is if the lead lender should fail. Do the participants have a direct property right in the loan, or are they merely unsecured creditors of the lead lender?

As far as is known, there has been no test case to settle this point, but there may be occasions when the subject is worthy of discussion with the bank's attorney.

* William M. Issac, "Loan Participation's and the Securities Laws," *Journal of Commercial Bank Lending,* October 1975.

CHAPTER 8

Acquisitions and Mergers

Acquisitions and mergers may be accomplished by using funds raised on the assets of either or both the company making the acquisition and the company being acquired. When done carefully and constructively, it may achieve marvelous results for all concerned.

However, there are numerous credit, tax, and legal problems that must be handled expertly; otherwise, they may lead to difficult and sometimes insurmountable problems that not only may consume vast amounts of time, but also may result in lawsuits and losses. These problems may entangle the lender as well as the buyer.

As a general rule, it is not good financing to rely principally on the funds raised on accounts receivable and inventory to "swing the deal." These assets are short-term in their nature; if, in the future, receivables or inventory should be reduced, funds borrowed against the new levels might not be adequate to meet the monthly or quarterly principal payments called for by purchase agreements. The ideal structure is one where acquisition financing is arranged by raising about 75 percent of the amount needed through a combination of the equity investment of the buyer, and fairly long-term loans on chattels or real estate. The lender's regular advances on receivables and inventory might raise the 25 percent needed to complete the purchase, as well as provide the working capital for future operations.

Because no two acquisitions are the same—and all usually are complex—no attempt is made here to discuss the many legal and tax matters that are involved. In general, when purchasing assets, it is important to comply with bulk sales laws (Article 6 of the Uniform Commercial

Code, "Bulk Transfers," deals with the subject). When purchasing stock, be sure that the liabilities of the company are fully disclosed and understood. Beyond this, it is strongly urged that the lender work closely with attorneys and tax accountants who are thoroughly experienced in this type of transaction.

CREDIT CONSIDERATIONS

Whether or not the assets of both companies will be used to raise funds for the purchase, it is important that the buyer supply the following information to the lender:

1. A firm estimate of the cash that may be contributed to the purchase by the buyer. An equity investment by the purchaser of at least 25 percent usually will make the transaction possible, although the amount may be somewhat less, or more, depending on the overall strength of the deal. Because the lender generally provides the bulk of the funds needed for an acquisition, using the assets of both the buyer and seller as security, this type of financing is often referred to as *bootstrapping* or, more facetiously, as "buying a cow with its own milk";

2. Certified financial statements for at least the previous three fiscal years of both companies. These naturally would include complete profit and loss figures and any notes and comments made by the companies' accountants;

3. A pro forma statement showing the condition of the surviving company after the acquisition;

4. A cash-flow projection to show the ability of the new company to meet its normal debts and its term obligations to the lender. Cash-flow projections should be analyzed carefully. They may be prepared by the same people who initiated the acquisition, and therefore may contain some of the same enthusiasm that triggered the idea of acquisition in the first place. Cash flows always should provide for contingencies that may result from such things as disruptions of sales, collections, or production, all of which are inherent in the everyday conduct of business. Projections also should include an estimate of interest charges covering the entire financing package. This item may be substantial, especially if as much as 75 percent of the purchase price is borrowed;

5. A statement from an authorized officer of the company being acquired, to the effect that all assets are worth as much as shown on the latest financial statement and that these assets are not encumbered

by any attachments or liens other than disclosed in the statements. This warranty also will represent that the company has no liabilities other than those shown on the statements;

6. Specifications of indemnities, in the event that there is any breach of warranties, and a statement of reserves that are to be set up against such contingencies;

7. A statement from the seller's attorney that the acquisition is in compliance with the company's charter and with all applicable state and federal laws.

Once the acquisition is financed, the lender enters the most critical period of the loan. It has been our experience that the initial financing package usually fully utilizes the assets of either or both companies; therefore, the lender's credit exposure is greatest during the first few months (and sometimes years) of the new owner's operation.

STUDY OF BALANCE SHEET AND PROFIT AND LOSS ITEMS

The lender's scrutiny of the concept of the acquisition, the persons involved, the assets to be pledged, the liabilities involved, and the profitability of the seller must be complete and in depth. There also should be serious consideration of how the loan might be liquidated without loss in the unhappy event that the new concern fails any time after the beginning of the loan arrangement.

The following are balance sheet and profit and loss items that should be studied by the lender:

Cash. This should be confirmed with bank depositories.

Accounts Receivable. The accounts receivable should be studied for age, contras, concentrations, consignments, and poor credit risks. Accounts receivable turnover should be calculated for the previous two or three years to determine if it is normal for the industry. A sufficient number of accounts should be verified to determine their validity and collectibility. The returns and allowance accounts should be scrutinized. This will assist in evaluating the quality of the product produced or sold, and in determining the probable cash value of the receivables.

Inventory. A physical inspection of the inventory and inventory records is imperative in order to evaluate them both quantitatively and qualitatively. Inventory turnover should be calculated for several years to determine its relationship to sales and to compare it with inventory turns considered to be standard in the industry. If inventory turns slowly, it might indicate a temporary excess of goods on hand. This is possibly a positive factor, because the oversupply can be sold off, thus helping in the overall acquisition financing. On the other hand, a slow turn in inventory might mean a build-up of slow-moving or obsolete inventory.

Prepaid Items. Many companies show prepaid items as a current asset. This practice, although usually not significant in the overall financing requirement, may involve a substantial amount of money. Prepaids may include utility and airline deposits, insurance, and rent. These are easily verified with the companies involved.

Machinery and Equipment. As has been noted, it is desirable that a significant portion of acquisition financing be secured by fixed assets, and that the loan be geared to a term that will comply with the buyer's cash flow projections. In order to determine the amount that may be prudently loaned on machinery and equipment, a professional appraiser should be employed (at the borrower's expense) to establish a knock-down, forced-sale, or auction value. When a formal appraisal is made, it often is surprising to find that some machinery is missing or has been cannibalized, or that machinery is on the premises that was thought to have been sold. The term of the loan should be geared to the expected life of the asset and should be amortized monthly, together with interest on the declining balance.

Real Estate. If the building occupied by the seller is owned and unencumbered, it sometimes may be the source of a good portion of the funds needed. Even if the building has a mortgage, it may be possible to remortgage it for an amount sufficient to complete the acquisition. However, if the present mortgage is an old one and carries a low interest rate, remortgaging at today's higher rates does not create any enthusiasm on the part of the buyer. On the other hand, this possible increased cost must be weighed against the potential profitability of the acquisition.

During periods of tight money, the mortgaging or remortgaging of buildings may be difficult, particularly if the property is entirely or mostly owner-occupied. Obviously, a building that is multi-tenanted, where leases may be assigned to support any loan, is a more attractive collateral package.

If real estate financing can be handled by a savings bank, it seems desirable to permit it. Commercial banks and finance companies are basically short-term lenders and cannot usually provide the terms or rates that are offered by savings banks. There are occasions, however, when it makes sense for a commercial bank or a finance company to make the real estate loan in order to complete an acquisition within an allotted period. In such cases, an agreement may be made with the buyer that he or she is free to seek a more favorable mortgage, and that when it is consummated, that portion of the loan may be repaid to the original lender without penalty.

If one financing source is to handle the entire financing package, an inspection of the property, as well as a professional appraisal, should be made. The appraiser should be requested to give estimates based on both *forced-sale* and *market-value* bases. The former contemplates sale of the property by an auctioneer or at a sacrifice price to a private party, and the latter assumes a negotiated price between a willing buyer and a willing seller.

Notes Payable—Bank. Any notes payable to a bank—whether to the bank that will become involved in the acquisition financing or to another bank—will have to be paid off with part of the proceeds of the new financing package. This especially is true if the notes payable are unsecured. If secured, payments will probably have to be restructured to conform with all other aspects of the new financing plan.

Notes Payable—Other. These notes will have to be studied to determine whether terms accelerate in the event of the sale or acquisition of the company, or whether the noteholders will simply rewrite the notes for the balance outstanding on the same terms and conditions as extended to the original debtor.

Accounts Payable. An up-to-date aged list of accounts payable should be obtained from both buyer and seller, along with agings for comparable periods in prior years. This is very important information, which not only lists the company's sources of supply, but also reveals the paying habits of the acquirer and any concentrations of payables with one or only a few suppliers. Concentrations may present a problem if such suppliers have any concern about extending the same lines of credit to the new entity as they did to the old one. This point should be verified early in the negotiations in order to assure a predictable overall line of trade credit.

Taxes Payable. When reviewing tax liabilities—whether excise, real estate, withholding, or income—prior income tax returns should be secured for at least the past three years. The returns should confirm the amount of tax liabilities or accruals shown on balance sheets and income statements; these also should check out with the company's books and records.

Very often the major reason for an acquisition is the loss (or losses) that can be carried forward or carried back. When such considerations exist, a professional tax accountant should be consulted to be sure that there is every reasonable expectation that the use of a carry-forward loss is legitimate or that a carry-back will result in a cash refund. Also in this connection, warranties should be secured from the seller that if the favorable tax status is not realized, the seller will either adjust the acquisition price or make a refund.

Retained Earnings. One of the earliest determinations that must be made in any acquisition is whether the debt assumed by the buying company will totally or substantially absorb the new entity's surplus account. If so, the specter of creditor's rights comes into being and must be considered carefully by the buyer and the buyer's attorney and accountant.

In addition to closely reviewing all items on the seller's certified financial statements, the buyer should require a statement certifying that no contingent liabilities exist except for any schedules submitted, such as for contracts signed but not started, contracts being worked on, union agreements, leases, or purchase agreements.

After all agreements have been signed, the funds have been advanced, and the acquisition has been made, the lender should follow the progress of the new entity. Great care should be taken, however, not to assume a dictatorial role in the conduct of the business. It is not unknown for a lender to be charged with liability to creditors in the event that a company fails and creditors suffer. There is a very narrow path to walk in situations of this kind. Frequent visits are necessary to keep up to date on the company's affairs, and a certain amount of counseling is inevitable. Any strong recommendations made which approach the form of directives should be avoided, particularly those made in writing. For this reason, too, the lender should reject any offer to be a director in the financed company.

CHAPTER 9

Liquidations

Up to now this book has pointed out many hazards of accounts receivable financing and has suggested supervisory techniques to preserve the value of collateral in the event liquidation takes place. The full repayment of a loan, particularly under unfavorable conditions, is truly the bottom line of lending; in regard to a secured loan, it is the acid test of the effectiveness of the control maintained over collateral. In spite of all due diligence, however, it is inevitable that losses will be realized in some liquidations.

Liquidations are a hard, distasteful, and emotional part of the lending business, but they are a factor that always has been and always will be present. Certainly, the lender must try to show compassion for a borrower who has tried his or her best and failed, but it also must be remembered that the size of the loan requested by accounts receivable and inventory borrowers is always larger than can be granted on an unsecured basis. This presupposes that if the loan gets in trouble, the lender is entitled to take whatever steps are necessary to liquidate the security with firmness and dispatch. To do less would be a dereliction of the bank's obligation to its stockholders and depositors.

It has been said that the four fundamentals of secured credit lending are (1) character, (2) financial responsibility, (3) purpose of the loan, and (4) collateral. Under liquidation conditions, you may forget about numbers two and three. You may only hope that the character of the borrower is what you originally appraised it to be, and that the collateral will stand up under the many pressures that may be exerted against it.

At a Robert Morris Convention in San Francisco, the National Commercial Finance Conference presented a panel to discuss the subject, "How to Realize on Collateral." Mr. Louis Rubin, President of A. J. Armstrong Finance Division said, as part of his presentation:

> If an account is in trouble, rule number one is not to rely for the time being on what the borrower or the administrator has told you concerning the facts. Do not assume that anything in your files or anything you have heard or believed in connection with the account is, or ever was, accurate. Instead, start from scratch and conduct a complete independent loan review. You must reinvestigate and construct a current picture, especially of the collateral, so that you may then realistically and intelligently deal with the situation from an objective point of view.... This is when you have to stop eating the baloney the borrower has been feeding you and find out for yourself what is really happening.

CHOOSING A COURSE OF ACTION

An element of urgency is present whenever one is confronted with a liquidation situation. More harm may be done, however, by flailing around aimlessly than by taking time to carefully assess the problem and choose a course of action that will yield the best results to the bank, the unsecured creditors, and the borrower. There are two factors to consider in any liquidation. First, what is the *necessity* for the liquidation?

1. Is fraud involved?
2. Is management ill, old, or sick of business and simply wants to cash in on assets and retire?
3. Has the business suffered steady losses and is liquidation the means to realize on assets before further deterioration takes place?
4. Is the borrower no longer able to meet payables, and has he lost creditor support?
5. Is there a possibility of bankruptcy—either voluntary or involuntary?

The second factor to consider is what *type* of liquidation is indicated.

1. Is there any indication of fraud? If so, a prompt meeting with the bank's attorney should be arranged for the purpose of deciding what action will best protect the bank's interest. Where fraud is suspected, speed is essential to determine the extent of the fraud and the collectability of the collateral. This kind of situation usu-

ally dispenses with any business niceties and concentrates on the bank's legal rights to collect as much of the loan as it can and in the shortest possible time.

2. Does management appear honest, friendly, and cooperative with the bank, and are there indications that this attitude will continue? If this is the situation, it might be best for all concerned to defer notification and let the collections apply to the loan balance as they are received until it is repaid in full. The bank, of course, retains the right to notify at any time.

3. If collateral pledged to the bank includes inventory, can it be sold through a private sale or will it have to be auctioned off?

4. Will liquidation take place under bankruptcy proceedings?

REVIEW OF COLLATERAL AND DOCUMENTS

As soon as it appears that liquidation of collateral is a possibility, the department head and the bank's examiner should bring accounts receivable records completely up to date. Starting with the balances shown on the last aging of accounts receivable, they should do the following:

1. Add all new sales to the previous month's balance;

2. Deduct all remittances;

3. Deduct all credit memos;

4. Review returned goods reports, if any, to determine what credits will have to be issued. If inventory has not been taken as collateral, be sure such goods are segregated from other inventories and are held for disposition by the bank;

5. Review recent correspondence to determine whether there are any major complaints that might result in large credits to receivables.

Inventory

If inventory has been taken as collateral, whether or not the bank has made a loan on it, the bank should determine as quickly as possible what goods are on hand and what procedures should be followed to bring in the greatest revenues.

For example, the bank should insist on a physical inventory unless the volume of goods is extremely high or widely dispersed. In such instances, inventory should be heavily spot-checked with emphasis on the goods that are most readily salable and of highest value.

Inventory may be taken by the borrower, but a member of the bank's staff or a disinterested warehouseman should be present. If the product involved is in cases, barrels, boxes, or other containers, a sufficient number should be opened to be sure that the goods as represented actually exist.

The bank also should be sure that all records are current. Much of the posting and inventory taking will have to be done on the borrower's premises. Loan agreements should give the lender the right to do this, and when dealing with a friendly borrower it should present no problem. In any event, the department head and the bank's attorney should carefully review all documents to ascertain all of the bank's rights and to determine that they may all be exercised. Under certain conditions, it is not always possible to take advantage of all the rights included in agreements. In this respect, it is important that legal guidance be secured.

POSSIBLE LIQUIDATION PROCEDURES

When deciding on a course of action in regard to liquidation, any one or all of the following should be considered:

1. Seizing control of all collections on the borrower's premises and of all bank accounts;
2. Notifying all account debtors to make payment directly to the bank;
3. Notifying the post office to direct all of the borrower's mail to the bank. If a change of address form was obtained at the time of signing loan agreements, it need only be filed at the post office. If not, the department head or the bank's attorney should secure the borrower's permission to redirect mail to the bank;
4. Establishing a custodian on the borrower's premises. If the borrower objects to this, never force entry onto the premises, but consult promptly with the bank's attorney for guidance in asserting the bank's rights;
5. Locking up all valuables or movables on which the bank has a claim. These could be precious metals, gems, tools, or dies;
6. Not starting any new contracts that cannot be completed in a short period of time. This holds true unless there is every indication that more will be realized by completing contracts than by abandoning or selling semi-completed units;
7. The bank starting to approve credit on any new sales;
8. Not allowing the borrower to continue selling to slow-paying customers;

9. Changing all locks on the borrower's premises with keys to be controlled by the bank. If the borrower occupies rental space, work with the landlord to confirm your right of entry during any reasonable hours. It is hoped that you have previously obtained a Landlord's Waiver—particularly if inventory is involved;

10. Being very careful about increasing your dollar exposure. It is sometimes necessary to advance moderate amounts to cover payroll for people needed to finish work-in-process or to remove a tax lien that has been placed. Otherwise, every attempt should be made to keep the total loan well within the expected recovery from collateral. The old adage of throwing good money after bad is never better illustrated than when a lender tries to keep a shaky borrower alive by spoon feeding small amounts to meet continual crises.

The degree to which these considerations should be enforced will be greatly influenced by the relationship of the bank to the borrower. For example, if the borrower is unfriendly or uncooperative, if there is any suspicion of dishonesty, if he has died, or if he has left town, the bank has every right to take a hard line, using whatever measures are available to best protect its interests.

Notification Considerations

When considering the problem of whether or not account debtors should be notified to pay the bank directly, it must be recognized that there is a prime advantage as well as a prime disadvantage in so doing. The advantage is that the bank gains direct control over remittances and eliminates the possibility of the diversion of funds by the borrower. The disadvantage is that when an account debtor is alerted to the fact that he is about to pay his last invoice to his suppliers, he knows that further adjustments or credits may be difficult or impossible to get. Naturally, he will want to take time to inspect the last goods he bought or to review services rendered to be sure that any credits due or to become due will be given to him.

If it is decided that notification is in the bank's best interest, the form of notification should be made or approved by the bank's attorney. The form should state clearly that the invoices or the balances shown have been assigned to the bank and should be paid directly to the bank in the self-addressed stamped envelope that accompanies the form.

Options for payment by check may be given to the account debtor. The check may be made out in favor of the bank; the check may be drawn to the order of *both* the bank and the borrower; or the check may be made out only to the borrower. In any event, the check should be sent only to the bank. The account debtor should be warned that if payment is sent to the borrower and it is not subsequently received by the bank, it may make the account debtor legally liable for duplicate payment.

If notification is to be made around dates when the borrower's larger customers pay their bills, it is sometimes advisable to call them on the telephone and tell them of the assignment and what has happened to their supplier. This will forestall such checks going to the borrower. Another alternative with larger accounts is to send notification via registered mail with return receipt requested. This gives proof that the notifications have been sent and are actually in the hands of the customer.

Correspondence and telephone calls resulting from notification, however, inevitably will uncover differences between the borrower's and the customers' records. Communication with customers will also uncover a fair amount of chiselers who want very generous allowances if they are to keep the goods. Some of this negotiation is legitimate; there are also buyers who know that a lender does not have an intimate knowledge of his borrower's business and who know that the lender does not have the time to enter into long negotiations or the ability to store merchandise. Such buyers consider lenders fair prey and will exert all possible pressure to secure larger allowances. If the borrower is still friendly at this point, he may help immeasurably in judging the fairness of claims and in negotiating reasonable settlements. Even if the borrower is not entirely friendly, he may be influenced to help, providing that personal guaranties were secured when loan agreements were signed. It should be evident that every dollar collected is one dollar less of personal liability.

It is suggested that all allowances be recorded on a master sheet, to prove and support any settlements made with customers. Correspondence pertaining to allowances should be filed with the master sheet.

Account debtors sometimes will require that the lender submit proof of assignment or proof of delivery. This simply involves sending a copy of the appropriate assignment schedules and, if necessary, copies of invoices or bills of lading. This requires that the lender take possession of copies of invoices, credit memos, shipping documents, and any other data that the lender does not have already and that will support the claim.

There is hardly any aspect of receivable and inventory financing that calls for such quick decisions and prompt action as liquidations. This is especially true if you hear that an involuntary bankruptcy is imminent or if you have an inkling of fraud. In such cases, either the department head or the examiner, or both, should go immediately to the borrower's office because *at that moment* there could be $10,000 worth of checks in the office which are going to be disposed of one way or another. At the same time, credits for returned merchandise may be picked up. Collections or pertinent data in the hands of the bank rather than an unfriendly trustee could reduce or eliminate many arguments. Possession greatly improves the bank's bargaining position relative to a receiver or trustee in bankruptcy.

FURTHER DISCUSSION OF LIQUIDATION TECHNIQUES

In an address to the Buffalo chapter of Robert Morris Associates, Roger K. Soderberg, President of Ursus, Inc., Salem, Massachusetts, spoke on the subject of assistance to financially troubled companies. Mr. Soderberg is an attorney and a business consultant who is frequently called upon by banks and commercial finance companies to assist in rehabilitating ailing businesses, or in liquidating them.

Mr. Soderberg's remarks were subsequently published in the *Journal of Commercial Bank Lending*; the portion entitled, "The Question of Liquidation" follows.

> There is inevitably, in any discussion of the handling of troubled companies, the absolute necessity of considering the problems of liquidation. Many businesses are beyond help when they are first brought to the attention of someone who could help them or are, by their nature, not viable businesses or are owned by management which is unwilling or unable to either admit or correct its mistakes. The most important thing to keep in mind when considering a liquidation is that, even though it represents the end of this particular business, it is in fact a business operation and must be handled in a business-like fashion. Too often, liquidations are left to lawyers or to courts or to others who are not essentially businessmen. The same principles prevail in a liquidation as do in any other situation. You must know and understand what you are selling, you must know and understand the market to which you can sell that product and you must be prepared to demand and expect a fair price for the product. In addition, reasonable control must be established to enable you to know what has been sold and what is still on hand and where it is located. Protection against pilferage must be considered. Packaging, although on a slightly different than normal sense, must be considered. A clean, well-lighted,

well-maintained warehouse will be helpful in selling an inventory even in a liquidation.

The valuation of inventory and equipment

Obviously, a major aspect in the success of a liquidation is going to be the original valuation that was placed on the collateral. Most of you consider and evaluate collateral every day, so I will not go into any of the more obvious considerations and pitfalls, but there are a few that we have come across that are sometimes not given the attention and consideration that they deserve. In the case of both inventory and equipment it is necessary to know something about how the borrower's price for that property was originally arrived at. A company which, because of its cash position, must buy in small quantities and which does not have an ideal credit record with a vendor may well pay up to 15% or 20% higher than another customer purchasing the same product. In addition, in many industries, dealers, wholesalers and other middlemen customarily take discounts on their selling prices. However, in an economy where materials are in short supply, such discounts are no longer available. Accordingly, in a liquidation where a major source of customers may be dealers, it may be that the dealer's cost for new fresh goods from their suppliers is already 30% below your borrower's cost.

Secondly, many companies refer to items as raw materials which for liquidation purposes should really be considered goods in process. For example, we have done business with a manufacturer of safety toe caps. They buy steel from a service center already slit to a width which they use in their manufacturing operation. They consider coiled steel to be a raw material. However, only they and their one competitor have any efficient use for that particular raw material slit in that particular width. Liquidation prospects would be very slim even though an inventory which consists of true steel raw material should be very salable. This can be true in a number of other items that we tend to think of as almost commodities.

Preliminaries of liquidation

Before the principal portion of the liquidation can be undertaken, several aspects must be taken care of:

The job of handling a liquidation begins the moment you decide to foreclose and ends when your loan has been repaid. Someone must go directly to the premises to do all of the things required in taking possession, including changing locks, dealing with the local police and fire departments as well as the alarm company, dealing with utilities that must be continued through the term of the liquidation, considering preventative maintenance that should be taken if equipment values are to be maintained while the machinery is not being operated, such as draining cooling systems, oiling equipment, removing harmful chemicals and the like. Also, someone must deal with the landlord, and I might mention that typically we have found the landlord to be the most difficult person to deal with in a liquidation. Both internal and external security protection must be provided. Employees often feel justified in walking off with small tools or other valuables if the only one that is going to suffer is the bank, and an empty building is an invitation to thieves and vandals. Fire and theft and other casualty insurance must be considered. It's likely that the borrower's insurance would have been cancelled for nonpayment of premium, and new insurance must be placed on the equipment. We carry a floater policy for use in these situations and will put equipment under its coverage at the start of a liquidation. Only when all of these details have been taken care of and a system set up for seeing that they continue to be taken care of, can we turn to the central part of the problem, that is, actually selling the property to be liquidated.

Four ways of conducting a liquidation

I would like to discuss four common ways of conducting a liquidation. The first is the sale of inventory to the borrower's regular customers. The highest price which you will be able to get for inventory is the price that the borrower normally gets from his customers. Accordingly, if you can fill orders at regular prices or at small discounts, you can recover a significant amount of your advance against a relatively small amount of inventory. In the liquidation of many manufacturers, a work-out of in-process goods makes sense. Our first step is to analyze the goods in process as well as the components on hand to determine what part of the inventory should be finished. Then we retain a sufficient part of the borrower's work force to complete the inventory on which the finished value will be very high in relation to the costs that must be incurred in finishing it. Generally, we will not incur costs which would be more than 50% of the liquidating sale value of the finished goods, and in most cases, the added value ranges in the area of 15-20%.

Where the defaulted borrower is a distributor of some sort, you often have an excellent chance of selling a significant portion of his inventory to his regular customers. In some cases, where it will not be easy to replace the defaulted customer as a source of supply, it makes sense to send a general mailing to his customers advising that he is going out of business and suggesting that they stock up to the greatest extent possible immediately. We handled the liquidation of an outboard motor manufacturer not too long ago who had a fairly large inventory of spare parts. We wrote to all the dealers and advised them that they should stock up because it would soon not be possible to purchase parts. We took a full year, but finally sold the inventory at 50% over book value. In situations where the company's goods bear a very high mark up, it is sometimes desirable to let people come in and "cherry pick" the inventory by offering a mark down from the normal selling price, which may still bear a very good relationship to the cost of the goods. In a retail business, we are really talking about a going out of business sale. The same principle can be applied to a wholesaling business and a manufacturing business.

Another desirable way to conduct a liquidation is to find a purchaser who is interested in purchasing the assets for the purpose of conducting a similar business. Other than the company's own customers, this type of purchaser will probably pay the highest price for the collateral you are liquidating. For this reason, I emphasize the necessity of obtaining patents where they are part of a business and, in addition, I would emphasize the necessity of obtaining a lien on all tools, dies and so forth. In selling a facility, you are actually selling a business. Although purchasers will be little interested in the other company's overhead structure or management arrangements, they will be very interested in the cost of goods sold and all of the direct manufacturing costs. Obviously, one of the difficulties of completing this kind of sale is that good cost figures will probably be hard to come by and must often be assembled by the person conducting the sale.

Thirdly, a reasonable method of conducting a liquidation is simply a series of individual sales. You put a good horse trader in the middle of a factory or warehouse, you get the word out that things are for sale, and you work out the best deals you can in each instance. This process is time consuming and requires the services of good people who know the value of what they are selling. The individual people who come in to buy will, in most cases, be very knowledgeable about what they are seeking. If the person who is negotiating with them is less knowledgeable, he will clearly be taken advantage of.

Lastly, we get to what is probably the most common way of conducting the liquidation, an auction. Too often lenders will automatically liquidate by holding an auction even when another method would produce a greater recovery. Auctions do have the advantage of getting rid of all the collateral at once and of eliminating potential claims by a debtor that private sales were not commercially reasonable. But, they often result in a low recovery. The difficulty of getting a good price is generally more pronounced in the case of inventory.

With equipment, there is no question but that sometimes an auction becomes necessary and, in certain circumstances, it is a reasonably good way of conducting a liquidation. However, a great care should be used in selecting the auctioneer and in working out an arrangement with him. A variety of deals can be made with auctioneers, and the typical arrangement in which you guarantee to the auctioneer that his expenses and his fee comes out first and you get whatever is left by no means has to be the kind of deal you make. Obviously, auctions are subject to certain things beyond your control, such as weather keeping attendance down, but a well-run, carefully planned auction clearly has a place in the various devices which should be considered in conducting a liquidation.

Summary and Conclusion

In all areas of dealing with troubled companies, whether on-going operations, unwinding operations or liquidations, a high degree of expertise and professionalism is necessary and a little imagination often helps too. There is clearly a financial aspect to dealing with these problems, but there is also a very real operational aspect to handling these situations properly. One cannot deal effectively in this area by reviewing financial statements.

We were asked some time ago to look at a situation to justify a trustee's position in accepting an offer to purchase a division from a bankrupt company. The offer had been made by the manager of the division. When we visited the plant, we found that the man's desk drawer was stuffed full of orders and his warehouses were stuffed full of merchandise ready to fill those orders. We told the trustee that a liquidation would bring more than the offered price. He hired us to do it, and recovered three times more than he had been offered. This, by the way, was a situation that was not being handled by rank amateurs or inexperienced people. It was a major publicly owned company, the lead bank was one of the largest banks in the world and many of the major commercial law firms in New York were involved in the situation. However, none of them had the type of approach or the kinds of people essential to deal with these things well.

Success in handling a problem, whether it be measured in terms of turning the company around and rehabilitating it or in liquidating the company for the maximum possible recovery, will occur only where a number of factors are handled correctly. Management of the company must swallow that inherent difficulty we all have in admitting our limitations and accept such useful assistance as is available. Trade creditors and their lawyers must evidence a desire to cooperate in the resolution of the problem without acrimony or vindictiveness. The lender must maintain the delicate balance of offering constructive help where possible and financial accommodations where reasonable while, at the same time, protecting his lending institution and applying a measure of discipline to the customer.

Lastly, the person handling the situation, whether original management of the company or an outside party, must tie all of the elements together and exhibit enough control and progress to give all of the other parties a new incentive for cooperation. With the right combination of skills, a great deal of hard work and sometimes a little luck as well, many situations can be saved and every situation can be improved. If a liquidation cannot be averted, it at least can be handled well.

The banker's role in this situation is not only difficult but in many cases it is central. The banker not only has to consider his obligation to protect his institution but also his institution's responsibility to and its reputation in the business community. By fully utilizing those tools which are available to him, whether they are resources within his institution or are drawn from outside agencies such as lawyers, accountants, consultants and the like, he can often be the difference between an orderly, sound and constructive approach and utter chaos.*

BANKRUPTCY—LIQUIDATIONS AND REORGANIZATIONS

The Bankruptcy Reform Act of 1978

Bankruptcy proceedings and their impact on secured lenders always have been an integral part of accounts receivable and inventory lending, but this area of law took on additional significance for the secured lender with the passage of the Bankruptcy Code of 1978. This comprehensive revision of bankruptcy law became effective on October 1, 1979, with major repercussions for accounts receivable and inventory lenders.

This review of bankruptcy law explains some of the principal provisions of the Bankruptcy Code, as they apply to a secured lender. By no means is it a complete review of bankruptcy law, a subject which would require an entire book in itself, nor is it in any way a substitute for able counsel.

The Bankruptcy Code is a federal statute providing for a variety of proceedings under which a distressed debtor may obtain relief from his creditors and the creditors may impose supervision on the payment of indebtedness. Under the Bankruptcy Code of 1978, the proceedings that directly affect secured lenders are those set forth in Chapter 7, Liquidations, and Chapter 11, Reorganizations. A proceeding under Chapter 7 is intended to bring about the disposition of all of the assets on an equitable basis according to the rules set forth in the Bankruptcy Code. Chapter 11 provides the sole proceeding for the reorganization of a debtor. Proceedings under this chapter are intended to give the debtor the opportunity to reshape its business if necessary, to compro-

* Roger K. Soderberg, "Assistance to Financially Troubled Companies," *Journal of Commercial Bank Lending,* November 1974, pp. 50-54.

mise its outstanding indebtedness, and ultimately to remain in business.

Bankruptcy proceedings take place in federal bankruptcy courts, which are adjuncts to the district court in each United States judicial district. These courts are presided over by bankruptcy judges. Since the Bankruptcy Code is a federal statute, it takes precedence in cases where conflicts arise between it and the provisions of state law. In many cases, however, the Bankruptcy Code incorporates and applies state law by its own provisions. For example, for purposes of determining whether a transfer of ownership is complete and irrevocable or whether it may be set aside in the bankruptcy proceeding, the Code applies the test of whether or not the transfer of ownership had been completed under applicable state law. (As used in the Bankruptcy Code as well as in this discussion, the term *transfer* includes any sale, conveyance, assignment, or other disposition, whether absolute or conditional, of any property or any interest in property such as a mortgage or a security interest.)

The bankruptcy court relies heavily on general equitable principles, and often will resolve matters of discretion in favor of the least protected party. The secured lender should not expect the court to take a protective posture with respect to its rights. The court assumes that it must protect the debtor and the unsecured creditor, and that the secured creditor should protect itself.

Bankruptcy is a specialized area of law, and it is prudent for a lender whose borrower has gone into a bankruptcy proceeding to retain the legal representation of an attorney who has experience in this area. Such an attorney's knowledge of the specialized legal issues and of the other specialists who will be involved is very helpful.

Liquidation proceedings and reorganization proceedings both may be initiated on either a voluntary basis or an involuntary basis. That is, either the debtor may itself bring a petition for the proceeding, or the petition may be brought against the debtor by three or more creditors holding aggregate claims of $5,000 or more. If the total number of claim-holders is fewer than twelve, the proceeding may be initiated by the petition of one claim-holder having a claim of at least $5,000.

The purpose of a Chapter 11 proceeding is to permit the debtor to continue in business while attempting to make an agreement with creditors concerning the payment of old debts. To do this, a plan must be proposed and accepted by the court. A plan is a formulation of the manner in which the debtor will discharge the outstanding secured and unsecured obligations. The plan may deal with different classes of indebtedness differently; for example, secured claims almost always would be treated differently from unsecured claims. In most instances, the plan will stipulate the payment of some portion of the total amount of debt. Often the payment will be partly in cash and partly in deferred payments. Payment also may be made through a medium other than money. For example, common stock of either the debtor company or some other company may be distributed as part of the plan. The distribution of stock in this fashion is exempt from the normal registration requirements provided under federal security laws.

The plan may terminate the debtor's obligation under agreements requiring performance or payments in the future. An example of this would be the termination of a long-term lease. The plan also may contain provisions for continuing supervision of the debtor's affairs, either by the court or by representatives of the creditors.

In a proceeding for reorganization under Chapter 11, the bankruptcy court has jurisdiction over secured claims; the reorganization plan adopted by the proceeding *may impair and alter the rights of the holder of the secured claim.* The power of the court is not absolute, being defined by a number of limitations set forth in the Code, but the secured party is a real party in interest in these proceedings and must actively take part in the proceedings in order to protect its rights and its interest in the collateral for which it bargained when the secured loan was made.

When the plan has been formulated, it must be presented to the creditors for acceptance or rejection. Acceptance requires the affirmative vote of the holders of at least two-thirds of the dollar amount, and more than one-half of the number, of claims in each class.

The Code provides eleven tests that must be met in order for a plan to be confirmed. Confirmation is the order of the court that makes the proposed plan effective. Condition number eight of these requirements is that the plan be accepted by each class of creditors who would have its rights impaired by the plan. However, following the enumeration of conditions that must be satisfied to allow confirmation, there is a provision that permits the court to confirm a plan even though condition number eight has not been met. The court may do this if it finds that the plan does not discriminate unfairly and that the plan is fair and equitable with respect to each class of creditors who have not accepted the plan. This has been dubbed the "cram down" provision of the Bankruptcy Code. In a typical uncomplicated case, the claim holders might consist of only two classes: (1) the general, unsecured creditors, and (2) a single secured lender. The "cram down" provision acts to prevent the secured creditor from having a veto power over any plan. *It also extends to the court, within the limitations contained in the*

Code, the discretion to determine what is fair and equitable to the secured creditor. Many accounts receivable and inventory lenders will be uncomfortable knowing that someone else, such as a bankruptcy judge, should have the ability to make a determination so important to the operation of their business.

A proceeding which has been commenced under Chapter 7 may be converted to a reorganization under Chapter 11, and a Chapter 11 case may be converted to a liquidation under Chapter 7. The rules governing such conversions follow.

For converting a Chapter 7 liquidation to a Chapter 11 reorganization:

1. A debtor in a Chapter 7 proceeding has an *absolute one-time right* to convert to a reorganization proceeding (but only if the case was started as a liquidation proceeding; it may not be a conversion of a reorganization proceeding).
2. Any party in interest may *request* that a Chapter 7 liquidation proceeding be converted to a Chapter 11 proceeding. After a notice and a hearing the court decides whether to convert the case or not.

For converting a reorganization to a liquidation:

1. A debtor in possession *may convert* a voluntary Chapter 11 proceeding to a Chapter 7 liquidation proceeding.
2. In all other cases a Chapter 11 proceeding may be converted to a Chapter 7 proceeding *only at the request* of a party in interest and a hearing before the court. At the hearing, the court must consider any losses or diminution of the estate; the absence of reasonable likelihood of rehabilitation of the debtor; inability to effectuate a plan; unreasonable delay prejudicial to creditors; failure to propose a timely plan; a denial or revocation of confirmation of a plan; inability to effect consummation of a plan; material default under a plan; and termination of a plan by an event of default in the plan.

The plan in a reorganization proceeding may provide for the liquidation of the debtor, thus accomplishing the purposes of Chapter 7, while permitting the trustee and the court to exercise the powers made available under Chapter 11. The secured lender always should be prepared to face whichever proceeding might most interfere with its ability to maximize the protection afforded by the collateral.

The Bankruptcy Code gives to a trustee or to a debtor in possession extensive powers over property subject to a mortgage or security interest, in a reorganization proceeding in which no trustee has been appointed with respect to that property. Upon the filing of a petition under either Chapter 7 or Chapter 11, an automatic stay goes into effect prohibiting any action against the debtor or any of its property. This prevents the secured creditor from bringing any action to foreclose its lien; or otherwise to realize on collateral it holds, whether in the creditor's possession or the debtor's possession. A secured party has the right to request relief from the automatic stay any time during the proceeding. One of the grounds for obtaining such relief is the claim that a secured party does not have adequate protection. In the hearing to determine whether or not the stay should continue, the trustee has the burden of proving that the secured party is adequately protected. The statute specifically provides that the stay will terminate unless a hearing is held and a finding is made against the secured party. The court may have a preliminary hearing, however, at which time the final hearing may be further postponed. In the past, courts have tended to postpone such hearings despite rules designed to insure an early hearing for requests for relief from an automatic stay. The Bankruptcy Code attempts to insure that hearings will be held on a timely basis, but it remains to be seen whether this will occur.

The trustee has broad powers to use the property of the debtor during the pendency of a proceeding, notwithstanding any lien on that property. With the sole exception of cash collateral, a trustee may use any of the debtor's property, including accounts receivable and inventory. There is provision for a hearing at the request of the secured party to deny use or to impose conditions on the use of such property by a trustee; at such a hearing the trustee will have the burden proving that the secured party is adequately protected.

Subject to the ability to show, to the court's satisfaction, that the secured party is adequately protected, a trustee also may borrow against assets which already are subject to a lien. The Code provides that such new borrowing be secured by a junior lien if such financing can be arranged. If borrowing cannot be obtained with a junior lien, then the court may allow borrowing on an equal lien. If that cannot be accomplished, the *court may subordinate the existing lien and permit the borrowing to be secured by a senior lien on the assets.*

The Bankruptcy Code provides for a hearing to determine the actual value of the collateral held by the holder of a secured claim. If the actual value of the collateral is determined to be less than the total amount of the claim, the court will rule that the secured party holds a secured claim in an amount equal to the value of the collateral and an unsecured claim for the balance.

The secured party is left in a precarious position as a result of the trustee's power to use or borrow against assets, as long as the secured party is adequately protected, and the court's power to determine that a secured party may be undersecured. If the secured party argues too successfully that the value of the collateral is suspect and may be very low, the debt may be found to be partially unsecured. On the other hand, if the secured party argues too successfully that the value of the collateral is high, then the secured party may find that it has supported the trustee's case for using the property in question by establishing that the secured party is to be adequately protected.

In any bankruptcy proceeding a number of people are involved whose functions should be understood. First, of course, is the debtor and its counsel. Although their combined role is limited in a Chapter 7 liquidation proceeding, it is key in a Chapter 11 reorganization. In such a proceeding, they have the first opportunity to devise and successfully sell a plan. Parties other than the debtor may submit a plan only if the debtor has failed to submit one within 120 days after the proceeding has commenced, or if a plan has not been accepted by the creditors within 180 days after the proceeding has commenced. This is subject to the court's discretionary power to increase or reduce the time periods, and only if a trustee has not been appointed.

The secured lender and its attorney principally attempt to preserve the security they hold, and perhaps to obtain possession and control of that security. The secured party and its counsel normally will deal only with issues directly concerning their security.

The Bankruptcy Code provides for the formation of a creditors' committee to represent the general unsecured creditors. The Code provides that the committee of creditors appointed ordinarily shall consist of persons who are willing to serve and who hold the seven largest claims against the debtor. On request of a party in interest, the court may order the appointment of additional committees of creditors or of equity security-holders. The statute expressly provides that any of these committees may retain counsel. The creditors' committee and its counsel, together with other committees that may be appointed, will have the major task of working out a plan with the debtor. After the time periods referred to above, these committees may take the initiative and propose and present their own plans.

At any time during reorganization proceeding the court may appoint a trustee. The appointment of the trustee may be based on cause, that is, some showing of fraud, dishonesty, incompetance, or gross misman-agement of the affairs of the debtor; or the appointment may be based on a simple finding that such appointment is in the interest of cred-itors or other parties having an interest in the debtor. A trustee takes control of the debtor's assets, investigates the financial affairs of the debtor, and generally is responsible for the financial affairs of the debtor during the administration of the case. The court has the option of appointing an examiner instead of a trustee. An examiner will in-vestigate the acts, conduct, assets, liabilities, and financial condition of the debtor, and report both to the court and to the creditors on his or her findings.

Under a pilot program, created by the Code, trustees will not be selected by the bankruptcy judges for appointment in individual cases, but will be provided from an independent, salaried U.S. trustee staff. The Attorney General must appoint a U.S. trustee for each of ten pilot areas. The program is to be reevaluated by 1984, and at that time either discontinued or expanded to cover the entire country.

The meanings and relationship of the terms *priority* and *security* are often confused. The Bankruptcy Code establishes certain priorities among creditors. That is, it establishes an order in which debts are to be paid out of any free assets that are available to pay debts. These priorities and their relative order of payment are as follows:

1. Administrative expenses incurred while the case is pending. These may include the cost of the proceeding itself, and the ob-ligations incurred after the date on which the proceeding was commenced;
2. Unsecured claims incurred by the debtor after an involuntary pe-tition has been filed against it and before an order for relief has been entered;
3. Limited claims for wages. Claims are limited to $2,000 for each individual and must have been earned within the 90 days before the date of the filing of the petition or the date on which the debtor's business stopped, whichever came first;
4. Limited claims for contributions to employee benefit plans. These are limited to contributions arising from services rendered within the 180 days before the filing of the petition to the date on which the debtor's business stopped. They are further limited to $2,000 for each employee, less the amount paid to such employees under the third priority;
5. Deposits made by individuals for the purchase of goods or ser-

vices for personal, family, or household use, which goods or services were not delivered or provided. This is limited to $900 per claim;

6. Various federal, state, and local taxes.

These claims are to be paid exclusively from free assets, that is, unencumbered assets which the court has the power to distribute.

Security refers strictly to the recognition in bankruptcy of the effect of liens. Proceeds of encumbered property or the property itself will go to the lien-holder even in a bankruptcy proceeding. If all of a bankrupt's property is encumbered and there is no excess above the encumbrances to generate free funds, proceeds of the encumbered property will still go to the security-holder notwithstanding the fact that there are unpaid priorities. If a secured creditor holds a lien on some property but there is also unencumbered property, then the proceeds of the encumbered property go to the security-holder and the proceeds of unencumbered property are distributed in accordance with the rules on priorities. If the secured creditor has a deficiency after liquidation of the security, he is treated as a general unsecured creditor for such deficiency and is entitled to no priority.

Financing a Borrower Under Chapter Proceedings

When a proceeding for reorganization is initialed, the debtor should be dealt with as though it were a new company. If the lender is to continue financing a company's business operations under the jurisdiction of the bankruptcy court, new borrowing arrangements must be agreed to and new loan agreements must be executed, all with the consent of the court. The lender must treat the arrangement as an entirely new and separate loan transaction, and must carefully segregate both collateral and collections. Newly arising accounts receivable may not be used to secure the old indebtedness.

If the lender held a lien against inventory prior to the initiation of the bankruptcy proceeding, the agreement should cover the distribution of proceeds when that inventory is sold in the course of continuing operations. All too often, the debtor sustains further losses while operating under the jurisdiction of the court, and the losses are largely funded by a decrease in the inventory without a corresponding decrease in the bank's inventory loan.

It is unfortunate that most reorganization proceedings do not end with a plan. Instead, the efforts to achieve a reorganization fail and the proceeding ends with the debtor's company being liquidated. A secured lender must view realistically all of its actions throughout the proceeding, including its decision to finance the company, understanding that it probably is preparing for a liquidation.

The Bankruptcy Code confers upon a trustee the right to attack any flaw in the transfer of a property right, including a security interest, if a third party has such a right. For example, if a secured lender were to fail to file a financing statement, that fact normally would not affect the validity of the security interest of the lender. However, the failure to file a financing statement would make the security interest unenforceable against a subsequent lien holder who took a security interest in the borrower's property not knowing of the lender's security interest. The unperfected security interest also is unenforceable against a trustee, even though no such subsequent lien claimant ever actually existed. Accordingly, any potential defects in the lender's lien will face scrutiny in a bankruptcy proceeding.

Two important provisions, by which a trustee or receiver may examine and attack transactions that occurred prior to the initiation of the bankruptcy proceeding, are the provisions dealing with fraudulent transfers and preferential transfers. It is important to remember that the term *transfer* includes the creation of mortgages and security interests, as well as sales, conveyances, or other actual changes in ownership.

Fraudulent Transfers

A fraudulent transfer is one that was made within *one year* before the date of the filing of the petition, and made with an actual intent to hinder, delay, or defraud any present or future creditor of the debtor. A transfer also is fraudulent if the debtor receives less than a reasonably equivalent value in exchange for the transfer and if it meets one of the following tests:

1. The debtor was insolvent on the date that the transfer was made, or became insolvent as a result of it.
2. The debtor was engaged in a business, or was about to engage in a business, for which the debtor's remaining property was unreasonably small capital.
3. The debtor intended or believed that the debtor would incur debts that would be beyond its ability to pay as they matured.

Any transfer that meets this test may be avoided by the trustee. This means that the property that was sold or conveyed must be returned, and that a lien that was created simply would be voided. In addition, the Code allows trustees to bring actions under any state fraudulent conveyance laws. This has the effect of permitting the examination of a transaction which may have taken place more than one year prior to the filing of the petition, if the applicable state laws so provide.

One example of a potential claim of fraudulent transfer in which no one has any fraudulent intent is an acquisition loan where the acquired company's assets are used to secure the money borrowed for the acquisition. For example, if the purchaser agrees to purchase all of the stock of a company for its book value, he or she may find that the company's assets would support a secured loan for the full amount. However, the result of the transaction is to reduce the company's net worth to virtually zero, and probably to give it a negative working capital balance. The money borrowed on the company's assets does not stay in the company for business operations, rather it is paid out directly to the selling stockholders. Should operations become unprofitable and a bankruptcy occur, a trustee may claim that the company did not receive fair consideration for the lien it gave on its assets, because, when the transaction is viewed as a whole, the company incurred secured debt but received no benefit. Accordingly, the trustee might attempt to set aside the lender's security interest.

Preferential Transfers

A trustee may avoid as preferential any transfer of property that meets the following five tests:

1. It is a transfer to, or for the benefit of, a creditor.
2. It is a transfer for, or on account of, a debt owed by the debtor before the transfer was made.
3. The transfer was made within 90 days before the filing of the petition, or made between 90 days and one year before the date of the filing of the petition if the creditor was an insider and had reasonable cause to believe that the debtor was insolvent.
4. The transfer was made while the debtor was insolvent.
5. It is a transfer that enables the creditor to receive more than it would have were the case a liquidation and the transfer not made.

In the typical case in which a lender might have an unsecured loan for which it wishes to take security or for which it obtains an attachment, the test for a preferential transfer would be applied as follows:

1. The creation of the lien, whether by agreement or by attachment, would be a transfer made for the benefit of the lender.
2. In this typical case, the lien is obtained to secure a debt that was outstanding before the lien was created.

3. The timing aspect of the test obviously is critical. A lien obtained more than 90 days prior to the commencement of a proceeding against the debtor generally will not be subject to attack as a preference. However, if the creditor is an insider who had reason to believe the debtor was insolvent, then the time period is extended to one year prior to the beginning of the proceeding. The Code lists a number of persons who are to be considered insiders, including relatives of individual debtors, officers, and directors of corporate debtors. Anyone who is a control person is also considered an insider. The term "control person" is not further defined but some commentators have suggested that lenders, in some circumstances, may be control persons.

4. The debtor is insolvent if its assets are exceeded by its liabilities. This simple balance sheet test is all that is required, and it is immaterial whether or not the lender knew or had reason to believe that the debtor was insolvent unless the one year time period is being used.

5. The lien will be set aside only if it enables the creditor to obtain more against its debt than it would have obtained if it had gotten its unsecured distribution in a liquidation proceeding.

The Bankruptcy Code provides a number of exceptions and clarifications with respect to the preference test. The first is that a transfer is not a preference if it was intended as a contemporaneous exchange for new value, and, in fact, was substantially contemporaneous. This means that if a lender makes an advance against collateral, but incurs a minor delay in perfecting its lien, it may still be able to preserve its lien against an attack based on preference if perfection occurred "substantially contemporaneously" with the advancement of new funds.

In addition, the preference section of the Code includes a section dealing with the fluctuating values of accounts receivable and inventory loans. This section provides that a perfected security interest in inventory or accounts receivable, or in the proceeds of either, is not a preference—except to the extent that the aggregate of all such transfers caused a reduction, as of the date of the filing of the petition, of any amount by which the debt, secured by the security interest, exceeded the value of all security held for the debt at the beginning of the preference period. In other words, if a lender's collateral is not adequate to fully secure its loan to a borrower on January 1, but subsequent transactions reduce the deficiency and the borrower files a petition on April 1, the transfers (loan payments or collateral increases) which improved the lender's position are preferential transfers and may be set aside. If the lender were an insider, the appropriate comparison date would be the previous January 1. In either case, the test must be applied using the specific day that begins the time period in question. Apparently, improvements or deteriorations in the lender's position in the intervening days are of no consequence. However, you must recall that it will be the borrower or some group of creditors of the borrower who decide the day on which the petition is filed. The preference section deals only with the reduction or elimination of a deficiency between your collateral and your loan.

A similar provision concerns the right of setoff. Generally, the Code recognizes the right of a creditor to offset an obligation owed by a debtor in a bankruptcy proceeding against indebtedness owed to the debtor. Perhaps the most common example of this is the instance of a bank offsetting a loan against the debtor's funds on deposit at the bank. The Code recognizes the right of a creditor to do this, but limits the ability of a creditor to better its position with respect to other creditors of the debtor in the 90 days prior to the filing of a bankruptcy petition. You only may offset an amount that leaves a loan balance of no less than what the loan balance would have been had you offset on the day that was ninety days before the filing of the petition; if no loan balance was outstanding following a setoff on that date, then the first date thereafter, on which a remaining loan balance would have resulted, applies. In other words, if a borrower has a loan balance of $100,000 and a deposit account balance of $50,000 on January 1, and if the bank offsets on March 15 when the respective balances are $100,000 and $80,000 leaving a loan balance of $20,000, and if a petition is filed on April 1, the bank may be liable to return the $30,000 by which its position was improved.

This has been a general introduction to some of the areas of bankruptcy law with which secured lenders often come into contact. The most important thing for a lender to know about bankruptcy is that it is a relatively complex area of law. Expert legal advice is necessary any time you think your actions may be covered by any aspect of the Bankruptcy Code.

CHAPTER 10

Marketing

Accounts receivable and inventory lending is an exciting and powerful factor in the financing of a large segment of American business. The rewards to both the lender and the borrower may greatly offset the costs and problems inherent in handling this type of business. In fact, the hazards and precautions detailed throughout this book may be comfortably handled as part of the job, and should be neither onerous nor difficult.

ADVANTAGES TO BANK

The advantages to the bank of providing receivables and inventory financing are great and, whenever possible, should provide a strong adjunct to full service lending. Almost every bank wants to establish and promote its image as a full service bank. Of course, there are many banks that because of size or location should not attempt receivables and inventory lending; but there are many others which have the capabilities and which owe it to themselves and their communities to offer this tremendously vital service.

By providing a good accounts receivable and inventory lending program, the banks will service another layer of industry, and will provide funds for qualified borrowers which have been going to competitors or which have not been able to get adequate financing from others.

Perhaps a bank already makes loans on receivables and inventory based on procedures established more by circumstances than by design.

In that case, a tighter program will allow larger and more useful loans to be made—not only more prudently, but also more flexibly.

It has been the author's experience while in commercial financing that the average life of a receivable and inventory account is between two and three years, after which a great majority of borrowers graduated to a bank or to the equity market. A very small percentage went the bankruptcy route. Because of this, it only seems reasonable to believe that banks should have similar results. When receivable and inventory accounts improve sufficiently, they should be moved from secured lending to the more conventional forms of financing.

Not the least among the reasons for providing a program of accounts receivable and inventory financing is that it is a continually exciting and dynamic method of lending. In many types of financing, a loan officer structures and makes a loan and then becomes a spectator, waiting to see how the deal turns out. When a receivable loan is structured and the initial loan is made, the program has only just begun. From this point on, the bank becomes a part of the borrower's team and has a daily interest in the borrower's sales, collections, profits, or losses, as well as interest in its annual and interim progress. The bank should not become a part of management, but it should work closely with management and cooperate in every way possible to contribute to the borrower's well being. Although this is a laudable objective, it is also common sense. The more prosperous the borrower is, the less the bank has to worry about repayment of principle and interest. In any event, when success is achieved—or even when disaster merely is avoided—an accounts receivable and inventory lender can feel a proprietary interest and some pride in the result.

ADVANTAGES TO BORROWER

The advantages arising from borrowing on the security of accounts receivable and inventory are clear, and they are easy to sell to qualified borrowers. Its extreme flexibility allows the business to handle seasonal fluctuations of regular growth, or to buy time if it is a company that has run into adversity. There is no regular repayment schedule on an accounts receivable loan because reductions come from the application of receivables collections to the loan. The loan becomes quasi-permanent by continual advances on new sales and by the application of customer collections to loan balances.

Another advantage is that a receivable and inventory arrangement is simple for the borrower and the bank. Both can tell on a day-to-day basis how much may be borrowed, and the borrower can instruct the bank to deposit the required amount into his or her account. This eliminates a great amount of negotiation time for both parties. Interest is charged only on a per diem basis, so that borrowers never pay for any funds not in use.

Accounts receivable and inventory loans may be combined with fixed asset loans, to provide a borrower with adequate financing to meet ongoing needs, and with a repayment schedule geared to the borrower's ability to pay. A final selling point for this type of service is that the bank's compensation should be based only on the borrower's daily loan balance; therefore, the borrower should not be required to maintain any compensating loan balance.

FINDING AND DEVELOPING THE MARKET

The principal problem in building up a satisfactory volume of loans for an accounts receivable and lending department is to identify the market and to select the most efficient ways of soliciting this type of business. The actual selling of the program is simple because of the many obvious advantages to the businesses that can use it.

To begin with, everyone connected with commercial lending should become acquainted with the basic concepts of accounts receivable and inventory lending, and should refer all prospects to the head of the receivables department. Emphasis should be placed on the fact that the bank wants to solicit only *good* business—companies with a good track record and from which the bank may get a satisfactory rate of return. Volume for volume's sake is a very dangerous policy. Credit losses suffered in the early life of a receivable department may sour the bank's management on the real potential of receivable and inventory lending. In this respect, the department head should evaluate all leads submitted by other loan officers and should explain to them the reasons for whatever rejections are made. Over time, an understanding will be reached regarding the general type of loans that the bank will find acceptable.

On a continuing basis, particularly after it has shaken down to a comfortable routine, the department and its loans should be included in the agenda of the bank's meetings of loan officers, branch managers, credit officers, and trainees. The discussion of loans, both good and bad, will help to educate bank personnel about the value and the hazards inherent in making revolving secured loans.

Aggressive solicitation of receivable business should be deferred until the department's personnel are sufficiently acquainted with their duties and routines to handle any appreciable increase in business. When the department is ready, the following methods should produce loan applications.

Personal Solicitation

Every loan officer should be required to solicit likely prospects within the bank's service area. Prospects may be selected from lists of manufacturers, wholesalers, and selected retailers whose annual volumes range from about $600,000 to approximately $10,000,000. Companies in this range should produce receivable loans from about $60,000 to $1,000,000. The most likely prospects are those that show a third grade or worse paying record; this indicates that for one reason or another the company's working capital is insufficient to handle the business it is doing.

The most useful lists are those which focus on the greatest number of prospects. For example, there is no value in getting a general list that includes multi-million dollar companies or, on the other hand, companies with little or no net worth. It is suggested, therefore, that lists be confined to three main targets: (1) types of industry or wholesalers within the bank's service area with which the bank would like to do business; (2) lists of manufacturers or wholesalers (an exception to this might be small department store chains within the area); and (3) businesses with a net worth of $75,000 or more, but with a third grade paying record.

Prospects with no net worth rating should not be eliminated from a list. The absence of a rating may mean only that the credit agency has not been given a recent financial statement on which a rating may be established. Selections actually should be weighted slightly in favor of reported paying habits rather than net worth.

Dun & Bradstreet is an especially good source for lists because they select names as outlined above and will provide three-by-five inch cards that show the prospect's name, address, telephone number, names of principal officers, type of business, and ratings. This kind of background information is very helpful in providing conversation openers for the solicitor.

*Direct Mail
Solicitation*

Prospects also may be gleaned from a direct mail program in which names are provided from purchased lists. No attempt should be made to make a mailing to the entire list at one time; this might produce a volume of leads that could not be handled properly by the receivable department or other bank personnel. Prospects should be organized by geographical areas, and only a certain number of mailings should be sent each week. In this way, a degree of control is maintained over travel time and distance, and the number of calls resulting from weekly mailings may be serviced better than if a complete mailing were made all at once.

Mailings to the same prospects should be made at least three times per year—with emphasis on the fall and winter months, but skipping the period around the Christmas holidays. All mailings should include a self-addressed stamped envelope and a return postal card on which the prospect can request that additional information be sent or that a loan officer call. When a request for a personal call is made, it should be given priority in order to maintain the prospect's interest and to show that the bank is sincerely interested in doing business.

When a brochure is requested, it should be sent with a simple cover letter; this should be followed up within a week to ten days to ask the prospect if he or she received the material and if there are any questions.

Direct mail advertising also may be sent to accountants, lawyers, and consultants. To a large extent, this is institutional advertising and thus may be done only once a year, just to keep the bank's name alive with this source of business.

*Statement
Stuffers*

Stuffers announcing the bank's accounts receivable program may be sent with monthly statements. These may be sent monthly for the first year and bimonthly thereafter. Stuffers should include a coupon to be returned to the department head. From an economic standpoint, stuffers are best directed to commercial accounts, but consideration should be given to occasionally including them with consumer statements as well. Many individuals having personal checking accounts are influential corporate officers in the companies for which they work.

*Prospect Leads
from Publications*

Magazines and business-oriented papers, such as publications of state commerce departments or city business development agencies, should be checked. Often they will produce leads since they report on companies that have moved into the area, or are planning to, and those already in the area that have purchased a new building, leased more space, put on extra shifts, or merged. Many of these activities will dilute working capital and thus will make the companies at least possible candidates for financing. This kind of a call almost invariably produces a courteous reception. The prospect is pleased that they made the papers and that a bank was motivated to do something about it.

Leads from Customer Accounts

Whenever customers of the bank submit schedules of accounts receivable, they should be reviewed not only for credit reasons but also as a source of prospective accounts. Checkings should be made of past due accounts to determine if they might be desirable accounts for the bank; it should be determined whether the bank could provide the working capital to enable the prospect to pay more currently. This has to be a *cold* call. However, the prospect who is already identified as being slow to pay almost always is interested in the bank's interest in calling.

Leads from Old Call Files

A good source of business, and one that is frequently overlooked, is old files on companies that have been called upon but with whom the bank did not choose or was not able to do business. The circumstances of most businesses change considerably from year to year; what might have been an unacceptable situation at the last discussion could very well be suitable now. This is potentially productive busywork and may be done when business is slack. It was our experience that this activity almost always produced enough new business to make the effort worthwhile. Even if no prospects are found, the review of old files may serve to clean them of dead prospects.

Newspaper Advertising

After the bank's receivables and inventory department has been in operation for a while, news of the department should be included from time to time in the bank's regular advertising in newspapers and periodicals. As a means of determining whether this source of marketing is effective, a reply coupon should be included in the advertising.

It is believed that this kind of advertising is more institutional than directly productive, but an occasional receivables ad will enhance the bank's reputation as a versatile, full service bank.

Public Relations   It is worthwhile for the department head, and perhaps other members of the staff, to join trade groups and to attend their conventions when it seems advisable. It is also helpful to seek speaking engagements at such organizations as Rotary Clubs, Kiwanis, and trade conventions. Occasionally the entire subject matter may be accounts receivable and inventory lending, but at other times, a simple reference to the fact that your bank now offers this service is more appropriate.

No one person in the bank can do all of the advertising and promotional work required to get an accounts receivable and inventory program off the ground; it takes a team effort. The entire commercial lending department, both at headquarters and in the branches, should cooperate with your marketing staff. Even in this era of frantic competition in banking, this kind of business is readily available; properly solicited and administered, it should prove to be a significant profit center for the bank.

CHAPTER 11

Conclusion

Accounts receivable and inventory lending has demonstrated for many years that it is a vital means of financing, unique in its ability to provide funds for thousands of borrowers who do not qualify for unsecured loans. In many cases it is the *only* financing program that can supply adequate funds for rapid growth, high seasonal factors, periods of adversity, or acquisitions, and still can provide the bank with security for its loans.

America has become great through the vitality of its business and industry, and a significant part of its growth may be accounted for by the ever-increasing availability of commercial financing and factoring. The following figures, provided by the National Commercial Finance Conference, New York, represent the volume of dollars employed by banks, commercial finance companies, and factors over the past three decades, in supplying financing and factoring to American businesses:

Growth of Commercial Financing and Factoring
(amounts in billions of dollars)

Year	Commercial Financing[1]	Factoring[2]	Total
1940	$ .41	$ .79	$ 1.2
1950	4.00	2.70	6.70
1960	10.06	4.91	14.97
1970	21.92	10.13	32.05
1975	36.34	18.23	54.57
1978	57.6	26.1	83.7
1979	66.6	28.1	94.7

1. Volume figures shown are made up substantially of loans made on the security of accounts receivable and inventory.

2. Factoring volume substantially represents the total of receivables purchased by factoring firms.

Many fine businesses of national prominence have grown to their present stature through the use of receivable and inventory financing. Many companies that have suffered reverses have recovered by pledging assets for loans that otherwise could not be obtained. In addition, thousands of acquisitions and mergers have been accomplished by providing experienced and talented businessmen and women with opportunities to make such transactions through loans on the assets of either the buyer, the seller, or both.

Throughout this book there are many caveats regarding the possibility of fraudulent acts by the borrower, or the possible diminution of the collateral held by the bank in support of its loans. The list of admonitions is long because there are many ways that fraud may be perpetrated, and many ways for collateral to lose some or all of its value. All of these caveats must be kept in perspective. The book would not be complete unless they were listed, but, happily, the great majority of borrowers are honest and earnest persons who are striving hard for success and who have more at stake, on a personal level, than does the bank.

Deliberate frauds are a rarity; through the bank's close cooperation with a borrower and its understanding of the collateral pledged to the bank, the value of receivables and other assets should be maintained to cover any loan made against them. The work involved in receivables and inventory lending is demanding but the rewards are commensurate with the effort. Every bank located in an area where it is even suspected that this kind of business may be generated will do well to study and consider it carefully. The business will fill an important need for both the bank and the community, and will help to promote the bank's image as a dynamic and full-service organization.

Index